YOUR HATE MAIL WILL BE GRADED:

A DECADE OF WHATEVER, 1998–2008

ALSO BY JOHN SCALZI

Old Man's War

The Ghost Brigades

The Android's Dream

The Last Colony

Zoe's Tale

YOUR HATE MAIL WILL BE GRADED:

A DECADE OF WHATEVER, 1998–2008

JOHN SCALZI

Foreword by Wil Wheaton

TOR®

A TOM DOHERTY ASSOCIATES BOOK
NEW YORK

DEDICATIONS

This book is dedicated to the following:

To those who blog, for giving me things to read when I should be writing.

To H.L. Mencken, who I'm sure would be either amused or appalled by the dedication.

To Ghlaghghee, Lopsided Cat, Zeus and the dearly departed Rex, my cats, because dedicating a book of online entries to cats is the ultimate in petblogging.

Finally, to Joy. Just because.

ACKNOWLEDGMENTS

Thanks to Bill Schafer and all at Subterranean—publishing a book of online entries is still a new enough idea that this qualifies as a grand experiment. Thanks for being experimental.

Thank you to Kristine and Athena Scalzi for making my life more than the grand sum of what I write online.

Thank you to the readers of Whatever. Reading this book provides you with only half the experience of the site—the other half comes from the witty and sometimes remarkable responses the entries garner from the readers. This is why I encourage you to come read the site after you read this.

Thank you to Tim Berners-Lee for inventing this whole Web thing. It's awfully handy.

FOREWORD

By
Wil
Wheaton

t seems like everyone knows a blogger these days. Many people *are* bloggers. It's like being part of a secret club that anyone can join. All they need are computers and opinions.

I've been around this blogging thing for a long time, almost as long as John Scalzi has. I can recall with some amusement when newspapers, magazines and "real" journalists and writers laughed at us. Many of them treated us like we were a bunch of amateurs playing with the latest passing fad.

I can recall with a great deal of amusement when these horrified "real" journalists realized that the blog-o-sphere (a term we all hate but continue to use, because nobody has come up with anything to replace it) was not only here to stay, but was forcing them to join us or perish.

I can recall with supreme amusement when they finally *did* join us, and then started whining that we didn't play by their rules. We were raw, we gave things away (for free! as in beer *and* speech, thank you very much), we spoke truth to power, we were outspoken and impolite. There were regular calls by these established media personalities and companies for panels on blogger ethics. Sales of clutching pearls, smelling salts and fainting couches skyrocketed.

Eventually, the old guard got over themselves and accepted that we weren't going anywhere. These days, blogs and bloggers are squarely in the mainstream. Every news outlet in the world has several blogs. Bloggers regularly sit beside credentialed journalists at press conferences (and often ask better questions). When Scooter Libby was finally put on trial in 2007 for outing CIA agent Valerie Plame in 2003, the most comprehensive coverage came from a group of bloggers who were covering the story from inside the courtroom. Countless writers—including the author of this book—have subverted the traditional publishing process and released entire novels on their blogs. An entire generation is growing up in a world where blogs have always existed and are just as relevant to them as magazines and newspapers were to their parents. The Internet, originally designed to facilitate the easy sharing of information (not porn, as it's turned out—not that I'm complaining), has finally realized that intention. Blogs and bloggers are here to stay, until they unplug the Internet and turn out the lights on planet Earth.

So what you're holding here is more than an entertaining collection of essays, stories and insights about everything from parenting to politics to publishing. You have a piece of Internet history, and it is your solemn duty to preserve it for the ages. Oh, sure, you can read it. You can even read it twice, if you want. You can probably share it with your friends and family (I'm sure John and everyone at Subterranean would prefer you bought them their own copy, but I won't tell on you if you don't) but when you're all finished, it should really be placed in a climate-controlled nitrogen-filled museum display, or at least watched over by top men, because John is an OG blogger, and Whatever is an OG blog. The Internet is serious business, people, and you'd be wise to remember that, or I'll throw you off my digital lawn and Skype your parents.

Some of you may know John as the award-winning author of novels such as *Old Man's War*. Others among your number may know John as the guy who wrote *The Rough Guides* to *Science Fiction* and *Space*. But I'm willing to bet the cost of this book that most of you know John as the guy who taped bacon to his cat and put a picture of it on his blog.

I know John as all of these things, plus a few more that shouldn't be disclosed…but certainly merit a mention in passing, if only to inflate the myth behind the man and impress you with my implied proximity to his greatness.

Regardless of how *you* came to know John and his work, though, you don't really *know* him unless you've read his blog. That is where this book comes in.

John is one of a handful of people who have been blogging since the beginning. This is an impressive feat all by itself, but what's truly remarkable is how consistently entertaining and *readable* he's been for the last decade. I've been blogging since 2000, and I've been a more-or-less full-time writer since 2004, so I know how hard it can be to populate a blog with consistently worthwhile entries for a few weeks at a time, let alone a decade.

I started reading Whatever about three years ago, because our mutual friend Mykal kept telling me about something funny or insightful his friend John had posted. It's been a daily stop for me ever since. It's been hugely entertaining to come across some of my favorite entries in this book. (I especially like the posts where John shares practical advice for guys like me who hope to achieve some small portion of the success John's made for himself, with Fred the Cult Leader and Super Gay Happy Fun Hour! coming in tied for second.)

If this is your first time reading John's blog, however, you should know a couple of things before you read any further, lest it all end in tears.

John ignores the oft-given advice to avoid discussions of parenting, religion and politics, and posts about these topics frequently. Unlike most who tackle these topics, John addresses them intelligently, with great humor and insight. However, if you're very sensitive or easily offended, John's going to mock you as he skins and barbecues a barn's worth of sacred cows. I speak from experience on this point. John once wrote about one of my most beloved movies of all time, thusly: "*Star Wars* is not entertainment. *Star Wars* is George Lucas masturbating to a picture of Joseph Campbell and conning billions of people into watching the money shot." My natural geek instinct was to grab a pitchfork and convert a slide rule to a torch, but before I could summon my fellow outraged Jedi (or find a slide rule), I read the rest of John's post. Goddammit if he didn't make a lot of sense. Sure, it helped that John hated the prequels as much as I did, but his larger point about what *Star Wars* really *is*, versus what a lot of us want it to be, was made with humor and logic, and I eventually put my lightsaber away. I don't know if fundamentalist Christians (John calls them "Leviticans") or asshole parents are as easily mollified, so you should absolutely track one down, give the poor devil a copy of this book and grab some popcorn.

I'm close to my maximum word count (we bloggers struggle with this limitation when we write things that will be printed on dead trees; we're just not used to having space-based limitations) so let me get to the bit that I hope will be quoted on the jacket: *This book captures everything I love about blogging. This book is filled with awesome. In the vernacular of the damn kids today, this book is made of EPIC WIN. John is funny, John is sarcastic, John is thoughtful, John is insightful, John is provocative…in other words, John is John, and I hope he never stops writing about and within Whatever.*

Finally, I would like to note, with glee, that most of this introduction was written on a laptop while in a coffee shop. Contrary to what John says, I'm pretty sure I fooled at least one person.

Wil Wheaton
actor, author, blogger
Los Angeles, CA

AUTHOR'S NOTE

Hi there. This is the part of the book where I get to explain to you what the hell this book really is.

In one sense it's simple enough: This is a collection of selected entries from "Whatever," an area on my personal site where I write daily on whatever subjects catch my eye (hence the name). I started writing it in 1998, which in Internet years means I began writing in the Cretaceous Period—a time so far back in the mists of the Internet that the word "blog" wasn't in common use. We called these online daily writey thingies "online diaries" or "Web journals." I could tell you stories, but I sense your eyes glazing already. Let's move on.

People who aren't familiar with blogs/online diaries/Web journals, aside from being stuck mentally or otherwise in the early 90s at best, still tend to think of them as written by one of three types of people: Frothing political junkies, angst-filled teenagers, and people unnaturally obsessed with their cats. I wouldn't deny you can find all three, of course (often in tantalizing car-wreck combinations), but there is naturally more to the world of online writing than that. Several million people "blog" in one form or another; tens of thousands of people do it on a more or less daily schedule. Many of these folks are strictly amateur, but then many are not—along with the cat lovers and the angsty teens are scientists, academics, lawyers, sports enthusiasts and others who write intelligently and knowledgeably about their primary subjects and write entertainingly on others. There are even folks who started out as writers in other fields and found themselves pecking away online.

I'm one of those. A few years before I began writing "Whatever," I had been a newspaper columnist, and then after that I had written a column for America Online. In 1998, I was, shall we say, between column gigs, and decided that I need somewhere to write daily to keep sharp. You know, just in case someone came banging down my door, demanding I start up my column writing ways again.

In this respect "Whatever" was a miserable failure: Look, ma! Still not a newspaper columnist! However, the Whatever was directly responsible for my publishing four books (including this one) and indirectly responsible for several more, and it's helped me land a number of writing gigs online and off. And it in itself has become popular enough that it's afforded me a certain narrow level of online fame and celebrity—not to be confused with *real* fame and celebrity, mind you (there's very little money involved, alas), but still interesting to have. In short, it's been incredibly useful in ways I couldn't have imagined when I started it in the hopes of getting a column. It is a prime example of something that John Lennon once said: "Life is what happens to you when you're busy making other plans." A decade on, I can't imagine not writing the Whatever.

The Whatever selections you'll find in this book can be approached in several ways. For the sociologists, it's an example of early American online writing: The "blog" in the first decade of the form. You'll find this particular blog does in fact read a bit like a newspaper column, because that's where some of my early writing experience was. However, these entries differ rather a bit from most newspaper columns as they exist today, primarily because there's no set topic or length: I can write 250 words on politics or 2,000 words on the meaning of life (or vice versa). No newspaper editor in his or her right mind would give a columnist that sort of flexibility; one may argue this is to the detriment of newspaper columns, but I think it's more accurate to say that's just the difference in the medium and let it go at that.

For the historians, this is a time capsule: observations on the great events between 1998 and 2008 (as well as many not-so-great events), including a three presidential elections, 9/11, gay marriage, Hurricane Katrina and the Iraq War. It's also a personal history, because interesting things happened in my life as well, and while I avoid going into embarrassingly personal detail, either in the book or in Whatever generally, nevertheless this is a very personal mode of writing, and there's no avoiding the fact this is—to get Mailer on you about it—me observing me observing life, the universe and everything. I can be cranky sometimes and sentimental other times. Humans are like that.

But since most readers aren't sociologist or historians, there's another approach, which is reading it for the fun of it. The selection of entries you'll find covers a wide range of topics, tones and time, but the idea for all of them is that they are (or should be) entertaining—because if they're not keeping your attention, why would you come back to read any more? I'm not a precious writer; I don't usually write for the art's sake, because I'm really not that good. I write because among other things I like the idea of people reading my stuff. I write to be read. This is not to say that I write blandly to keep from offending—with a book title like *Your Hate Mail Will Be Graded* that should be obvious enough—but I do try to write so that even if people disagree vehemently with me (and if you read the comments at Whatever, you'll see that they do), they'll still get something out of the reading experience. It's my hope that even when I write something that pisses you off, you'll still get some enjoyment out of how it was phrased.

Time capsule, new media, entertainment: However you approach the writing in the book, I hope it speaks to you. And remember that if you like what you read, there's more where that came from: http://whatever.scalzi.com. I'll be there. Swing on by.

Until then: Enjoy.

John Scalzi
May 11, 2008

A Note on the Organization of This Book

As you flip through this book you will notice that the entries are apparently not organized in any particular order: entries from a decade ago butt up against entries of recent vintage, and there is no rhyme or reason to why one topic follow another. But in fact there is a reason: Because arranging it so is very much how things are at Whatever. The whole point of the site is that I write whatever I want, whenever I want, however I want to. Readers never know what they're getting next (and for that matter I generally never know what I'm going to write next). As goes the blog, so goes the book. I hope you have fun with it.

DISCLAIMER

Mar
1
2003

For everyone who needs one, the following disclaimer:

1. Everything here is my opinion, and mine alone.

2. Occasionally, I am completely full of shit.

3. Well, all right, fine, more than occasionally.

4. On occasion I will also opine on things I know little or nothing about.

5. Which is fine, because the US Constitution says I can.

6. So there.

7. I'm not interested in being fair.

8. I am occasionally petty, nasty, snappish and rude. I'm also occasionally a tremendously sweet guy. You never know which you're going to get.

9. Unless you have been told specifically by me otherwise, no, as a matter of fact, I *don't* care what you think about me or my opinions.

10. I do try to be polite when I tell you that.

11. But I can't promise anything.

12. This is done by me for the purposes of my own amusement, and exists and updates entirely at my whim. If I decide to go away for a day, or a week, or forever, then I will.

I think that's it for now.

JESUS' DICKHEADS

Jul

13

2007

A Hindu chaplain was called to offer a prayer at the US Senate yesterday; the response of some Christian nutbags was to slip in and disrupt the prayer because the Hindu chaplain wasn't giving his shoutout to Jesus. They were trundled out, the prayer was given, and yet, somehow, the Republic did *not* fall. I think we can all thank Vishnu for that.

Look, this one is simple: Some people really and truly believe that what Jesus wants is for them to be *dicks* to everyone who isn't their particular, mushy-headed stripe of Christian. And if it's what Jesus wants, then it can't be wrong. Now, I'm entirely sure that in their minds they can come up with a better explanation for their activities than "Jesus wants me to be a dick"—they may actually be able to find some internal calculus that has them being a dick out of love for us godless idolaters and saving our worthless heathen souls, even—but the rest of us can call it for what it is. And also, of course, when these Dicks for Jesus try to offer up some alternate explanation for their behavior, I think it's fair to remind them of a number of things:

1. Whatever the rationale, they're being dicks.

2. At no point in the Bible does Jesus say "be a dick in My name."

3. Lots of *other* Christians seem to get through life without feeling called upon to be a dick in the service of Christ.

4. Indeed, when many of *these* Christians discover to their dismay that they've been a dick about something, they will frequently fall to their knees and say, "Forgive me, Lord, for I have been a total dick."

5. And He *does*.

6. That's a hint.

Now, the chances of any of this penetrating the mental shield of righteousness is pretty low, so you shouldn't expect anything more than a slightly befuddled look that shades into the growing suspicion that they're jeopardizing their very souls conversing with one such as you, you and your *heathen logic*. But it's worth a try, and if it doesn't work, at least they know what you think of their somewhat less-than-Christlike behavior. Because nothing digs at the heart of a Christdick more than the knowledge that someone thinks they're doing their Christianity *wrong*. Gets 'em all defensive and huffy, which is better than them being smug and self-righteous, in my book.

HOLDEN CAULFIELD IN MIDDLE AGE

Jul

18

2001

Holden Caulfield turned 50 this last week, and if the imaginary, fictional world in which he lives has any parallel with ours, right about now, he's got a kid who is now the age Holden was in *The Catcher in the Rye*, and that kid is *just driving him nuts*. Wouldn't that be a kick.

I never got Holden Caulfield anyway. This partially due to having my own reading tastes bend towards science fiction as a teen rather than the genre of Alienated Teen Literature, of which *Catcher* is, of course, the classic. If you were going to give me a teenage hero, give me Heinlein's Starman Jones: *He* traveled the galaxy and memorized entire books of log tables and became captain of a starship (for procedural reasons, granted). All Holden did was bitch, bitch, bitch. Put Holden at the controls of a starship and he'd implode from stress. Not *my* hero, thanks.

(Actually, if you're going to give me a teenage hero, give me Joan of Arc. There's an achiever for you: Kicks English tail and saves France, despite suffering from profound schizophrenia (Shaw argues that the voices were an expression of the "Evolutionary Appetite," but in truth, there's no reason they couldn't be both). Thank God she wasn't born in the 20th century; they would have medicated her ass into catatonia, and then the Germans would have been able to roll right over the French forces at the start of WWII! Hmmmmm.)

But it's also partially due to the nature of Holden, and my own nature as well. Holden is justly famous in the literary pantheon as being the first major teenage literary character to be allowed to note that the world was a tremendously screwed up place, and to have an intellectually appropriate response to that fact. All the other literary teens of the age were solving low-grade mysteries or having boy's own adventures or what not, and, golly, they were always polite and respectful to their elders. Holden was the proverbial turd in *that* punchbowl, and arriving as he did in the early 50s, just in time for rock n' roll and the first mass teen market, he offered the blueprint and pathology for teenage sullenness that's still fervently followed to this day (although, admittedly, the tattoos and piercings these days are a new touch).

However, I was not especially pained as a teen, and all attempts in that direction ended up as sort of twee, rather than genuinely dark and isolating. It was too bad, really, since I was all set up to accept Holden as a soulmate. I mean, *I* went to boarding school, *I* was somewhat sensitive, *I* had all that bundled up energy of wanting to change the world and not knowing quite how to do it. But I just didn't have that certain *something*—mistrust of society, desire for someone to encapsulate all my inexpressible teenage emotions, basically suspicious and snotty nature, or whatever—that would make me go cuckoo for Caulfield. I suppose it's a shortcoming. I failed angst in high school. They let me graduate anyway.

Fact is, I liked neither Holden nor the book. One can recognize the book has a certain literary merit without needing to like the thing, of course. But it's more to the point to say that Holden has a certain fundamental passivity that I dislike—the desire for people and things to be different without the accompanying acceptance of personal responsibility to effect those changes. To go back to Heinlein and his juvie novels, his teenage characters are not very big on internal lives, but they're also the sort who go out, do things, fail, do things again, and eventually get it right. Holden merely wishes, ultimately a man of inaction. He's a failure—a particularly attractive failure if you're of a certain age and disposition, admittedly, but a failure nonetheless. I remember reading the book as a teen and being irritated with Holden for that reason; I couldn't see why he required any sympathy from me, or why I should empathize with him.

It's been a fortunate thing that Salinger has sat back and rested on his increasingly thorny laurels for the last several decades, because in doing so he's spared us inevitable *Catcher* sequel, in which we learn whatever happened to that freaky Caulfield kid. Here's what I think. After a certain amount of time faking being deprogrammed, Holden goes to Brown and after graduation eventually gets a job at an ad firm, where, thanks to his ability to pitch products to "the kids," he does very well. He gets married, has a couple of kids, gets divorced, becomes a high-functioning alcoholic but is nevertheless eased towards the door with a generous buyout, and after that—well, after that, who cares? Sooner or later, the rest of one's life becomes a coda.

Big Holden fans will no doubt be upset with the life of hypocritical mediocrity I've provided for their anti-hero, but really, unless he committed suicide shortly after the end of the novel (not at all unlikely, given his creator's literary tendencies), he has to have caved. He was too passive to do otherwise. No Holden fan would be at all satisfied with this, of course—which may be one of the reasons Salinger packed it in. It's better for everyone involved if Holden's life coda begins before he's out of his teens. Everyone walks away happy, except, of course, for Holden himself. But that's as it should be.

HOW TO SEND
ME HATE MAIL

Mar

7

2002

Got some hate mail yesterday for my column about a cartoon from liberal Ted Rall, who attracts frothing conservatives like Angelina Jolie attracts questioning co-eds. However, it wasn't really *choice* hate mail, so I think it's a good time to offer up a primer on How To Send Me Hate Mail. Please pay attention, since these are valuable tips for composing winning hate mails that will stand out from the crowd.

First off, let's be clear that I *do* make a distinction between hate mail and people who disagree with me and e-mail to say so. E-mail me with a legitimate comment or question, no matter how negative, and I typically respond civilly. In Scalzi's World, it's not a crime to disagree with me, even if it does speak poorly regarding your judgment. However, if you just e-mail spew, I consider it hate mail and respond as such. Now that we're all clear, here are my Hate Mail Tips:

1. Don't Expect Too Much.

The fact is, hate mail really doesn't bother me, since fundamentally, if you're not my wife, a member of my immediate circle of family and friends, or a client, I don't actually give a damn about what you think of me. Life's too short to sweat other people's opinion, especially the sort of algae-grazers who have nothing better to do than write hate mail. Really, what *useful* person has the time for that? So, despite your best efforts, I'm just not likely to collapse into a heap of self-loathing on the basis of your hate mail. Sorry to disappoint; it's just the way I am.

Since I don't take hate mail to heart, what I'm looking for in hate mail is pure entertainment value. Which brings us to point number 2:

2. Be Creative.

Honestly, if you're going to take the time to tell me how much you *hate* me, make some effort to do it in a way that's not going to *bore* me. I've been called an "asshole" so many times in hate mail that it's just lost all its charm, as have all the major profanities. So, I take points off for profanities, unless they're used in really new and exciting ways. Here's a quick workshop on that, using that old reliable, "Fucker":

"Fucker"—No good. Plain. Uninspiring. Trite. Hardly registers a blip. Needs oomph. Needs…a modifer!

"Toad Fucker"—Better. "Toad" is not the usual modifier here, so that's good, and of course it's an interesting mental visual. But let's assume that any single modifier of "Fucker" is already old news, especially when it involves a noun springing from the animal kingdom. What we really need to do is to fuse "Fucker" to a string of truly interesting words. Like:

"Choad Mongering Krill Fucker"—*Now* we're talking. This insult works on so many levels. "Choad," of course, is a great piece of slang, not nearly utilized to its full potential in everyday invective, so it's still a nice fresh slap to start the insult. "Mongering," likewise a *great* verb: Sounds great, first off, but also obscure enough to thrill—after all, who mongers very much anymore? "Krill Fucker" implies that you're so hard up you'd screw a baleen whale's morning snack *and*, inasmuch as krill are microscopic shrimp, it also says you have a dinky little wanger (otherwise, of course, how could you fuck a krill? It'd just break apart). Finally, the phrase lends itself to multiple variations: "Dick Whoring Shrimp Porker," for example. The possibilities really are endless.

(While we're vaguely on the subject of animals, if you're going to compare someone to an animal, remember that lower orders of primates are intrinsically funny. Some of my favorites phrases: "Trepanned Lemur," "Ass-Mastering Aye-Aye," and "Enema-swilling Loris." Best of all, you don't even have to modify "bush baby.")

Remember, I get a lot of hate mail. To really register, you have to do the work. The satisfaction of knowing I'm really paying attention makes it worth the effort.

3. Prepare to Be Graded.

If I don't think your hate mail is up to snuff, I'll send it back with the suggestion you try harder. For example, yesterday someone sent me a message which was, in its entirety: "You're a prick, an' so's your little fuckin' friend" (referring to Ted Rall). I sent back, asking if that was *really* the best this guy could do, mentioning that I'd gotten better insults from retarded monkeys (as you can see, I don't respond back to such slack efforts with my "A" material).

The response: "Go fuck yourself, you nitwit." Again, not especially compelling. "A trepanned lemur could do better," I gently suggested, bringing out the lemurs in a bid to inspire my correspondent. "Please try again." He countered by saying Ted and I were "tremendous fucking idiots," which, in my book, was still rather disappointing. To his credit, however, he did appreciate the lemur reference. Which just goes to prove my point.

Look, I don't think it's too much to ask for a little effort when it comes to hate mail, so if I don't think the effort's there, I'm going to call you on it. On the flipside, if you come up with a choice piece of spew, I'll compliment you on your form, and if it's *really* good, I'll probably start using it as a .sig quote for my e-mail. Here's one of my favorites:

"You can continue to be a negative force in the universe, spewing putrid venom, childish disdain, and unmitigated disgust for everyone who doesn't offer you sex or money—or whatever else it is that you might like."

I mean, how can you *not* appreciate the craft? I used that as a .sig quote for months.

4. Be Accurate.

The hate mailer in the first part of tip 3 called me a "fuckwit cartoonist," which would be a passable insult ("fuckwit" is okay) were it not for the fact that I'm not a cartoonist nor have I ever been. The guy just assumed that since I was talking about Ted, I was a cartoonist my-self. I pointed out his error and the guy got all huffy—like his errone-ous assumption was somehow *my* fault! Just remember that when you assume, you make an "ass"-mastering aye-aye out of "u" and "me." I'll be watching for those little slip-ups.

Hopefully these tips will inspire those of you who aspire to write me hate mail to new and ever more creative heights. Good luck! I'll be waiting to see what you come up with—and I'll be sure to let you know just what I think of your efforts.

THE CHILD ON THE TRAIN

Jan

1

2003

About a week after Krissy completed the first trimester of her pregnancy, she went in to the doctor to have a routine checkup for herself and her baby. While she was being examined, the doctor had difficulty finding the baby's heartbeat. This in itself was not unusual—at just over three months, a fetus is still a small thing. The sound of its nascent heartbeat is easy to lose in the other sounds of the body. But by the next day, Krissy had begun to spot and bleed, and shortly thereafter she miscarried. As with nearly a quarter of all pregnancies, the processes that form and shape a life had stopped at a certain point well short of completion, and for whatever reason this child would not be born. It was a death in the family.

By and large, we kept the matter to ourselves, telling the people who needed to know—family and close friends—but otherwise saying nothing. I had written about Krissy's pregnancy on my Web site, as I had written about Krissy's first pregnancy—and why not, since a pregnancy (at least in the context of a happily married and financially secure couple) is a happy thing. For a writer, there's a lot of material to discuss, so long as it's done in a tasteful manner that doesn't have one's pregnant wife planning to beat one in the head with a pan. But a miscarriage is obviously something different. There's no way to write on one's Web site, in a breezy and conversational style, that a pregnancy has ceased.

Even if there were, the event was too close and too personal to share in that way. Celebration should be public, by definition, but grief is a fragile thing. Grief is a small, difficult and necessary visitor that dwells in your home for some little time, and then has to be gently encouraged to depart. Crowds make it nervous and inclined to stay put. We didn't want that. We figured anyone who learned of it later would understand. We held our grief close and then after enough time, bid it farewell and set it on its way.

And it *is* gone; its time in our house was brief. Our friends, our family, and most of all our daughter helped see to that. One cannot stand in the face of such fortunate circumstances as we have and wish to cling to grief. There is too much that is good in our lives together to stay sad for long. So we didn't.

Were you to express your condolences to us today, we would of course thank you for them—we know they're sincere and we know they're meant from the heart. But we would hope you would also understand when we said "thank you" and then chatted with you about something else entirely, it's not because we are pained about revisiting the grief. It's that the grief is like a shirt that is six sizes too small. It fit once, but it doesn't fit now, and trying to get it back over our heads would be an exercise in futility.

I mention the miscarriage now primarily because this is around the time that Krissy would have been due, and various correspondents have been asking about it. When I write back that Krissy has miscarried, they're all deeply apologetic for bringing up what they (not unreasonably) assume is a painful topic. And of course, it's not their fault at all, since I mentioned the pregnancy but not the miscarriage. I really don't want anyone else to feel horrifyingly embarrassed because of *my* decision not to discuss certain information.

I also want to avoid scenes like that one I had in October, in which I was standing around with a circle of casual acquaintances. One of them was discoursing about the danger of asking other casual acquaintances about their personal lives, since there's always something horrible that's happened—and no sooner did this acquaintance finish saying this than she asked me how Krissy's pregnancy was coming along. Rarely has someone posited a statement and proved it with such brutal efficiency. I felt bad that my omission put her in such a situation. So now it's out there.

I should mention that the fact that we've left behind the grief of the miscarry does not mean the event is forgotten; or perhaps it's better to say that the child we lost is not now nor ever will be forgotten by us. It is, as I've said, a death in the family, and while the small absence it created is small indeed, it is yet still an absence. It doesn't go away, and even though we see it without grief, we recognize it exists. It would be wrong to pretend it does not.

If I could describe to you what a miscarry feels like from an emotional point of view, I would ask you to imagine a dream in which you are standing on a train station platform. While you are waiting, you look through the dirty windows of the train car in front of you and see a small child looking back at you. The child's face is indistinct because of condition of the windows, but what you can see looks achingly familiar. For a moment, the child is separated from you by only that single, dirty pane of glass. Then the train starts to move, and the child starts to move with it.

And you realize that the reason you're on the platform at all is because you're waiting for your own child to arrive, a child you have yet to meet. And you realize that you could have claimed that child as your own. And you know that whatever child eventually comes to you, you will love that child like the sun loves the sky, like the water loves the river, and the branch loves the tree. The child will be the greater whole in which you dwell.

But it will never be that child, the one you could only glimpse, the one who went away from you. All you can do is remember, and hope with everything in your heart that the child who went away from you finds another who will love it as the sun loves the sky, the water loves the river, and the branch loves the tree. You pray and you hope and you never forget. That's what you do. That's what I do.

UNFAIR

One of the nice things about writing something mildly controversial, such as the Big Bang and Creationism or Confederate idiocy, is that it brings in a number of new readers, many of whom are not familiar with my rhetorical style and are therefore shocked about how mean and unfair I am to whatever position it is that they have that I don't. So let's talk about being "fair" for a moment.

Basically, for the purposes of the Whatever, I'm wholly uninterested in it. Complainants about my unfairness have suggested that as a journalist (or having been one in the past), I should know something about being fair and objective. Well, I admit to having been a journalist now and again, although when I worked at the newspaper I was primarily a film critic and a columnist, jobs which were all about being subjective. So I wouldn't go entirely out of my way to trumpet my own rich personal history of journalistic endeavors. I can do traditional journalism, and when I do it, I do a very good job of it. But it's never been my main thing; opinion is what what I got paid for in my time as a journalist.

This space is not about journalism; never has been, never will be. It's about whatever's on my brain at the moment (hence the name), and it makes no pretense of being anything else. This gets written in the interstitial time between paid writing assignments; it's meant to be a venting mechanism and a practical way to keep writing in a certain style—the writer's equivalent of doing scales—so that when I do this sort of thing on a paid basis (it does happen), I'm ready to go.

But ultimately it's all about me: I pick the topics, I comment on the topics, and the basis for the comments is whatever I'm thinking about the subject. I. Me. Mine. It's all me, baby. What's going on in my head is inherently unfair because it comes from my own, singular point of view; I don't try to consider every point of view on a subject when I write about something here: I don't have the time, for one thing, and for another thing I don't have an inclination.

If you have your own opinion, don't expect me to air it for you, unless you understand that typically when I present other people's points of view here it's to point out why they are so very wrong wrong *wrong*. Expecting me or anyone to validate your point of view out of the goodness of our hearts seems a dangerously passive thing to do. You have a functioning brain and an Internet connection; get your own damn Web page. Don't worry, I won't expect you to be "fair," either.

But I doubt that many of the people who want me to be "fair" are actually asking for actual fairness, anyway. What they want is some sort of murmured polite dissent to whatever beef-witted thing they want to promulgate, something that implicitly suggests that their ideas have legitimacy and should be discussed reasonably among reasonable people.

To which my response is: Well, no. Your opinion that whatever it is you want to foist on the world is reasonable does not mean that I have to agree, or treat it with the "fairness" you think it deserves. Rest assured that I am "fair" to the extent that I give every idea I encounter the respect I think it rates.

To take the two most recent examples of this, by and large Creationism (from a scientific point of view) is complete crap; therefore I am rightfully critical of attempts to teach it (or its weak sister "intelligent design") in science classes. Likewise, denying that the Confederate flags represent evil is pure twaddle and I'm not required to treat the idea that they don't with anything approaching seriousness. You may not like this position, but ask me if I care. If you want me to treat your ideas with more respect, get some better ideas.

(Somewhat related to this, I've noticed that most of the people bitching about "fairness" to me tend to be conservative in one way or another.

This makes sense as the topics I've been writing about recently fall into the conservative camp. However, inasmuch as conservatives have written the manual on how to demonize those who hold unconforming views—please refer to Newt Gingrich on this—this position strikes me as awfully rich. Not every single conservative person can be held responsible for the rhetorical attack-dog manner of many public conservatives, of course. But on the other hand, I'm not particularly moved by complaints of my mild version here. It's like someone from a family of public gluttons castigating someone else for going back to the buffet for a second helping.)

I'm likewise not responsible for your reading comprehension of what I've written. I do of course try to be coherent—it's a good thing for a writer to attempt—but what I write and what you think I wrote can be two entirely separate things. More than one person saw what I wrote about Creationists the other day as a general broadside on Christians and Christianity. However, had I wanted to do broadside swack at Christians in general, I would have written "Christians" rather than "Creationists"—the two words not being synonymous, after all.

Another good example of this is when I mention a particular stance is likely caused by ignorance. Well, no one likes to be called "ignorant," since the common opinion is that people who are ignorant are also typically dumber than rocks. However, ignorance does not imply stupidity; it merely implies lack of knowledge. Ignorance is correctable; stupidity, unfortunately, is typically irreversible. The good news is that rather more people are ignorant than stupid, which means there's hope. So if you're ignorant, congratulations! You can work on that.

I'm happy to clear up any misunderstandings or offer any clarifications if you have questions; send along an e-mail, I'll respond if I can. But generally, in terms of my writing here, I tend to be a strict constitutionalist—what I mean to say is usually in the text itself.

I recognize that a lot of people will consider my utter lack of concern regarding "fairness" here as proof that I'm unreasonable or disinterested in hearing other points of view, but again, that's another assumption over which I have no control. Likewise people may assume that I'm exactly like I write here, which is also not entirely accurate; what's here is just one aspect of my total personality, not the complete picture. It does no good to assume that people are only what they write, but I'm not going to lose sleep over it if you think that about me. I can accept a certain amount of unfairness. Life, after all, is famous for not being fair.

THE INEVITABLE BLACKNESS THAT WILL ENGULF US ALL

Mar

30

2007

Adam Ziegler, who I think really needs a hug, asks:

The world is a sad place. One can argue that some things have improved in recent centuries and decades, yet with every turn of the sun, parents lose their beloved children, innocents are maimed or forced in slavery, wars rage, and most people on this planet endure grinding poverty. We live atop a mountain of sorrows, made higher still by our ongoing misery.

But you are fortunate. By luck of birth and the skill of your hands, you have escaped the fate of most. You earn a generous wage as an entertainer. You have a beautiful family, your health, a comfortable home. But all of it could end tomorrow.

Even if you are one of those rare individuals who can live every moment in the present; even if you know in your bones that life is what you make of it, you are still an intelligent person who knows the state of the world and how fortunate you are to have your fragile place within it. You know that, in the end, most of what you say or do will matter very little. You know that you, your family, everyone you know and everything you have worked for must someday come to ruin and dust.

My question: Does it make you sad? How do you deal?

Well, I deal with it, first, by not thinking about it all a tremendous amount. I do that largely by keeping busy. It's funny how just the simple act of answering a day's worth of e-mail will keep the crushing inevitability of the entropic heat death of the universe at bay for a good half hour to an hour. *There, I've tidied up my inbox. Take that, proton decay!* Having an eight-year-old in the house—while certainly increasing entropy—does also help to keep me sufficiently distracted. I'm surely aware this sounds like a dodge—fiddling while Rome pops out of existence one sub-atomic particle at a time—but it really *does* work, and if you are the sort to obsess about everything eventually turning into dust, then keeping busy is a good make-work solution for being overwhelmed by the ennui that comes from recognizing that nothing you do will matter 500 years from now, anyway. And this way at least all your e-mail gets answered.

The second way I deal with it is to have a sense of perspective about the matter. Look, at the end of the day, trillions of years from now, *everything* in this universe is going to disappear. It's right there on the label marked "quantum physics." Long before this happens, just five billion years from now, the sun will turn into a red giant, likely swallowing the Earth and reducing it to a cinder. Long before that—billions of years before that—changes in the sun's internal workings will render our planet uninhabitable. And long before *that*—in the relatively short period of time of a few million years—it's very likely we'll be extinct because unless you're a shark or an alligator, the chance that your species will simply peter out after a few million years is really rather excellent. We're likely with the majority there, even if we weren't busily altering our environment so rapidly it's like we're daring future generations of humans to survive.

With the exception of the very *last* of these, there's not that much to be done about it; the universe is not notably sympathetic to our cries that we should be special and eternal. *It's nice you feel that way,* the universe is telling us, *but one day I'm going to end and I'm going to take you with me.* Once you wrap your brain around this simple and unalterable fact—the fact that not even the *universe* is getting out of here alive—the rest of it comes pretty easy. And you realize that to some extent worrying about enduring when your genome will dissolve, your planet will dry up, your sun will engulf your home and every single thing that ever was in the universe will randomly pop out of existence, a particle at a time, is a little silly. This frees you to stop freaking out about what will happen in the future and focus on what the hell's going on now.

Yes, tomorrow I die in any number of ways; tomorrow anyone I know and love could do the same. 50 years from now I have a very good chance of being dead; 60 years from now it'll be a near-certainty; 100 years from now it's unlikely that anyone alive will be reading my work. Honestly, have *you* read a book from 1907? That year, the best selling book was *The Lady of the Decoration*, by Frances Little; prior to just now looking up this info, I'd not heard of either the book or the author. Nor, prior to just now, had I heard of *The Port of Missing Men, Satan Sanderson, The Younger Set* or *Half a Rogue*, best sellers all, or of Meredith Nicolson, Hallie Erminie Rives, Robert W. Chambers or Harold McGrath, their authors. These were the *best sellers* of the year. My books sell just fine today, thanks, but if I can't be bothered with *Half a Rogue*, it seems doubtful the citizenry of 2107 will have much use for *The Last Colony*.

Does this make me sad? Not really. Sure, it'd be nice to be remembered eternally, or, at least as long as people read, but that's not really up to me, and I just think it's dumb to spend much time worrying about it—and indeed, for as much as I *like* like my writing, I think I'd be a little worried for the future if 200 years from now I was hailed as one of the great literary lights of our age. It would make me wonder what really interesting selective apocalypse occurred that only my work and work inferior to it survived.

My work is meant to be read *now*. If it survives and is enjoyable 20 or 40 years in the future, excellent; I'll be happy to enjoy the royalties and the low-to-moderate notability it provides. But I don't worry about writing for the ages; the ages will decide what they want to read by themselves, and I won't be around to care either way. I think intentionally writing for the ages is a fine way to psyche yourself out and assure whatever it is you're writing is stiff and pretentious, and frankly there are very few writers who are so preternaturally good at this gig that they should flatter themselves that the contemporaries of their great-great-great grandchildren will give a crap. Ask Frances Little or Harold McGrath about this one. I want to give people a good read that doesn't insult their intelligence and also pays my mortgage. If eternal art comes out of these desires, groovy. If not, then I still get to eat.

Moving away from my work to more ineffable aspects of my personal life, yes, I'm aware of the fragility of life and the suddenness with which circumstances can change. Today my life is good; there are any number of ways it could go crushingly wrong. Aside from basic and laudable prophylaxis, however (i.e., pay bills on time, live within means, buckle seatbelts, teach child basic moral standards, etc) I'm not sure that there's much benefit in thinking too much about all the ways things could get horrible, fast. So I don't. Being capable of understanding the downside—to anything—does not suggest that one is obliged to model it in one's head more than is absolutely necessary. Short of actually experiencing horrible wrenching change, I believe I am as prepared as a person can be for its possibility. Worrying about it beyond that point is useless overthinking; I've got enough stuff to do already.

Finally, in the larger sense—the one in which I am a citizen of the world, that I like no man am an island, blah blah blah blah blah, it becomes a matter of asking one's self first whether one wants to be engaged in the world, and then if so, how best to be of utility. I do enough things that I feel engaged in my world and I feel like I'm trying to do beneficial things (or at least I'm doing as little harm as possible). I think it's my responsibility to try to make the world a better place than it was before I got here; I don't feel obliged to be heart-rent at every thing that's wrong with the planet. One person can make a difference in the world, so long as that one person realizes that one person can not do everything or be actively concerned with every damn thing. I pick and choose; everyone does. I focus on what I think I do well and where I think I can do good.

Now, I understand that these answers would suggest a certain and elemental shallowness to my nature—a willingness *not* to think about topics or issues that are weighty in themselves and worth thinking about. What I'm leaving out here, for the space of relative brevity, is a detailed examination of processes by which I came to this intellectual methodology, generated through years of self-examination and self-realization via intentional and unintentional experiential phenomena, to produce the robust heuristic structure through which I filter data. As regards that, let me just say that I've had a life, and I've paid attention, and this is what works for me.

I don't discount that in the end, everything I do, say, write and am will amount to a whole lot of not much; I just don't think it's a relevant metric. The relevant metric is: Have I constructed a life that gives me happiness, allows me to *give* happiness, and allows for this life to have meaning within its admittedly limited context? If I am succeeding in this particular metric, I think I'm doing pretty well. Yes, one day my species will be replaced by hyper-intelligent squids, the earth will turn into a charcoal briquette and the universe will end in an increasingly thin proton soup. But that's all waaaaaay in the future. Right now, things are good.

How DRM
is Like
Guantanamo

Jan
17
2007

How is Guantanamo like DRM, you ask? They're alike in two ways: First for what they are not, and then for what they represent.

Let's begin with the first: Both are used by the people who have created them for purposes other than what they're ostensibly used. In the case of DRM, it exists not primarily to combat piracy but to amputate the right of "fair use." In the case of Guantanamo, it isn't primarily for harboring dangerous terrorists but for concretely embodying the extra-constitutional idea of expanded executive powers.

Both represent different immediate aims, but both are *bad* for precisely the same reason: they're about taking a society based on rights and turning it into a society based on access. In the case of DRM, the idea being posited is that we don't have fair use, or the right to personal copies of work we've purchased—the originator of the material has every right to the work, in perpetuity, and access to that work is given on sufferance. In the case of Guantanamo, the idea being posited is that the executive has the ability to create a new framework of rights, irrespective of those outlined in the Constitution, which means that the executive, not the Constitution, is that from which our rights derive, and access to those rights is given on sufferance. And in fact in both cases there are no *rights* at all for the individual or the public. There's only *access*, controlled by entities whose list of priorities are not notably congruent to those of the public, and are likely to become less so over time, so that access is progressively more strictly managed.

None of this is new, of course, and it's axiomatic that yesterday's freedom fighters are today's rights pocketers. Hollywood—where the push for DRM is based—was founded by pirates who fled the east coast and the monopoly imposed on film by the Edison Trust. The Bush Administration—which has vigorously attempted to expand executive power—is the final reduction of a political movement begun in part as resistance to the expanded executive powers assumed by FDR. But just because these are merely This Year's Model of rights arrogation doesn't mean they don't need to be fought against.

One of the interesting things about right *now* is that I think we're in the (very) early days of the pushback. People are better educated about how DRM messes with their ability to do what they want with the stuff they own; people are fatigued with and suspicious of the Bush Administration and its goals and motives. Naturally neither DRM promoters nor the executive ascendancy crew are going to go down without a fight; the question is whether now being on the defensive makes them more canny in achieving their goals or will simply cause the backlash to be even more intense. I have no idea, personally, although I suspect things aren't going to get any easier for either group from here on out.

I'll tell you what I hope for, however. In the case of DRM, I think the entertainment companies will eventually recognize it's bad business. I have nothing against renting when I'm actively renting (I love my Rhapsody music service for a reason), and I think DRM is perfectly fine there. When you buy something, however, you shouldn't need permission to do what the hell you want with it. I personally ignore or break DRM when I come across it on things I buy, and if it's not possible to do either I don't buy the product. In the case of executive overreach, naturally I'd like to see that reined in by more active and engaged Congress and courts, and by members of all political persuasions who at least temporarily will put the text of the Constitution ahead of political expediency. I suspect by dint of its sheer incompetence, the Bush administration has admirably exemplified why the executive branch should not be legally ascendant above the other branches of government; this may indeed be the only useful thing to come out of this administration. But as in all things we will have to see.

I will say I'm looking forward to the day that DRM and Guantanamo—and the philosophy of rights they symbolize—plop onto the dustbin of history. That'll be a good day for me, and for us.

LEVITICANS

Feb

24

2004

On occasion people ask me what, exactly, it is I have against Christianity, inasmuch as I seem to rail against it quite a bit. My general response is: I have nothing against Christianity. I wish more Christians practiced it. The famous bumper sticker says "Christians aren't perfect, just forgiven," but I often wonder just how often they check in with Christ about that last one. I look at the picture I saw recently, of a kid with an allegedly Christian group protesting the gay marriages in San Francisco, wearing the shirt that has "homo" written on it with a circle and slash through the word, and I try to find some of Christ's teachings in that. As you might imagine, I'm finding very little.

If that kid were hit by a bus and got to meet Christ shortly thereafter, I do imagine the conversation would be a sorrowful one, as the homo-negating young man would have to try to reconcile his shirt with the admonition to love others as one loves one's self. I would imagine at the end of that conversation, the young man would be looking to see if Christ were holding a lever, and if there were a trap door under the young man's feet.

In a recent comment thread, one of the posters wondered why many fundamentalists spend so much time in Leviticus and so little time in the New Testament, and I think that's a remarkably cogent question. Indeed, it is *so* cogent that I would like to make the suggestion that there is an entire class of self-identified "Christians" who are not Christian at all, in the sense that they don't follow the actual teachings of Christ in any meaningful way. Rather these people nod toward Christ in a cursory fashion on their way to spend time in the bloodier books of the Bible (which tend to be found in the Old Testament), using the text selectively as a support for their own hates and prejudices, using the Bible as a cudgel rather than a door. That being the case, I suggest we stop calling these people Christians and start calling them something that befits their faith, inclinations and enthusiasms.

I say we call them Leviticans, after Leviticus, the third book of the Old Testament, famous for its rules, and also the home of the passages most likely to be thrown out by Leviticans to justify their intolerance (including, in recent days, against gays and lesbians—Leviticus Chapter 18, Verse 22: "Thou shalt not not lie with mankind, as with womankind; it *is* abomination").

To suggest that a Christian is actually a Levitican is not to say he or she is false in faith—rather, it is to suggest that their faith is elsewhere in the Bible, in the parts that are easy to understand: The rules, the regulations, all the things that are clear cut about what you can do and what you can't do to be right with God. Rules are far easier to follow than Christ's actual path, which needs humility and sacrifice and the ability to forgive, love and cherish even those who you oppose and who oppose and hate you. Any idiot can follow rules; indeed, there's a good argument to made that idiots can *only* follow rules. This is why Leviticans love Leviticus (and other pentateuchal and Old Testament books): Chock full of rules. And you can believe in rules. That's *why* they're rules.

So, back to the guy with the "homo" shirt. Is he a Christian? Well, on the basis of his actions, it would appear not. But he's undoubtedly a Levitican—a Levitican is just the sort of person who would go to the San Francisco City Hall and yell at gays and lesbians for having the temerity to want the same rights as the rest of us. Fred Phelps and his merry band of followers who picket funerals of gay men with "God Hates Fags" signs are Leviticans through and through—not a drop of Christ in them, but they sure are full of their Bible books. John Ashcroft: Filled with the Levitican spirit and not terribly shy about it. Pat Roberts and Jerry Falwell showed their Levitican membership cards right after 9/11 when they suggested that America invited the terrorist attacks by being tolerant of "the pagans, and the abortionists, and the feminists, and the gays and the lesbians who are actively trying to make that an alternative lifestyle." The guys who shoot abortion doctors: Leviticans to the core. Judge Roy "Put those ten commandments in the rotunda" Moore: Levitican. Hardcore.

Let's be clear: Not every Christian is a Levitican, not by a long shot. Not every fundamentalist Christian is a Levitican. And not every person who believes that allowing gays and lesbians to marry is morally wrong is Levitican, either. (Also to be clear: Although Leviticus is part of the Torah, I don't see too many Leviticans among the Jews, who in my experience see the Torah as a jumping off point to engage the world rather than a defense against it.) People of good will can disagree, vehemently, about what it right and what is wrong, what is moral and what is immoral, and what should be done about it. What makes a Levitican, in my book at least, is the willingness to transmute one's beliefs into hate and intolerance, to deprive others of rights they ought to enjoy. Leviticans have ever been with us. They quoted the Bible to justify slavery. They quoted the Bible to try to keep women in the home. They quoted the Bible to keep the races pure. They quote the Bible to try to keep gays and lesbians from the benefits of marriage. And each time, after they've quoted the Bible to their satisfaction, they go out and use that justification for their hate to do terrible things.

In my opinion, the best thing Christians can do is recognize this group within their host—one that reads the same book, purports to follow the same teachings and alleges to worship the same Christ, but through its actions proves itself time and again to be something other than Christian. And I think Christians should ask these people: Who *are* you? Do you follow the loving example of Christ or do you follow the rules of Leviticus? Do you use the Bible to illuminate your love or justify your hate? When Christ comes back, how will you show that you've followed his path? By the number of people that you've loved, or the number of the people whom you have "righteously" opposed? Do you love Christ or do you love rules? Are you a Christian, or are you a Levitican?

As for the rest of us, I propose we do our best to separate the Christians from the Leviticans in our minds. I see no reason to blame those who genuinely follow Christ for the actions of those who merely use Christ as a shield for their own hates and fears. And when a Levitican comes across your path, politely point out to him or her what he or she really is: Not a Christian, merely a Levitican.

Most likely, the Levitican will hate you for it. But that just goes to prove the point.

A Quick Note to About-to-be-Married Gays and Lesbians

May

17

2004

I have married nine people. One of them I am married to; the other eight I have married to each other (two at a time). So I have some experience on the whole wedding and marriage thing. Please allow me the honor of sharing some of it with you.

Remember to breathe.

It's all right if you stumble over words during the vows, but don't screw up the name of your spouse.

If you feel yourself crying, go with it, but remember to sniffle strategically—tears are endearing in a wedding ceremony, a runny nose less so.

Don't lock your knees.

The old saying that if the ring gets jammed as you slip it on it means it'll be a troubled marriage is a contemptible lie, so don't let it worry you. But strategic use of talcum powder wouldn't hurt.

You will almost certainly have trouble focusing on anything but the face of your beloved during the ceremony; that's why there's a third person up there to direct traffic.

Even if you've written your own vows, you'll barely remember what you say. So don't sweat most of the words. It's the "I do" that counts.

Speaking of which, I think it's always better to say "I do" than "I will." You're going to be married in the future, but you're *getting* married *now*.

But remember, it's *your* wedding. Anyone else's opinion about what the two of you should do or say during the ceremony is strictly advisory.

When you're told to kiss your spouse, do it like you mean it.

Be aware that this last piece of advice will be almost entirely un-necessary.

When you plan your wedding, try to cover all contingencies. When the one thing you forgot could go wrong *does* go wrong during the wedding itself, accept it and keep going. Weddings are often imperfect, like the people in them. It doesn't mean they're not still absolutely wonderful (like the people within them).

Before the ceremony, pee early and often. I know. But look, you want to be up there with a full bladder? You'll be nervous enough.

Some people don't think you should invite your exes to the wedding. But I think it's not such a bad thing to have one person in the crowd slightly depressed that they let you get away. They'll get over it at the reception. Trust me.

There will not be nearly enough time at the reception to spend all the time you want with all the people you want to. They'll understand and will be happy for the time you can spare them.

Smashing wedding cake into each other's face is strictly amateur hour.

It's your best man's (or the equivalent's) job to remind people that at a wedding reception, as at the Academy Awards, speeches are best very short. You didn't spend an obscene amount on the catering just to have it grow cold as Uncle Jim blathers on.

Remind the DJ or band that they work for you, and they'll damn well play anything you want. For some reason I think this may be less of a problem at gay weddings. Thank God.

There will be drama of some sort at the reception. If the wedding party lets any of it reach the newlyweds, they haven't done their job.

Don't fill up on bread. You'll have to dance later.

The first dance should be a song people expect from you. The second dance should be a song they absolutely don't. It gets things going.

Try to remember as much as you can. Don't worry if you don't; what you absolutely *will* remember is how it feels to be with those who love you, who are pouring their love and happiness over you. Weddings are testimony to your clan of family and friends. You put them on to give them a chance to share your joy. They come to them to remind you that they already do.

In case this is in any way an issue, let someone else clean up the reception hall. You have better things to do on your wedding night.

There are very few things in the world that are better than the very first time you wake up next your spouse.

In some ways, your marriage will be like every other marriage out there. In other ways, of course, it won't. Those of us who are married now will certainly offer you advice, whether you ask for it or not. But there are some things where you'll be the first married people to experience them. In some ways, those of us who are married now will be glad we don't have to go through them. In other ways, we're deeply envious.

Marriage is work. It never stops being work. It never *should*.

I'll be married nine years next June 17th. During all that time, there hasn't been a single day where I haven't said "I love you" to my spouse—several times if at all possible. The two facts are related.

Other short phrases which also occasionally come in handy: "I'm sorry," "You're right," "I'll get that" and "Of course I'll go down to the freezer and get you some ice cream, even though it's 3 am and you woke me from a dead sleep. There's nothing I'd rather do." Okay, so that last one is not that short. Think about all the times *you're* entirely unreasonable, and then go get the ice cream.

The thing about marriages—even the really good ones—is that human beings are in them. And you *know* how people are. Keep it in mind.

I have no advice to give you for the people who have decided that your marriage threatens their own. Only remember that some of us out here would wish to give you the strength to endure them.

I cannot speak for all married people, but I can speak for myself. Marriage has been so good to me that I cannot imagine not sharing it with anyone who wants it. I celebrate your weddings, and I offer the greatest gift I have: That you receive in your married life the joy I have had in mine, and that you share that joy, every day, with an open and loving heart. You're about to be married. There is nothing better.

To those about to be married: Welcome, friends. It's good to have you here.

THE
PERMANENT
UNDERCLASS

After bagging on *Salon* so much in recent weeks, here's a plug: An article today on author Barbara Ehrenreich's descent into the underworld of the just-above-minimum-wage worker, the folks who are making $6 - $8 bagging your groceries or trimming your lawn or dusting your mantle or whatever. Ehrenreich did these gigs to see how people get by near the bottom of the economic ladder, and her conclusion, which comes to no surprise to anyone who has ever actually had to work in a Joe Job: A lot of these people aren't actually making it at all—they just live in a sort of limbo in which they make just enough to get to choose between eating and paying the gas bill every few months. And God forbid any of them ever get sick. Then they're really screwed.

The article struck a chord because, not to put too fine a point on it, I come from fairly white trashy background. We're talking a real live welfare cheese eater here, folks (it comes in a metal can the size of a tom-tom. So does welfare peanut butter). I'm not ashamed of my welfare days—among other things, it's not as if I had a choice in the matter—but I'm also fairly pleased that I'm no longer dragging along the bottom of the social net.

However, I'm also aware how little it takes to get trapped into the permanent poverty cycle. If you ever want to know what the real difference between being poor and not being poor is, the answer is truly and astoundingly simple: It's education. It really is. I'm the walking, talking, Web-writing proof of this. I'm the first person in my immediate family to finish high school, much less college. Consequently, I make more than all the other adult members of my family combined.

To be sure, there are other factors involved, relating to personality and particular circumstances. However, ultimately, the only difference that counts is that I had a college diploma to wave around when I first went looking for jobs. Simply put, if I hadn't gone to college, I wouldn't have gotten a job working at the *Fresno Bee*—you can't get a job at a newspaper of any size without a college degree anymore. If I hadn't had a high school diploma, well. I can't even imagine. The world would be full of jobs I couldn't have. There are millions of Americans, with no handicap other than the lack of one or two of these diplomas, who open the want ads and see nothing but jobs that someone else will get. So, damn it, kids, stay in school.

Every time I hear a well-fed conservative fart about how there's no need to raise the minimum wage, I have to fight the urge to give him a punch right in his fat face. I dare any of them to make a go of it at $17,229 a year, which is the official US poverty level for a family of four. That comes out to $8.61 an hour, presuming a 40-hour work week and 50 weeks of work a year—well above minimum wage. Find an apartment ('cause you certainly couldn't afford a house), find a car that you can afford that won't crap out on you and whose tank you can afford to fill, pay your gas and electric bills, pay for food and for clothing, and hope you don't fall ill, because there isn't a chance in hell you can afford health insurance.

If you can manage *that*, then try it on the *actual* Federal minimum wage, which is $5.15 an hour ($10,300). Anyone who thinks the minimum wage is adequate for anything but beer money has simply never had to exist on it.

W

Ironically, while I have immense sympathy for the poor schmucks who earn $6 an hour washing cars or whatever, I find that I am utterly and entirely intolerant of college-educated people who gripe about their finances. A friend and I were e-mailing each other about it the other day; she wrote "If you're able-bodied and have a college education, there should be no whining allowed," and I have to say that I agree with this philosophy completely.

Despite the downturns in the new economy sector of things, unemployment nationwide is still at really low rates, 4.5% or something like, and unemployment for the college-educated is of course, even lower. Generally speaking, there is *no* reason a college graduate cannot work and make enough to get by pretty well. Even those people with useless degrees. After all, I have a degree in philosophy. What the hell am I ever going to do with *that*?

I cheerfully note that "get by pretty well" is an economic standard, not a mental happiness standard—i.e., lots of college-educated people make enough money but are desperately unhappy with their jobs because the jobs "aren't them," or however you want to phrase it. I'm actually very pleased whenever someone tells me they're unhappy with their job for a reason like this—it means the economy is so good that people can allow themselves self-pity because all their job gives them is money. You know that in the Depression, people weren't bitching about the fact their lousy jobs didn't allow for self-realization. *Eating* takes precedence over self-realization. If shallow 20- and 30somethings can gripe about needing to find themselves in their work, you're in good times. Live it up.

(I'll also cheerfully note that I was one of those shallow 20somethings—I left my job at the *Fresno Bee* specifically because they cut my humor column and wanted me to do more straight-ahead reporting, and—stomp stomp pout pout—I didn't *wanna*. It was '96, the beginning of the 'Net boom. Would I have done the same thing five years earlier, when there was a recession and college grads were begging for jobs? Hell, no. Timing counts.)

Be that as it may, the initial theory still applies—college degree, no whining. And, to be entirely honest, I think this goes double with "creative" types, who nobly starve for their art. Two words: Day Job. A Day Job is a (not-yet-digustingly-successful) creative person's best friend. Very few people are insanely creative 24 hours a day (and those that are often have more emphasis on the *insane* than the *creative*), so why not fill those hours in which you'd otherwise be agonizing over your personal sense of self-worth with cash-generating busywork?

I think college is the best thing that can happen to someone economically, but I also believe that with that diploma you agree to throw certain things out the window, among them the right to garner sympathy for your financial position. If you're educated enough to get a degree, you're educated enough to make money (I say "educated" rather than "smart," since lots of smart people are unfortunately not educated). If you're educated enough to make money, then go out and make it. Really, it's not that hard. At least, not right now. And thank God for that.

THE TERROR OF
BAD CHOCOLATE

Apr

22

2002

Some people believe bad chocolate is like bad sex: Even when it's bad, it's still good. This formulation is nonsense at its root. Bad sex is definitely *not* still good. It's actually tremendously depressing, sort of like getting all worked up go to Disneyland just to find that the only ride open in the whole park is the monorail to and from the parking lot—and that the monorail seats smell kind of funky.

Secondly, bad chocolate is *worse* than bad sex. We accept that sex may occasionally be bad—it's the inevitable side effect of being human and letting hormonal surges replace rational thought—but chocolate is supposed be above that. Chocolate is supposed to be an absolute good. Occasional bad sex is regrettable, but bad chocolate is a betrayal.

What's even worse is when you see a Bad Chocolate Moment coming, and yet there's not much you can do about it. One of those happened last night, when Krissy tossed me a small plastic tub of something pink and asked me to open it for her. I looked down at the tub, and saw that they were, in fact, Frankford MarshMiddles Chocolate Crème-Filled (artificially flavored) Marshmallow Eggs, inexplicably left unopened during the orgy of Easter candy.

Immediately, several issues presented themselves:

1. For people over the age of 10, marshmallow candies are not meant to be eaten so much as they are to be used for various scientific experiments, generally involving microwave ovens, liquid nitrogen and/or Bunsen burners. That's because people over the age of 10 generally understand that marshmallow comes from gelatin, which comes from something that was scraped off a rural route with a shovel or that once participated in the Kentucky Derby and finished somewhere between 8th and 12th. Also the freshness of marshmallow candies has a half-life shorter than even the most unstable of transuranic elements. The tub proclaimed it was a "Resealable Stay-Fresh Tub!" which was nothing more than a contemptible lie. A stainless steel holding chamber filled with inert helium can't keep marshmallows from going stale. All told, there are better ways of getting a sugar high than tolerating stale sugar suspensions whose origins inevitably lead back to something with a mane, big soulful eyes, and a small Guatemalan in checkered pants sitting on its back.

2. "Chocolate Crème"—"crème" in the context of candy almost always means "unnatural chain of sucrose polymers." It's edible only to the extent that your white cells won't actively attack it as it courses through your small intestine.

3. "Artificially Flavored"—Artificially flavored chocolate is to chocolate as grape soda is to grapes, which is to say a concoction whose only relation to its natural analog is that it is within ten Pantone strips of being the same color.

4. On top of this the marshmallow eggs looked like decapitated Peeps, and that's just *wrong*.

The artificial flavor theme was reinforced when I cracked open the tub, exposing myself to the sort of chemical smell one typically associates with killing weeds.

I looked over to my wife. "Sweetheart," I said.

"Yes?"

"This might not be an optimal chocolate experience," I warned.

She looked at me blankly, as if *this might not be an optimal chocolate experience* were words from a Tristan Tzarza poem, pulled out of a hat and set down in random order and thereby devoid of all semantic value. Then, "Why did you say that? Did you *eat* one?"

No," I admitted, with my voice providing a subtext there signifying that while I might smear one across a new picture to stop the photographic development process, I wouldn't actually put one in my mouth. "It's just a feeling I have. I just don't want you to be disappointed."

My wife gave me a look as if to say, *you dear, silly man, give me the chocolate before I am compelled to gnaw on your aorta.* So I did, and went back to the magazine I was reading.

For this reason, I missed the part where Krissy gagged and actually spit the chocolate crème-filled marshmallow egg back into her hand rather than have it inhabit her mouth any longer. However, I didn't miss the part where she picked up the small tub they came in and stuffed it as far down into the trash as it would go. Then she looked over with a face that suggested that she'd just been fed the rancid gut of a raccoon (which, considering what gets used to make gelatin, there's a small possibility she had). But more than that, it was a tragic look of betrayal. Chocolate isn't supposed to do *that* to your mouth. Thus the quick trash stuff. It was too late for Krissy's innocence about chocolate to remain unshattered—but *not* too late to spare our daughter. By plunging the Pink Menace into the garbage, Athena might be spared the same horrible fate. Krissy did it for the children.

As for my Krissy, I just happened to have a bag of Cadbury solid chocolate candy eggs, so quickly enough the crisis had passed. But I guarantee you from now until the end of time, I could say to her, "hey, remember those chocolate crème-filled marshmallow eggs," and it will generate a hearty shudder. It was Bad Chocolate. And you just don't forget a thing like that.

THE EXISTENTIAL PLIGHT OF CHESTER CHIPMATE

Feb
12
2007

The cereal box on my breakfast table features someone named Chester, the mascot for the "ChipMates" line of cookie cereal. On it, you can see him doing his thing, opening his arms wide in celebration of the cereal brand which he is exhorting you to enjoy in all its flavorful, vitamin-enriched kidtastic goodness. He is cute and non-threatening, particularly for one who is clearly meant—by attire and accoutrements—to be a pirate. As required by the National Code of Cereal Mascots, his eyes are wide and unlidded, his eyebrows arched with pleasure and his mouth ever so slack, showing just a hint of tongue, as if to imply the joy of consuming the cereal is so great that one's brain simply cannot ask one's jaws to clamp down and risk not tasting the powdery, particulate fragments that hover in the air above the bowl, jostled up after the cereal has tumbled the distance from the box to the bowl's concave surface. He is everything a cereal mascot is meant to be.

And yet.

What do we really know of Chester? What is his story? What are his motivations for presenting this bowl of cereal to us? To which of the two great cereal mascot archetypes does he belong? Is he a Taster, one of the lucky mascots, like Tony the Tiger or Toucan Sam, who gets to enjoy the product he is so assiduously pitching? Or is he a Chaser, one of those poor bastards like the Trix Rabbit, doomed to the Sisyphean task of promoting a cereal he himself is never once allowed to enjoy? The pirate garb suggests he is a Chaser; after all, pirates spend their time chasing booty, which they may or may not ever get. But on the other hand, perhaps this pirate already has his treasure—these dun, chocolate-spotted discs of corn and oats—in which case, like Lucky the Leprechaun, he would be tasked with keeping said treasure from cute but frighteningly rapacious children who chase him about trying to get it for their own. Which would put him solidly in the Taster camp. Fact is, Chester could swing either way. We don't know.

And we can't know. And that is because Chester is the mascot not for a national brand of cereal, but for a store brand (or, as those in the industry call it, a "private label" brand), made for the Krogers supermarket chain here in America's heartland. As a mascot for a private label brand, Chester finds himself in an uncomfortable position. His job performance is hampered, not because of his lack of skill in his job, but by the simple mechanics of private label distribution. None of his efforts, for example, will ever get ChipMates into a Food Lion or a Safeway. They have their own private label cookie cereals, possibly with their own mascots—an excitable giraffe, perhaps, or maybe a baker out of his mind with cookie-based rapture.

But more than that, as a store brand mascot, Chester is denied the vehicle that would allow his character its narrative: The commercial. Everything we know of all the major cereal mascots comes in 30-second animated snippets; it's how we know Tony the Tiger is an excellent lifestyle coach, or that Snap, Crackle and Pop have virtuoso comic timing, or that the poor Trix Rabbit is in desperate and immediate need of therapy. We will never have these brief windows into Chester's soul; store brands aren't given commercials of their own. At best, they get a picture in an advertising circular or a second or two on a local TV ad, as the camera pans across a collection of private label items and some droning announcer declares the remarkable savings they afford. Two seconds of being panned across is not enough time to develop a coherent backstory. All Chester gets is the cereal box, and a single, ambiguous pose.

And, of course, he's lucky to get even that. Some mascots don't even get a box; think back on the humiliation visited upon Schnoz the Shark or Mane Man as they tried to entice consumers to their cereal in flimsy plastic bags, shelved, as they always were, on the bottom shelf of the cereal aisle. Think also on the extremely high rate of unemployment among cereal mascots. When was the last time Baron Von RedBerry got work? Or Twinkles the Elephant? Or Dandy, Handy 'N Candy? The dirty secret about being a cereal mascot is that if it doesn't work out—if your cereal flops or management decides to make a mascot change—you're through. You can't get work again. No other cereal will hire you. The best you can hope for is that somewhere along the way some advertising whiz kid decides to run a nostalgia campaign, and then you get trotted out again, gamely smiling for the camera and pathetically grateful that the income will help you get your meds (cereal mascots are ironically susceptible to several diseases related to vitamin deficiencies). Say what you will about the ignominy of being a store brand cereal mascot, but at least it's steady work. Creating new mascots for a private label brand is money the grocery store companies simply aren't going to pay.

Be that as it may, spare a moment for the existential plight of Chester Chipmate, a mascot without voice or history or personal motivation, an enigma wrapped in a mystery, coated in sugar and fortified with minerals. Who knows what wisdom he might impart to us if he had just one 30-second animated commercial? An exclamation that his wares are chiptastic? A promise that his cereal is good to the last crumb? An admonition that in this life we all have to make choices, and some choices come with their own pains, which we must accept with eyes wide, eyebrows arched, jaw slacked and tongue slightly visible? Perhaps all these things. Let us enjoy a bowl of ChipMates and think on it.

BEST CALENDAR
OF THE
MILLENNIUM

Dec

16

1999

The Mayan Calendar. I'm writing this on December 16, 1999—on the Mayan calendar, it's 12.19.6.14.6. That's right, only 5,485 days until the next baktun! Better hit the mall now!

Typically speaking, calendars do two things (beyond, of course, giving "Far Side" cartoonist Gary Larson a way to recycle decade-old cartoons for ready cash). First of all, they provide us with the ability to meaningfully note the passage of time. For example, today is the 226th anniversary of the Boston Tea Party, the 55th anniversary of the Battle of the Bulge and the 78th-month "anniversary" of my first date with my wife (we were obviously not married at the time). One week from today will be my daughter's first birthday. Send gifts.

All these events are contingent on our calendar for their notability relative to the time in which I exist; If we noted weeks and months differently, it might be the anniversary of something else entirely different. Months and weeks have no basis outside us: We made them up, or, if you prefer, God made them up, and we went with his basic plan (don't we always).

The second thing calendars do is notify us of the cyclical nature of our planet. Thanks to a more or less fixed tilt of the earth's axis and a regular period of revolution around our sun, our world gets hot and cold on a predictable schedule, and the patterns of life take note. Flowers bloom in the spring. Animals hibernate in the winter. Leaves fall in autumn. We get re-runs in the summer. It's the circle of life. For various reasons primarily relating to food, the planting and harvesting of, we've needed to know when to expect the seasons to come around again.

The problem has always been that humans have picked bad ways to note that passage of time. The biggest culprit has been the moon. It has a cycle, of course, about 29 days from new moon to new moon. Alas, that cycle has no real relation with the earth's position in its orbit. So while creating months relative to the moon (the word "month" is in fact etymologically descended from the old English word for "moon"), is perfectly fine for recording subjective blocks of time, it's rather less helpful in keeping track of when the seasons are coming. Sooner or later you'd get snow in July. And that would just wreak havoc on your baseball schedules.

Some of your smarter civilizations switched to a calendar in which the year was demarcated by the path of the sun (in the case of the Egyptians, they used Sirius, the Dog Star. Those crafty Egyptians). This was better, as there was, in fact, a direct relation of the sun's path and our year. But the rotation of the earth does not correspond exactly to its revolution. There's an extra quarter of the day (but not exactly a quarter of a day) thrown in for chuckles. Give it enough time, and your seasons and your months will still get away from you.

So you keep fiddling. Our current Gregorian calendar deals with it by inserting a leap day every four years, except in years that end with double zero, except those years which are cleanly divisible by 400. Like 2000. Don't worry, scientists are keeping track of these things for you. Be that as it may, there's *still* slippage. Calendars aren't an exact science.

Enter the Mayans, who, it should be noted, were the kick-ass mathematical minds of the pre-computational world (they used zeros before zeros were cool!). While everyone else was looking at the sun or the moon as a guidepost for the passage of time, the Mayans looked a little to the left of the sun and discovered…Venus, which as it happens, has an exceptionally predictable path around the sun that takes 584 days. Five of these cycles just happens to coincide with eight 365-day years. Thrown in a couple of additional formulae, and you can keep time that's damn near perfect—The Mayan calendar loses a day about once every 4000 years. Consider *we* can't go four years without having to plug in a day, and we've got atomic clocks and everything.

So why don't we switch to a Mayan calendar? Well, this is why:

First bear in mind that the Mayan kept track of two years simultaneously: the Tzolkin, or divinatory calendar, which is comprised of 260 days, demarcated by matching one of 13 numbers with one of 20 names (13x20=260—you can do at least *that* much math), and also another calendar of 18 months of 20 days, with five extra days known as the "Uayeb," for Days of Bad Omen (probably not a good time to do much of anything).

These two calendrical systems linked together once every 18,980 days (that's 52 years to you and me): this period of time was known as a "Calendar Round." Two calendar rounds, incidentally, make up another time period in which the Tzolkin, the 365-day calendar, and the position of Venus sync up again. Think of this as a Mayan century, if you will.

With me so far? Okay, because, actually, I lied. There's another calendar system you need to keep track of as well: The Long Count. Here's how *this* one works. You start off with a day, which in Mayan is known as a kin. There are 20 kin in a unial, 18 unials in a tun, 20 tun in a katun, and 20 katun in a baktun (so how many days is that? Anyone? Anyone? 144,000—roughly 394 years). Each of these is enumerated when you signify a date, with the baktun going first. However, remember that while kin, tun, and katun are numbered from 0 to 19, the unial are numbered from 0 to 17, while the baktun are numbered from 1 to 13. So if someone tries to sell you a Mayan calendar with a 14 in the baktun's place, run! He's a bad man!

And thus, combining our Long Count calendar with our Tzolkin and our 365-day calendar, we find that today (12/16/1999) is 12.19.6.14.6, 6 kan, 12 mak. Now you know why we don't use the Mayan calendar. And the next time you plan to cheat on a math test, sit next to a Mayan.

What happens after you reach the 13th baktun? I don't know, but it's going to happen pretty soon —the Mayan calendar rolls over on December 23rd, 2012. Maybe then we'll get a *real* apocalypse. Until then, let's all party like it's 12.19.19.17.19.

THE STUPIDLY OBVIOUS PHRASE OF THE DAY

"The Poor Suffer the Most"

Used, for example, in this news header today in a story about food shortages: "As a brutal convergence of events hits an unprepared global market, and grain prices go sky high, the world's poor suffer most."

Really? The *poor* suffering the most? It's hard to imagine. Because, you know, usually when there's a major global crisis of any sort, it's the poor sitting there on the sidelines, going *whew, dodged **that** bullet*. How *strange* that the people the least economically, socially and educationally able to deal with wrenching change should suffer the most. How *odd* that the rich should so often be able to shield themselves from the ravages of events. It's almost as if they have some *advantage* over poor people, although off the top of my head what it might be escapes me.

Which is not to say that the rich always get off scot free: who among us can forget The Great Davos Lobster Bisque Inconvenience of '04, in which the victims, none with a net worth of less than $15 million, suffered a small amount of gastric distress due to too much heavy cream in the soup? The poor escaped *that* with hardly a cramp. Good for them. The poor did have that tsunami that year, though. Killed a couple hundred thousand of them. But in terms of *aggregate worth*, it all evens out, you see. Intestinal discomfort for the rich, death by wall of water for the poor. Seems fair.

A tip for news writers: it'll be news when the poor *don't* suffer the most. "As the mysterious Billionaire's Virus decimates Aspen, the world's stinkin' rich suffer the most." *That's* a news head worth writing.

TEN YEARS AGO TODAY

Mar
10
2008

In February of 1998, my wife and I decided that it was time that we take the plunge and perform that quintessential act of Great American Dream-ism and buy our own house. At the time I was working at America Online as its in-house writer/editor, and we were living in an apartment in Sterling, about three miles from AOL's corporate offices. We liked the area and most of our friends lived nearby; it was a good place to put down roots. So we started house hunting and near the end of the month found a place we really liked. Back at work I told a co-worker that we were likely to make an offer on the house the next day.

My immediate boss, who had the cubicle next to mine, suddenly popped her head up and asked to talk to me privately. "Don't make that offer," she said.

"Why not?" I said.

"I can't tell you yet," she said. "Just don't."

Two days later the reason became clear: The group I was in at AOL was being disbanded, and while everyone else in the group was transferring into other departments, no one wanted me. The reason for this was somewhat ironic: As AOL's in-house writer/editor, I was used as a company-wide resource—but no one wanted someone who was a company-wide resource on their department budget. I wasn't being fired, I was told, I was being laid off. It was a layoff action of precisely one person. Also ironically, the layoff was coming about a week before my two-year anniversary at AOL. In one of the nicer things they could have done, AOL decided to make the termination date one day after my two-year anniversary—which meant I could vest stock I had in the company. My official termination date: March 10: Ten years ago today.

How did I take the layoff? In a word: *badly*. Up to that point my professional career had been fairly charmed: I helped pay my way through my senior year of college by writing music features and concert reviews for the *Chicago Sun-Times* and the *New Times,* and then got a very sweet job as a full-time newspaper movie critic at a time when most newspapers weren't doing much hiring. Then at the very upswing of the 90s Internet explosion, I was hired by America Online as their first in-house writer and editor. Basically everything was going great, I had no reason to think it wouldn't continue to go great, and if I hung around AOL long enough my stock would make me a millionaire and then I really wouldn't have to worry about much. So, yeah, charmed career, and I was pretty cocky about it.

Given my high opinion of myself and my career, the layoff was a smackdown of monumental proportions. Because my career had been so charmed, much of my self-worth was invested in my work; not to have that work anymore left me spinning. Adding insult to injury was the fact that Krissy and I had been planning to buy a house; in the space of a day we went from young people who had the means to get a nice house in a nice area to people who couldn't get a house on their own—no bank would have lent us the money with me being laid off and Krissy, who worked part-time, making the income that she had.

While I was literally stunned into immobility, Krissy took control of the situation and did the smart thing: She started to downsize us. We looked at the jobs in the area that I could get; none of them at the time seemed likely to pay what AOL had been giving me. That meant not only was a house out of the question, but the apartment we were currently living in was probably too expensive. Krissy started looking at cheaper places for us to live, made appointments for us to view them, and dragged me along to look at these new places.

And thus it was, standing in the living room of a cheap apartment that we were being shown in Leesburg, Virginia, I had what I expect was the lowest moment of my adult life. I was standing in the living room with gray walls, gray carpet and gray window blinds, on an overcast day, listening to my wife ask about the much reduced amenities relative to the apartment we lived in at the time, and it felt like my life had hit some sort of rewind—that I had managed to come so far, and now this was the bend in the curve, where things started their downturn.

Note, if you will, the possibility that in my depressed state I may have been being overly dramatic about this. But I'm telling you how I felt, and this is how I felt: Low, depressed, and like all the forward momentum I had had in my life —and especially in my personal life—had smacked up hard against a wall. And it had landed me here, in this crappy apartment that I might be living in from now on because it's what we were likely to be able to afford. How low was I about this? Let's just say that on our drive back to our soon-to-be ex-apartment, Krissy was vaguely concerned that I might open up the passenger side door and toss myself into traffic.

I spent another couple of days being blackly, blackly depressed, and then something interesting happened, which was that I had one of those epiphany moments you hear about people having. And the epiphany was this—that how I and Krissy reacted to what was happening to us right now was going to echo through how we faced the rest of our lives, individually and together.

In this case, there were two ways this could play out. We could play it safe, take that depressing-but-affordable apartment, live within our reduced means and grind it out. Or we could say *screw this*, go back to house hunting, buy a house, keep moving our lives forward, and have faith in ourselves that we would find a way to make it work.

Now, I'm sure you think you know what I was going to choose. But I want you to remember two things. The first was that for the very first time in my professional life, I was hit with a setback, and it hit me incredibly hard. Not only in the ego department, but my decision-making. I'd never even considered that I would ever be laid off for any reason at all, and I was clearly wrong about that. What else could I be wrong about? I was uncertain and I was gun-shy. The second thing is that it would be one thing if it were just me going for broke. But I was married, and whatever happened to me would happen to Krissy, too. If I screwed up, I would take her down with me. It was bad enough I was already laid off; this added another layer of complications to things.

So despite what you think you might know about me, you should know that my decision could have gone either way. This was a time in my life that I was really and truly without a compass. I didn't know what to do. So Krissy and I sat down to talk about what we would do next.

And it was Krissy who said, "Well, *I* want a house."

Which was enough for me. Because while Krissy wanted a house, *I* didn't want to live in that damn, gray apartment. So we called our real estate agent and told her we were ready to look at houses again.

"You got a new job!" our real estate agent said.

"No," I said.

"Oh," she said. "Well, that will make things difficult."

"Let us worry about that," I said.

Here's how we did it: With help. I called my Uncle Gale and Aunt Karen asked for their trust and their signatures as co-signers on our mortgage loan. They gave us both. And like that, we were back.

And we were back in more than one way. Krissy and I decided to have faith in ourselves and in each other and to find a way to make it all work—to live the lives we wanted to live, not lives dictated by circumstances outside our control. And almost as soon as we made that decision about our lives, things suddenly got better. Krissy's job, frightened that she would leave and they would have to hire two people to do what she was doing, put her on full-time status with health benefits, replacing the benefits I'd lost at AOL.

On my end, it turned out that people at AOL suddenly realized that when I wasn't around, their writing wasn't getting done; all the various departments that didn't want me on their head count were happy to hire me as an outside contractor. That started happening almost as soon as people realized I was gone. Shortly thereafter I was hired by Media-One—an early broadband company—to write music reviews for their online portal. And then I got a phone call from a marketing company; I had been recommended to them by a friend at AOL for a project. Would I take it on? Sure I would.

In sum, very quickly I was making more than I had been making at AOL, and actually working a bit less. And from home. Home being the house we bought shortly thereafter; on the day we closed, Krissy and I took the keys, walked into our new home, turned on a boom box, and danced around the place to Madness' "Our House." Because it was, and because we could.

Would have all this stuff happened if we decided to play it safe? Oh, probably, minus the house portion. But the point of it was how we reacted to it. When this good fortune came in, we didn't feel like we had dodged a bullet and had gotten lucky. We felt that it justified our belief that we could make it work, and that our faith in ourselves was not misplaced. And, yes, that made a difference in how we viewed the world, going forward. It still makes a difference now.

And this is one of the reasons why I tell people that being laid off from AOL was one of the best things that ever happened to me—because as much as it knocked me for a loop, it made me ask myself who I wanted to be in control of my life—and it made me make a choice about how my life would be. It was the right crisis at the right time; it was something I think was necessary for me. In a very real way, it's the moment I can point to and say "this is when I knew I was a grown-up." It's maybe a silly way to put it, but it was important all the same. So: Thanks, AOL, for laying me off. I appreciate it. It's done more for me than you know.

Oh, and there's one other reason to thank AOL for laying me off. On March 10, 1998, the actual, official date of my layoff, I was feeling understandably a bit low about it, even though by that time things were already beginning to look up. But still, waking up and thinking "I have no job to go to" was a little off-putting. So Krissy decided to cheer me up. Nine months later: Athena. So, yes, this day ten years ago was a life-changing day in more ways than one.

FRED THE CULT LEADER

Jul

10

2001

Consider Fred. The unquestioned leader of the Scooby Gang, he's the one that directs the investigations ("Let's split up") and is therefore the one who explains the mystery at the end of each episode, pulling the rubber mask off Old Man Withers and explaining how he was trying to run everyone off the farm disguised as a banshee in order to dig for the pirate gold (or whatever). No one ever questions his supremacy or his *diktat*—he's like a Teenage Stalin in a red cravat. One wonders what would happen to, say, Daphne, if she were ever to note to Fred that his plans almost always caused her to be snatched by the latex-faced villain. I see Fred turning an apoplectic red, quickly regaining his composure, and then making sure Daphne "falls" down a well. She's replaced by Janet, red-headed, spunky would-be mystery writer. None of the other Scooby gang members makes mention of the switch. None of them dare.

Why do the Scooby gang follow Fred in the first place? These are supposed to be teenagers, after all, and in terms of teenage dynamics, the Scooby gang is all wrong. Fred and Daphne make perfect sense, of course: Prom king and queen, quarterback and cheerleader, student body president and treasurer, take your pick of teenage upper-strata clichés. Daphne and Velma likewise make sense; from the top of her butch bowl cut to the bottom of her sensible shoes, Velma's relationship with Daphne screams "unrequited crush"; poor Velma's probably been carrying Daphne's books and writing her school reports since the second grade without ever quite figuring out why. As for Shaggy and Scooby, well, come on; stoner loner and his talking, possibly hallucinated dog. A perfect match.

But there's no way on earth that they should all get along. In the real world, Fred would barely tolerate the presence of Velma, whom he would intuit, in a dull, instinctual way, as a competitor for Daphne's affections; likewise Velma would be a gushing font of passive-aggressiveness regarding Fred, subtly talking him down to Daphne whenever he was not around (now you know why Fred takes Daphne with him whenever the gang splits up). Neither Fred nor Daphne would be seen near Shaggy or any of his ilk; we all know the natural antipathy that exists between high school royalty and the teenage equivalent of the raving homeless. Velma would hardly be a better match for the boy and his dog. While Velma's natural social standing is closer to Shaggy's than to Daphne's, as Daphne's minion, she's required to ape her social opinions. Put these five in a room, and you don't have the Scooby Gang, you have the Breakfast Club, minus the happy ending where they all sign a joint declaration to the music of Simple Minds.

So the idea of this group being a naturally occurring grouping of teenagers is out, way out—and enforced contact would result in somebody being bitten, not necessarily by Scooby. Fortunately, there's a much more rational explanation for this odd little grouping, led by Fred. It is: Fred is not the leader of a gang of friends, he's the leader of a cult.

Think about it. It makes perfect sense. The eerie lack of conflict within the group. The unquestioning adherence to Fred's declarations. The ever-repeating ritual of "solving" crimes, most of which play out exactly *the same way*. The creepy itinerant lifestyle that packs four teens and a dog in a van for weeks at a time without so much as a single change of clothes. Honestly—these are *teens*. Shouldn't they be in school at least part of the time? Why do they travel so much, anyway? Where are their parents? Aren't they concerned?

But these are the hallmarks of the cult life: The enforced separation from a previous life. The rejection of outside information in the form of education. The lack of any authority figures other than Fred and the occasional and all-too-complicit country sheriff. The Scooby gang doesn't travel because they are looking for crimes to solve. They travel because they're on step ahead of the deprogrammers. Somehow, Fred's got them all snookered. It probably has something to do with the Scooby Snacks.

WHAT MY JESUS WOULD DO

May
6
2005

Occasionally I am asked if I believe in Jesus. My standard answer to this is "as much as I believe in evolution," which serves the dual purpose of both answering in the affirmative and usually annoying the person who asks the question. There is no doubt that Jesus lived; I have no doubt Jesus died, and did so with the belief he was doing so for the sins of the world. Whatever one feels about the divinity of Jesus, this is a staggering assumption of moral responsibility, in the face of which one must feel humbled. I've read the words of Jesus, to benefit from his wisdom and also to try to understand this most influential of men.

I also read his words to understand the actions of some of those who claim to be his followers, and who are, at the moment and alas, trying to jam a certain suspect iteration of "Christianity" down the throats of all the rest of us—"all the rest of us" being non-believers, believers in other faiths and those Christians whose understanding of the teaching of Jesus does not appear to require such militant intolerance as is being practiced by this evanescently powerful minority.

As far as I can tell, the primary source of power for this group lies not in the teachings of Jesus, since what they do has little to do with that, but the simple fact that they feel they *own* Jesus, and have been reasonably successful in propagating the idea that their particular perspective on his teachings is both predominant and correct, neither of which is necessarily true. Nevertheless, by implicitly and explicitly claiming ownership of Jesus, these folks have made any attack on their agenda or their practices an attack on Jesus, using Him as a flak guard for policies and practices that would, frankly, appall this shepherd of all men.

Well, of course, these people *don't* own Jesus. He died for the sins of the whole world. Nor do they have a corner on the understanding of his words or his work. The Jesus *I* know and whose words I have read and striven to understand would not sign off on much of the agenda of those who now parade Him around like a fetish, and in doing so have created this *other* Jesus, a vacuous, empty vessel for an uncharitable worldview.

But this implicitly asks a question: What would the Jesus I know do, confronted by this Fetish Jesus? Would he fight him? Argue with him? Denounce him? Engage in a mystical battle of miracles?

The answer is: None of the above, of course. The Jesus I know would do the hardest thing imaginable: He would forgive.

He would forgive this Jesus, who inspires His followers to persecute those they fear.

He would forgive this Jesus, who would demand His followers declare some people unfit to love, to care for children, to serve their nation, or to be full members of their society.

He would forgive this Jesus, who appears happy not only to let His followers be blind to the natural miracles around them—the subtle handiwork of God that took billions of years to achieve—but also to force their blindness on everyone, in His name.

He would forgive this Jesus, whose followers reflect His high opinion of His own righteousness without the appropriate reflection or doubt, and who aren't shy about letting others know that fact.

He would forgive this Jesus the overweening pride He feels in saving His followers, and the pride His followers feel in being saved, a pride they believe sets them above all others, even though pride famously goes before the fall.

He would forgive this Jesus the idea that all of His flock must act, think, and vote a certain way at all times, without exception, or they are not one of His flock.

He would forgive this Jesus the small ways He tries, though His followers, to denigrate, isolate and diminish those who do not conform to His whims.

He would forgive this Jesus all *large* ways he tries, through His followers, to hurt, humiliate and destroy those who fight to keep their own point of view.

He would forgive this Jesus the fact that He has stood by while His followers have lost the view of the Kingdom of Heaven in a drive to gain treasure in this world—even as the least among them suffered.

And finally, He would forgive this Christ the loss of His divine self that comes from allowing His name to devolve into a shibboleth for grasping opportunists, a bludgeon to cow those who are doubtful of the wisdom of His followers' agenda, and a mask to hide unethical practices that have nothing to do with the Gospel and promises of the next world, and everything to do with mere, banal power in this one. He would forgive that this Jesus had diminished Their mutual name, the beauty of Their message, and the astonishing power of Their sacrifice two millennia in the past, a sacrifice for *all* people, not just this small and frightened tribe who demands that they and only they know Jesus and what He wants.

What an act of forgiveness this would be! And what an act of forgiveness for the rest of us to attempt to emulate.

This is what I will try to do from now on. When someone confronts me with the proposition that their faith in Jesus demands intolerance, ignorance or fear, I will simply say "My Jesus forgives your Jesus these things." And when they become indignant and retort that there is only one Jesus, I'll probably say "you don't say," and let it hang there in the air a good long time. And when they come back at me with more intolerance, ignorance and fear, I'll just remind them again that my Jesus forgives their Jesus these things.

At *no* point will I cede ownership of Jesus to these people, or the idea that the Jesus *I* know supports the intolerance, ignorance or fear they claim He does. They *don't* own Jesus, and I strongly believe He doesn't support their intolerance, ignorance or fear. And I think it's perfectly reasonable to let these folks know this, in a way that explicitly undercuts the proposition that they hold the monopoly on understanding Jesus.

If you feel the same way, then you might consider doing the same thing. Proudly proclaim your relationship with Jesus, in whatever form that may take, and let everyone know the Jesus you know is *not* who they claim Him to be; He's someone better. Reclaim Jesus for yourself. He's not private property, His words aren't copyrighted, and He's not the exclusive trademark of religious conservatives. He's yours if you want Him.

And when they get angry at you for doing it, the solution is simple: Forgive them. That's what the Jesus I know would do.

MEETING
AUTHORS
(AND ME)

Apr

3

2008

James asks:

> *I have bought tickets to Denvention and I am looking forward to seeing all of my favorite authors. My question is what is the appropriate way to approach an author? Ignore (or not) behavior like stalking and such (knocking on hotel door at 2 am) but how would you like to be approached? I'm fluctuating between, Ohmygod,ohmygod,ohmygod, it's Scalzi!!!!!! and a deep scary "it's good to meet you, John."*
>
> *Part of the problem is that I feel like I know you fairly well, because of how open and sharing you are here on the blog, but you know nothing about me. How do/should you (and us as your fans) manage this inequality?*

Yeah, it's interesting. One aspect of fame—even the rather meager portion of it that I and most authors have—is that more people know you than you know, and they have a relationship with you that you don't have with them. I can't individually know everyone who reads one of my books or reads Whatever; I'd have no time left at the end of the day. And once again it makes me feel sorry for people who are *genuinely* famous, who have this sort of unequal relationship with millions of people, not just a few sundry thousands.

I *do* think it's worth remembering that even though you've read our books (and our blogs) and feel friendly toward us, on our end of things you're a stranger, even if we've interacted with you through blog comments or e-mail or whatever. There are lots of regular commentors here on Whatever who, if they were to come up to me in real life and just start blabbering away, I would have not the first clue who they were, and I might even be a little alarmed (fortunately my regular commentors here are more socialized than that. Right? *Right?!?*). I'm glad you recognize this fact that our respective relationships are unequal in terms of familiarity, James, and I hope the rest of you internalize it too.

That said, you know: I'm just this *guy*. There's no great science to meeting me or any author for the first time. Presuming that you are adult and socialized reasonably well, the way to introduce yourself to me is the same way you would introduce yourself to anyone you've not actually met before in real life. You come up, make sure I'm not currently engaged in a task that needs my full attention, say "excuse me" or "hello" to get my attention, and then introduce yourself. Whereupon you and I will likely have a nice, brief chat, and after a minute or two we'll disengage and go about our lives. Pretty simple.

I do know that occasionally people are reluctant to approach me or other writers, because "oh, they get bothered so much, I don't want to bother them." Leaving aside the fact that authors are rarely bothered in this way because few people actually know what we look like, I think a lot depends on context. If you were to find me randomly out on the street or at a restaurant, this is not an inappropriate response; I probably *do* want to be left alone, because I'm busy having my real life. But if I'm at a convention (or book fair, or other public event), I'm generally there to be accessible to fans and readers, as are most authors who are there. I think we all generally *like* to be recognized in that context. Please feel free to come up and say hello; it's not a bother.

Bear in mind that it's not just fans and readers who get this way about writers; it's other writers, too (because we're fans and readers as well). I was at ReaderCon a couple of years ago, standing with a group of young writers, when China Mieville, who was the convention guest of honor (and who is a generally lovely person), paused nearby to look at some notes. And this is what happened:

> **Young Writer:** Oh my god, oh my god. It's *China*. God, I so want to talk to him. (nods all around)

Me: So call him over.

Young Writer: I can't! I'm too *embarrassed*. I wouldn't know what to say. That's *China*, man. And look, he's busy. Staring at *words*. I don't want to bug him. (more nods)

Me: You're all idiots. Hey, China!

China Mieville: (looks up) Oh, hello. (joins group to chat briefly, then goes about his business)

Me: See, that wasn't so hard, was it?

Young Writers: Oh my god! We talked to *China!* (neo-pro hands flutter, legs pump up and down with glee)

Okay, maybe they *didn't* giggle like Japanese schoolgirls at the end. But the rest of it is fairly bang on. Point is, *all* of us get a bit fannish and intimidated from time to time. But most authors, especially at conventions and seminars, are happy to say hello for a moment or two.

This does lead to another question: Is there a time at a convention when you *shouldn't* say hello to an author? Well, sure. Authors are often rushing from one panel or event to another (con organizers work us like dogs to keep you amused), so if you see an author with a *holy crap I'm late and I have no idea where my next panel is* look on his or her face, try to catch them some other time. Likewise, if you see an author trying to cram a sandwich down his throat like he's forgotten about the concept of chewing, it probably means he's only got a few minutes to fuel himself before he's off to something else. Give him a break, let him scarf, catch him later.

One other thing: Note the difference between public and private spaces, and public and private conversations. If you see an author at a con party holding court with a crowd of folks around, feel free to join in. If you see her talking very intently to one other person, over in the corner, you're probably not wanted. Likewise: author in the hotel bar, being loud and opinionated? Say hi. Author in the restaurant, having a quiet meal with spouse or friends? Catch them later. This is all common sense and common courtesy, and I'm sure you know all of this already. But feel free to pass this along to your more clueless friends.

So that's some general advice. Relating to *me*, here are some things you should know when coming to say hi.

1. I discover that as more people come up and say hi to me, and as my brain becomes more error-ridden as I ingest increasingly massive amounts of artificial sweetener, I am having a harder time remembering names and faces. So: Even if we've met before, I might not immediately recognize you by name or face. Just reintroduce yourself, at which point I will like say "Oh, *right*. Duh. Sorry," and we can move along. I'm generally very upfront about this inability to remember anything anymore, and hopefully I am so in a charming way, but what I'm saying is: don't be offended. It's not that you're not memorable, it's that my brain sucks.

2. I am generally very open to being approached (even outside conventions, in my real life), but occasionally you might come up to me when I'm in a conversation I'm really engaged in, or when I'm busy doing something, or even when, despite being in a public area, I just want to be left alone. When that happens I'll say something like, "Can I catch up with you later?", which will be your cue to step away. It does *not* mean "fuck off" (trust me, if I want you to fuck off, I will use words to that effect); it means "please catch up with me later." The upside to honoring this request is that when I see you again, I am likely to be happier to see you, because I know you're the sort of excellent person who leaves me alone when I ask to be left alone.

3. I am generally happy to sign books and take pictures. However, I don't want to read your short story, listen to an idea you've had we could collaborate on, go have lunch or dinner with you if we've only just met or go up to your hotel room for whatever reason you might contrive (and yes, people *have* tried to contrive, at least once, although not for the reason you're probably thinking). Thanks all the same.

4. Also, not that it's ever come up, or likely ever will, but just in case, here's the deal for groupies: You'll have to ask Krissy for permission. Good luck with that.

I think this covers most everything about meeting me.

WHY I BREED

Yet another irritating "childfree" whine generator erupted biliously toward me in e-mail recently.* This is not an infrequent occurrence, as my trolling of said population in the Whatever is apparently of some passing infamy in their small and angry circles. I don't mind at all, of course, since there's very little I enjoy more than afflicting the aggressively affrontable, which is what the "childfree" so frequently are. Short of slathering the childfearing in the collected mucus of an entire preschool, it's the most fun to be had out of these little, little people with their little, little hates. They're well up there on my List of People to Taunt, right along with creationists and Confederate sympathizers. If I could meet up one day with a Confederate childfree creationist, well, I don't know what I would do with myself. I expect I'd probably explode with glee.

The letter itself was not particularly noteworthy, just the usual child-free claptrap about how breeders are irresponsible, awful people to bring children into this terrible, feculent world and why couldn't we just have adopted if we wanted kids and there are too many people and we're all just gonna die in our own piles of misery and poo. Letters like this don't do much for me except make me glad that the senders have indeed cho-sen not to breed, because they'd righteously screw up their kids. But at the very end, the sproghater asked an interesting question, which was:

> Anyway, I have one question: In the light of 40,000 children dying every day and many more on the adoption lists, why did you feel the need to clone yourself (aka breed)?

My rather flip response in e-mail was "Because I rock, you silly person. There should be a million of me." The response was of course designed to enrage the recipient due to its potent combination of dismissive smugness, conscienceless ego and reproductive fervor. But in all fairness it's not a bad question and is worth a more responsive answer. Clearly, there are children to adopt; also clearly, lots of children die for various horrible reasons every day, all over the globe. With such a clear surplus of young humanity in the world, why add to their number?

Well, obviously, because I wanted to, and because I could. I wanted to for a number of reasons, some undoubtedly rooted in fundamental biology (living things naturally wish to make more of their number), but more—and more influentially—because of the conscious desire to *be* a father, which is something I've always had so long as I could remember thinking about the subject of breeding at all. This isn't to say I was in a *rush* to become a father—I didn't become one until I was 29, after all—merely that it was on the agenda of things to do with my life. On this matter, I was additionally helped in that a) I met a woman willing to conjoin her genetic material with mine and b) that said genetic material was up the task; i.e., my boys could swim.

But you say: I could have as easily been a father and experienced all the joys of parenting by adopting. That's true enough. And to be perfectly honest about it, I'm very big on the concept of adoption. My family, through my mother, has experienced adoption from both sides of the adoption coin: When she was 16, she put a child up for adoption (my brother Robert, whom I met when I was in middle school), and then when she was 54, she adopted a child of her own. I'm not personally opposed to the idea of adopting a child with Krissy, either. We've discussed it from time to time when we talk about whether we want to have additional kids. And who knows, one day we may adopt. Regardless of whether *we* do or not, I think adoptive parents make an unmistakably strong statement of parental love by affirmatively choosing their child to love and care for and as such have, and always have had, my admiration. So yes: Adopt, if you like. It's a good thing.

For all that, I think I can make a compelling case for making a child the old-fashioned way. First off, there are the economics. To be coldly fiscal about it, adopting a child costs a lot of money, whereas, assuming normal fertility, making one of one's own does not (and it's fun besides, which is an adjective I have yet to hear anyone apply to the adoption process). As a matter of policy, I would and do support ways to bring down the cost of adopting a child (bring on the tax credits!) to make adoption affordable for every family who wishes to adopt. But at the moment, we're not there.

Second, I believe that both my wife and I offer a compelling set of genes to the proverbial pool: Both of us are fit and intelligent and have no family history of inherited diseases or other afflictions, either physical or mental. It seemed likely that our offspring would also be fit, intelligent and healthy, and indeed, so she is. I would argue that the gene pool and the overall hybrid vigor of our entire species is incrementally enhanced by our contribution to it, and thereby the positives provided by such a genetic union rather greatly outweigh the negatives associated with bringing yet another human onto this groaning sphere.

To restate the above on a more personal level, I was also intensely curious to see what a child of mine would be like—and more specifically, a child of mine and Krissy's. Yon agitated childdespiser rather derisively asked why I would want to clone myself, and in fact I wouldn't. There's already been one of me, and I think we can all agree that one is sufficient. But in the entire history of the universe, there has never been someone like Athena, who is, for the moment at least, the summation of a couple billion years of evolution as expressed through the genetic lines which run through myself and my wife.

The combination of those lines results in an individual who is synergistic—more than the sum of her parts, and uniquely her own person thereby. To be sure, I see myself in her, as well as her mother. But mostly I see Athena. For herself alone, and not for the mere continuation of my own genetics, is her existence amply justifiable, and thus my desire to have her come into being. You are free to disagree, of course. But honestly, now. Ask me if I care.

As regards bringing children into the awful, terrible world: whatever. The toddlerkickers may believe it's a terrible time to bring a human into the world, but when has it not been? Pick a year, any year, that humans have deigned to grace with a sense of history, and you'll undoubtedly discover that it's an atrocious and utterly irresponsible moment to birth another generation of *homo sapiens*. Tell me that there are too many humans on this planet, and I'd agree—but then I'd ask you why it must then necessarily follow that I must volunteer my own genes for extinction. As far as I'm concerned, the issue is not only that there are too many people, but simultaneously too few like *me*. Breed a few more of my line, and then we might have enough people to vote in a President who doesn't think that providing birth control to third-world women who desperately need it is a moral evil—thereby reducing the human surplus far more effectively than by my falling on my genetic sword.

Agreed, too many children die daily. But this is not in itself an argument against my producing a child of my own. My child is almost certain *not* to die of starvation, or curable disease, or war, or neglect or ignorance or any of the reasons that the vast majority of those children die every day. This child is as safe from harm as any child not trapped in a plastic bubble can be. I can't save 40,000 children a day, but I can be a good parent *for* one every day, and I try to do that. Agreed, breeding is a selfish act, probably the fundamental selfish act—one is, after all, passing on one's genes. But I've read enough "childfree" griping about having to pay for schools with their taxes not to be *terribly* worried about these particular pots calling the kettle black.

So in summation: I breed because I can, because I want to, because I believe my doing so is a net benefit to humanity and planet (or at the very least presents no net damage) and because I expected to be (and am) fully pleased with the results. I realize these reasons are almost certainly insufficient to satisfy the babyslappers, but as there's not likely to be any reason that would satisfy them, I'm hard-pressed to be deeply concerned about that fact. Indeed, I wish I could say that I breed specifically to piss them off. Alas, I do not. It's merely a fringe benefit.

---

* Standard disclaimers: Not everyone who chooses not to have children is an obnoxious hater of the pre-adult; you are sensible people and know who you are. This taunting does not apply to you. The relevant

pathology of the unpleasantly childfree is not that they are childfree, but that they are unpleasant. They would very likely be unpleasant no matter what subject they chose to get worked up about.

Additionally: Not everyone who is a parent deserves to be; some—hell, many—need to be mulched in a wood chipper. And there are plenty of children who ought to follow their so-called parents right into said chipper. Just in case you thought I thought these particular populations were not capable of rank dumbassery.

Update: The sender of the original e-mail says (in a new e-mail): "Someone as arrogant as you does not deserve a beautiful child like Athena." Well, this is probably true. But as Clint Eastwood once said, deserve's got nothing to do with it.

POINT OF PRIVELEGE

Over the last week or so I've heard rumors of some sort of "privilege list," which was developed by some academics to make their students aware that whatever level of privilege they had before they got to college, they were all at the same place now (which is Indiana State University, apparently). I heard about it mostly via people being really pissed at its sloppy construction and slapping down a link to my "Being Poor" entry as a contrast, but tonight I finally got a look at the list itself. I have to say I'm really not at all impressed with the list, primarily because as indicators of class and privilege, many if not most of the things on the list are non-responsive in the real world.

If you're doing the exercise, you're supposed to take a step forward if one of the listed statements is true for you; the idea being, apparently, that any step forward is a mark of privilege, or a class indicator. Just for fun, I'll point out some of these statements, and why they aren't one or the other or both.

If were read children's books by a parent

As far as I can remember, my mother never read children's books to me. But that's because I learned to read when I was two; I read my own children's books, thanks much. My mother did, however, read to me books meant for adult readers. As it happens, I don't read children's books to Athena, either, because she learned to read almost as early as I did; at bedtime when she was younger, she insisted on reading her books to *us*.

The exercise also lists having books in the home as a mark of privilege or class, but inasmuch as I grew up poor in a house jammed with books, many bought for a quarter at a yard sale or thrift store, I would dispute that it's a mark of either. Clearly the folks who thought up this list are used to thinking of books as being expensive rather than really cheap entertainment.

If you went to a private high school

I went to a private high school; a really good and expensive one, too. And on vacations when my friends were going back home to big houses, I was going back to a single-wide trailer. Was I privileged? In one sense, certainly. In most other ways, well, no, not so much.

Going to a private school, incidentally, radically skews a number of other privilege indicators on this list. For example:

If you were the same or higher class than your high school teachers

Doesn't work, because while most of the kids who attended my school would have nominally have been of a higher social stratum than the teachers, we in fact had some very well-off teachers. My history teacher was a scion of the Fawcett publishing family; he donated the school library building. Named it after his mom, which was sweet. Why did he teach history at a high school if he could buy entire libraries? I would suppose because he *liked* it. By the strictures of this particular metric, however, many kids at my school would not have counted as "privileged," even the ones who got Mercedes for their birthdays.

Here's another non-indicator:

If you had your own TV in your room in High School

None of the very privileged kids in my high school had a TV in their room—because we lived at a boarding school, and TV wasn't allowed. They had all manner of very expensive audio equipment, though. Likewise, almost none of the kids at my high school had this ostensible privilege marker:

If you participated in an SAT/ACT prep course

Because my high school was a college preparatory school. You'd be getting the benefits of an SAT/ACT prep course just by going to your classes. And here's a funny one:

If your parents bought you a car that was not a hand-me-down from them

Because when your dad gives you his two-year-old BMW because he got a new one, you're not going to complain because it doesn't have that *new car smell*. One more, to bring the point home:

If your family vacations involved staying at hotels

Why on earth would you stay at a hotel if you had a vacation home?

Well, you say, at least all the rich kids can step forward for this one:

If the people in the media who dress and talk like me are portrayed positively

Clearly, these people have never seen *Pretty in Pink* or *Less Than Zero*, to use two examples from my day.

Somewhat unrelated, another silly one:

If you were unaware of how much heating bills were for your family

Leaving aside the idea that if you grew up in, say, Southern California, heating bills would not be a major topic, I can say that as a sometimes very poor child I rarely knew the sums of various utility bills, *because I was a kid*. I knew whether my mom was stressed about the bills, which I suspect is the point here, poorly worded. Be that as it may, a kid from an upper class situation might know the sums of her family's heating bills if her parents chose to give her an idea of family economics, to teach her to be fiscally prudent—which is not unknown behavior in those who are well off because they are smart with their money. Athena has asked about our bills, because she's curious; we've told her about them. I doubt anyone would suggest our spawn is not relatively privileged.

Well, you say, that's all just you, or specific people you know. Well, yes. This is my *point*. And for probably *any* person, there are things on this list meant to signify privilege that don't, or are meant to exclude privilege that could be signs of substantial privilege—just ask the boarding school student driving dad's old Beemer to the vacation house by the shore while his middle-class friends are stuck in an SAT review session. For nearly all of the "privilege markers" in this exercise, one can come up with excellent reasons why they are not an issue of privilege or class at all.

Which means that for the *purposes* of this exercise—showing indicators of privilege and class—this list is not actually useful, and indeed counter-productive. In this exercise, it's *entirely* possible for someone of a lower social class to appear more "privileged" than someone who is of the "rich and snooty" class. This doesn't create awareness of privilege; it does, however, create awareness of the essential lameness of this particular exercise. This may be why the exercise notes warn that "anger will be a primary emotion." I would be angry, too, if my time were wasted on an exercise like this.

(Don't even get me started on what a pile of crap the "Social Class Knowledge Quiz," also available at the link above, is. Some of us know what Choate *and* a "full pull" are.)

As an aside, one of the things that gets me about this "privilege" exercise is how actually divorced from class it is, primarily because so many of the privilege indicators are trivial consumer items well within the reach of all but the most poor among us. My gas station convenience store has pay-as-you-go cell phones for less than it costs to pay for an XBox game; at this point it's *not* a mark of privilege for a teenager to have one. I can go to Wal-Mart and pick up a TV for under $100 or a desktop computer for $300; not very *good* ones in either case, but that's not the point. My local mall has a Steve and Barry's in it; you have to work hard to buy something there that costs more than $15. Shopping in a mall isn't much of a class indicator, either. Hasn't been for a while now.

Elizabeth Bear, in commenting about this exercise, notes: "If I were writing it, it would have things like, 'Did you receive regular dental care and vaccinations as a child?' on it." She's spot on. The vector of privilege these days is not physical items, but how well one is cared for, or can care for one's self and family: Whether one has adequate health care, whether one has access to healthy food, whether one's housing and transportation costs are a not-onerous percentage of the household income, whether one has day care for children, whether one is free of high-interest consumer debt, and whether one can afford to save any money for the future. The privileged are those who have all of those things, or live in households that do. To suggest that having a TV in one's room as a teen is an indicator of privilege when the *real* indicator of privilege is whether that teen can get a cracked tooth easily fixed doesn't merely border on obtuseness, it's rather emphatically stomping over to the other side of the line and jumping up and down.

But perhaps one indicator of privilege is that one can creat an exercise like this and believe that it actually has anything to do with reality. Must be nice. I can only imagine it, myself.

Lazy People Irritate Me

Feb

7

2002

I don't know about anyone else, but I find it a bad sign when I come across not one but two guides on the same day on how to be poor. The first came from *The Stranger*, one of Seattle's alternative weeklies; in "The Power of Positive Poverty" (the *Stranger's* cover story last week, how depressing is *that*), writer Hannah Levin goes into great detail on how to have a life in Seattle with an income of about $10,000; it apparently involves trips to food banks and occasional groveling to the electric company to get your bill trimmed. The second comes from London, where writer Peter Tatchell reports that he's been living adequately, if not lavishly, for the last two decades at under 7000 pounds annually (which, as it happens, also translates to about $10,000 per year). Of these two situations, I would believe it's probably easier to live poor in London than in Seattle; London's probably a bit more pricey overall, but England also still has a more comprehensive safety net than the US, so if you really get screwed, you're probably better off.

No matter how you slice it, however, trying to make a go of it for $10,000 a year still pretty much sucks. Both Levin and Tatchell attempt make a virtue of their position—Tractell notes that the physical exercise required by poverty (no car) has kept him pretty well buffed even at age 50, while Levin touts a potluck congregation with other equally strapped friends as a reasonable social alternative to going out nights and getting trashed (which, I should note, it actually is). But neither of them, thankfully, is under any illusion that being poor is actually a totally positive state of affairs. "Poverty is embarrassing, frustrating, frightening, and depressing," Levin notes; Tatchell, who self-describes as not especially materialistic, still dreams of living in a nicer place than subsidized housing, but doesn't hold out much hope for it.

Reading both of these pieces, which are well-written and well-thought out, you can't help but ask yourself—hey, neither of these two people seem insane, utterly anti-social or entirely lacking in employable skills. So why are they living at or near the poverty line? The answer: Well, they're *writers*, of course. Levin makes what incomes she does make as a freelance arts writer. This means she makes diddly; then there's the fact that she's an arts writer for alternative weeklies, which takes her down to the "less than diddly" level. In Tatchell's case, his freelance writing is done to fund his gay activism campaigns, which are clearly the focus of his life, but which don't make him any money at all.

On the poverty thing, I'm ready to give Tatchell a pass; whether you agree with his brand of activism or not, activism takes a lot of time and effort, and the man's made the conscious decision to forego a more comfortable life in order to campaign on the issues that are important to him, which is not something everyone's willing to do. So, good on him—it sucks he's poor, but he's making a difference or at least pissing off a bunch of irritating straight people, which on most days can't be considered a bad thing.

Levin irritates me, however. The only reason she's poor, as far as I can tell, is that she's decided being an arts writer is the only thing she should be doing at the moment, and she's willing to deal with the poverty in order to have that self-affirmation. In a general sense, that's just fine: If you want to be poor in order to say you're a writer, instead having to assure the people whose food order you're taking that you *also* write, far be it from me to stop you. Go ahead and live off of Top Ramen if you want.

But here's the thing: Because she's self-selected to be poor, Levin also seems to assume that it's okay for her to graze off the food banks or get subsidized housing or apply for state-assisted health insurance. And that, my friends, is a big, steaming pile of crap. Levin's intelligent, articulate, almost certainly college-educated, and has skills that would allow her to get a job, would she deign to do so. She doesn't *need* any of this assistance, and every box of pasta she takes from a food bank, every emergency cut she gets off her electric bill and every handout she takes from charity takes away from people who honestly and legitimately need help. Not everyone has the *option* of being poor. Some people in this country don't have much choice in the matter.

Levin and others who are in her position should be ashamed of themselves. First off, writing doesn't have to be a vow of poverty, and I can speak to that fact directly. Even if writers don't make money hand over fist, they can make enough to support themselves just fine. Second, if I couldn't support myself with my writing—and Levin can't, as evidenced by the fact that she roots for handouts on occasion—I would get another job. I wouldn't stop being a writer, I would simply be doing something else as well. Certainly there's enough of a history of writers with day jobs to support that idea. This goes for anyone in any creative field or anyone who has a college degree.

Third, any person who *can* work enough to stay off the support net should do just that—and in fact they owe it to the people who actually *need* the support net. This is no joke: Some woman struggling to feed her children is going to wander into a food bank and miss out on something good for her kids because someone like Levin came through and took it first. Short of Levin's library card, there's hardly a service she mentions in her article that her using does not entail someone else losing out. I'd like to see her try to explain her "need" to that person.

In her article, Levin talks about having the "privilege" of being able to choose to be poor in order to pursue her goals, but I'd like to suggest to her that her "privilege" stops where someone else's need begins. What she needs to do is to get a job and start putting back into the support net what she's so obliviously taken out of it.

BEST VISION OF HELL OF THE MILLENNIUM

Nov

12

1999

I t comes from Hieronymus Bosch, the Dutch painter who lived in the 15th and 16th Centuries (although assuredly, not through them both entirely). Other people wrote about Hell, lectured about Hell, or simply feared it as the inevitable end to their sinful ways. Bosch *saw* Hell, like Walker Evans saw the Depression, and then reported on what he saw. It wasn't a very cheerful report, but then, what would you expect. Hell's not a resort filled with Payday bars and happy kittens. Unless you're allergic to nuts and cat dander. In which case, that's *exactly* what it is.

How did Bosch get this preview of Hell? It's not that hard to imagine. Sartre famously said that Hell is other people, and while he was probably directly referring to some annoying waiter at Deux Magots, the line has broader implications. People are flawed, and not in the Japanese sense of *wabi*, in which a slight imperfection merely accentuates the fundamental perfection of a thing. *Wabi* is the mole on Cindy Crawford's lip, the wheat bits in Lucky Charms, or the fact that Bill Gates' fortune is owned by him and not you.

No, we're talking about deep-seated incipient screw-upped-ness, the kind that puts you on the news as the helicopter gets a top down view of the police surrounding your home. For most of us, fortunately, it expresses itself in less virulent form, usually a furtive, opportunistic violation of one or more of the seven deadly sins when we think we won't get caught. Coupled with this is the dread knowledge that, not only do we *know* what we're doing is wrong, but we'll probably do it again the next time everyone else's attention is back on the TV. We're

all a country song waiting to happen. With that realization comes the grinding sound of Satan's backhoe scraping out space in our brain for another yet Hell franchise (six billion locations worldwide!). Hell is in *all* of us, not just the ones who use cell phones when they drive. All you have to do is look.

Bosch looked. A pessimist and a moralist (one can hardly be one without being the other), Bosch saw what evil lurked in the hearts of men, and then hit the paint. His friends and neighbors were no doubt unhappy to learn they were the motivation for Bosch's horrifying and fantastical canvases; it's difficult to live near someone who might paint your face onto a damned creature with Hell's staff fraternizing in what used to be its butt. But there's a story about another painter which could shed some light on what Bosch was doing. Pablo Picasso once painted a portrait of Gertrude Stein, only to have someone comment that Stein looked nothing like the painting. Said Picasso: "She will, soon enough." (And she *did*). Apply this same reasoning to a picture of yourself with imps in your ass. It might make you think.

Beyond the existential and theological nature of Bosch's work is the fact that, as paintings, they are just so damned cool. Bosch's paintings of Hell influenced two great schools of art: Surrealism and Heavy Metal. Surrealism got off on Bosch's vibrant and innovative use of color and his ability to combine the mundane and the fantastical to make bitter and intelligent social commentary. In fact Bosch had one up on most of the Surrealists in that he actually believed in something; unlike the surrealists and their kissing cousins the dadaists, Bosch's work is rooted in morality rather than running away from it. Bosch wouldn't have painted a mustache on Mona Lisa; he'd've had her devoured by a fish demon as a pointed warning of the dangers of vanity.

Heavy Metal artists dug Bosch, because, dude, he *totally* painted demons. Without Bosch, we'd have no Boris Vallejo airbrushings or Dio album covers, and it's debatable whether Western Culture would be able to survive their lack.

Some ask, does Bosch's work show Hell as it really is? No less an authority than the Catholic Church suggests that Hell is not so much a location as it is a state of being, an eternal absence of God's grace rather than a place where pitchforks are constantly, eternally and liberally applied to your eyeballs. In which case, Bosch's turbulent colors and troublesome devils are just another picture show, a trifle used to scare the credulous and the dim from indulging their baser instincts, like sex and thoughts on the possibility of even more sex.

It's the wrong question. It's not important that Bosch shows Hell as it truly is; it's entirely possible that, other than a useful philosophical construct, Hell doesn't exist at all. (This does not change the fact that the Backstreet Boys must somehow be eternally punished for their crimes.) But whether it truly exists or not, humans need the *idea* of Hell, whether it be to scare us into a moral life, comfort the smug ones who believe everyone *else* is going there, or simply to remind us that the actions of our lives, good or ill, live beyond those lives themselves, and the accounting of them may occur past the day we ourselves happen to stop. Bosch saw the importance of the idea and put it down in oil.

The question is not whether Hell exists, but rather: If we could see our souls in a mirror, rather than our bodies, would they be as Bosch painted them? If they were, we wouldn't have to wait until the next life for Hell. It would already be here.

POINTLESS IMPEACHMENT

I avoided the impeachment hearings yesterday because I couldn't see the point in bothering to watch them. I had things to do: We had a dinner party last night for about a dozen people, and I had to buy things, clean the house, try to start a fire in our wood-burning stove, keep the dog from freaking out when all these people showed up in her house, and so on. I didn't have time to listen to Ken Starr and all those Representatives posture.

The point is moot, anyway. They can impeach Clinton, but they sure as hell can't convict him. There wasn't any before the mid-term elections, and there's even less chance now; it's now all an exercise in futility and saving face. It burns and chafes a bunch of people that Clinton got away with it, including several pretty good friends of mine, but at this point, there's nothing to be done. Clinton's won this one, and the smart thing to do is to concede the point and move on to thwarting him in some other way.

Most of my conservative Republican friends are mystified that people are giving Clinton a flyer on this one: *So he committed adultery and had sex with a woman young enough to be his daughter. So what?* They just can't figure out why people aren't outraged. Well, most don't hate Clinton with every fiber of their being. This is really the key here. If Reagan had been caught getting serviced, you'd hear nary a peep out of the GOP; it would have been the Democrats attempting a neck-stretching.

And the other thing—look. Almost every heterosexual 50-year-old man in the United States would have sex with a willing 21-year-old woman *if they thought they could get away with it*. We're talking, no one would *ever* know. It'd just be you and this nubile ball of flesh (for the record, nearly every 60-, 40-, 30-, 20-, and 13-year-old would do it, too). This is not to say many of those men would not feel awfully guilty afterwards. But they would *still* do it—or at the very least be so extraordinarily tempted that they might as well *have* done it, for all the guilt they feel.

I think that, among men at least, a certain large percentage look at what Clinton did and go: *Good for him. He got some.* Another large percentage don't like it but know that in the same circumstances, they couldn't say they *wouldn't* do it. Yet another large percentage (this is where I fit in, mostly) simply don't care about a sex life that does not actively involve them. And so that leaves a certain small percentage who see what Clinton did, look inward to themselves to see if they might do the same thing in the same situation—and then lie to themselves, because their own image of themselves demands it. Those are the folks that want Clinton's head.

Now, I believe that it would never actually occur to *Ken Starr* to have sex with a 21-year-old woman. Ultimately, this is why most people don't really like *him*.

A Vegetarian Moment

Oct

20

1998

I could never be a vegetarian.

First of all, my heart just wouldn't be in it. I'm okay with the fact that what I'm cramming into my mouth was once a living thing, because with the exception of chewing gum (which is some sort of plastic, untouched by nature), everything you eat was once living. It's the way the whole digestive thing is set up. You can't live on chewing gum and multivitamins. I tried it my senior year of college, when I running low on rent money. It just doesn't work.

I feel bad for animals that they haven't managed to do what plants do, which is to create portions that can be plucked away, leaving the rest of the living entity intact. If God had created pigs that shed a fully-cured ham every three months, or cows that dropped sirloins from fleshy stalks, no one would find anything wrong with eating meat. But He didn't. And as bad as I feel, I don't feel bad enough, since I keep eating meat, and have no intention of stopping. I do draw the line at veal, though if I think about it logically, it's a questionable line to draw. Every calf I save from being penned is likely to go on to grow up to be several hundred quarter pounders. "Sooner or later" is the life story of a veal calf.

Another reason to avoid the meatless lifestyle is that if I became a vegetarian, I wouldn't be able to blithely note to the veggies that Adolf Hitler was a vegetarian (well, I *could*, but what would that say about me). Vegetarians hate having that brought up; it is, as you may imagine, a serious taint on the whole movement. You can often go for the double whammy by pointing out the Hitler also thought up Volkswagen, which will cause them to gnash their teeth as they grind their way back home in their 1970 VW bus. It never occurs to vegetarians to retort that Stalin ate *piles* of red meat; I wonder why that is.

But my lack of moral objections is not the real issue here. The real issue is that every once in a while, I get a hand-shaking, knee-buckling, mind-swishing urge for the flesh of an animal. My body, fed too long on cheap, cellophane-covered crackers and individually packaged Rollo candies, screams for the protein found nestled in the muscle and fatty tissues we generically call "meat." When I get to that point, it doesn't really matter what sort of meat product I devour. Porterhouse, chicken leg, hot dog—even a Slim Jim will work (though with the last one, you pay for it later, a point that ironically the Slim Jim folks are playing up in their most recent batch of commercials).

I was hit with one of those moments yesterday, around 3 o'clock in the afternoon—I had fed myself fat free, sugar free yogurt in the morning, and six or seven chocolate mint cups (think of Reese's Peanut Butter Cups, but with mint in the role normally played by the peanut butter), and my body had just had enough of that. *You've had your fun*, it said to me. *Now FEED me*. I barely made it down the stairs to the refrigerator.

Where I encountered a dilemma: There were no suitable meat products to be found in the fridge. I had expected to find a Cheddarwust—a summer sausage that, as you might have guessed from the name, was riddled inside with little pockmarks of cheddar cheese. As if you weren't already getting enough fat out of the sausage. But the Cheddarwurst was gone. We had used them all up. The only other meat product in the fridge was a package of turkey ham that had been sitting in the meat bin for longer than I could remember.

Which of course is a very bad sign. It was lying in wait to ambush me. It was the turkey's revenge—first it was killed, and then it was made to perform a carnivorous transvestite act, masquerading as the meat of a pig. Its only method of revenge was to lie in the meat bin past its due date and trick me into eating it then. Well, not *this* time, Tom. I passed it up (but I didn't remove it from the fridge and throw it in the trash, its threat then forever neutralized. No, I don't know why not. I suspect the decision will come back to haunt me).

The freezer held loads of meat, though, naturally, all of it was frozen and thus of little use to me in this moment of crisis. I looked into the door compartments, and found we had some frozen pizzas—cheese pizzas. I had eaten all the meat-flecked ones in earlier crisis situations.

But next to the pizzas: Corn dogs. Reduced fat corn dogs, yes, but it would do in a pinch. I grabbed one, nuked it, and tromped back up the stairs, happily munching on my dead animal fix.

I mentioned the Carnivore Moment to my wife when she came home. She looked at me blankly. I asked her why.

"Those were vegetarian corn dogs," she said. "There's not a speck of meat in them."

Vegetarians, start your abuse…now.

THE LIE OF STAR WARS AS ENTERTAINMENT

Oct
11
2006

Pyr Books main man Lou Anders points me in the direction of a call and response discussion on the topic of science fiction and "entertainment," as in, is written science fiction entertaining enough to capture the unwashed masses who watch it on TV and in the movies but don't bother to read the stuff. The first document in this discussion is an essay in *Asimov's* in which writer Kristine Kathryn Rusch says that the problem with written SF is that it isn't influenced enough by *Star Wars*, which to her mind is an exempar of good old-fashioned entertainment, and poses it in opposition to much of written SF, which is "jargon-filled limited-access novels that fill the shelves...dystopian novels that present a world uglier than our own, [and] protagonists who really don't care about their fellow man/alien/whatever."

This earns a whack from Ian McDonald, who both denies that the rest of SF ever abandoned entertainment ("It's as basic and primary as good grammar and syntax. It's not an end point. It's a beginning point"), and also decries the idea that entertainment is all there is, or that *Star Wars* is its apex ("Let me say, if that's the highest I can aspire to, if everything I have ever hoped for or dreamed of attaining, how I dared to touch hearts and minds, is measured against that; then the only morally consistent action I can take is for me to give up writing.")

For the moment I'm not going to go into the issue of whether written SF needs to save itself via being more entertaining, partly because I've discussed it before and partly because at the moment it's not an interesting subject for me. Suffice to say that I write books that are meant to be both entertaining and smart, because that's what I like to read. What I'm going to go into is the fact that much of the debate between Ms. Rusch and Mr. McDonald is irrelevant, because it starts from an erroneous premise. That erroneous premise is that the *Star Wars* films are entertainment.

Star Wars is not entertainment. *Star Wars* is George Lucas masturbating to a picture of Joseph Campbell and conning billions of people into watching the money shot.

There is nothing in the least bit "popular" about the *Star Wars* films. This is true of all of them, but especially of Episodes I, II and III: They are the selfish, ungenerous, onanistic output of a man who has no desire to include others in the internal grammar of his fictional world. They are the ultimate in auteur theory, but this creator has contempt for the people who view his work—or if *not* contempt, at the very least a near-austistic lack of concern as to whether anyone else "gets" his vision. The word "entertainer" has as an assumption that the creator/actor is reaching out to his or audience to engage them. George Lucas doesn't bother with this. He won't keep you out of his universe; he just doesn't *care* that you're in it. To call the *Star Wars* films "entertainment" is to fundamentally misapprehend the meaning of the world.

Which is not to say that the films can't be *entertaining:* They can be. George Lucas is an appalling storyteller in himself, but at the very least he has common tastes, or had when he first banged together the original *Star Wars* film. The original *Star Wars* is a hydra-headed pastiche of (as I wrote in my *Rough Guide to Sci-Fi Movies*) 30s adventure serials, 40s war films, 50s Kurosawa films and 60s Eastern mysticism, all jammed into the cinematic crock-pot and simmered in a watery broth made from the marrow of Campbell's thousand-headed hero. With the exception of Kurosawa, all of this was stuff was in the common culture, and Lucas did a decent enough job spooning out the stew. *Star Wars* also benefitted from the fact that it emerged at the end of a nearly decade-long string of heavy, dystopic SF-themed films, beginning with *Planet of the Apes* and gliding down toward *Logan's Run*. After a decade of this (and combined with the film's brain-jammingly brilliant special effects), *Star Wars* felt like a breath of fresh air.

But even at the outset, Lucas was about something else other than entertaining people. As he noted in a biography of Joseph Campbell:

"I came to the conclusion after *American Graffiti* that what's valuable for me is to set standards, not to show people the world the way it is...around the period of this realization...it came to me that there really was no modern use of mythology..."

What's interesting about mythology is that it's the residue of a teleological system that's dead; it's what you get after everyone who believed in something has croaked and nothing is left but stories. *Building* a mythology is necrophilic storytelling; one that implicitly kills off an entire culture and plays with its corpse (or corpus, as the case may be). It's one better than being a God, really. Gods have to deal with the universes they create; mythmakers merely have to say *what happened*. When Lucas started *Star Wars* with the words "A long time ago in a galaxy far, far away..." he was implicitly serving notice to the audience that they weren't participants, they were at best witnesses to events that had already happened, through participants who were long dead.

Why does this matter? It matters because Lucas' intent was to build an overarching mythological structure, not necessarily to make a bunch of movies. If you listen to Lucas blather on in his laconic fashion on the *Star Wars* DVD commentaries, you'll hear him talk about how he wanted everything to make sense in the long view—that all his films served the mythology. This is fine, but it reinforces the point that the films themselves—not to mention the scripts and the acting—are secondary to Lucas' true goal of myth building. Myths can be entertaining—indeed, they survive because they can entertain, even if they don't brook participation. These films *could* work as entertainment. But fundamentally they don't, because Lucas doesn't seem to *care* if the films work as entertainment, as long as they sufficiently conform to his created mythology.

This is especially evident in the prequel trilogy, which is designed for the specific purpose of consecrating the mythology of the Skywalker family; in essence, putting flesh on the bones of the myth, so that the flesh could then turn to dust and the bones could be chopped up for reliquaries. Because they're not designed as entertainment, it's not surprising they're not really all that entertaining; strip out the yeoman work of Industrial Light and Magic and what you have left is a grim Calvinistic stomp toward the creation of Darth Vader. Lucas was so intent to get there that he didn't bother to slow down to write a decent script or to give his cast (riddled though it was with acclaimed actors) an opportunity to do more than solemnly intone its lines. Lucas simply couldn't be bothered to do more; entertainment gave way to scriptual sufficiency.

Now that the magnum opus of the *Star Wars* cycle is done, we can see that any entertainment value of the series is either unintentional (Lucas couldn't suck the pure entertainment value out of his pastiche sources), achieved through special effects, or is the work of hired guns, notably Lawrence Kasdan and Leigh Brackett (those two wrote *The Empire Strikes Back*, the only movie in the series that has a script that evidences much in the way of wit, much less dialogue that ranks above serviceable. Kasdan and Brackett were clearly attempting to *entertain* as well as serve the mythology, showing it is possible to do both). It's clear that Lucas doesn't much care what people think of the films, and why should he? He got to make the films he wanted to make, the way he wanted to make them. His vision, his mythology, his *structure* is complete, and he doesn't have to rationalize the means by which the structure was achieved.

Ironically, I don't blame Lucas for this. He is who he is. Personally, I blame whatever jackass at 20th Century Fox agreed to let Lucas have the rights to the sequels and to the merchandising in exchange for Lucas lowering his fee to direct the first *Star Wars*. I don't know if the films of the *Star Wars* series would be better overall if there were real studio oversight, but I do know that each individual film would at least try to be entertaining. Because film studios don't actually give a crap about mythology; they give a crap about getting butts into the seats. Perhaps someone could have asked Lucas if maybe he didn't want to hand the script of Episode I over to someone who could, you know, actually *write dialogue*, or possibly if he might not be content to produce while someone else handled the chore of putting the actors through their paces, since clearly he found that aspect of filmmaking to be a necessary evil at best. In essence, people who would let Lucas fiddle with his myth-making, smile, then turn to a director and screenwriter and say "now, make this *entertaining*, or by God, we'll feed your testicles to Shamu." Oh, for a time machine.

Now, hold on, you say: If the *Star Wars* films aren't meant to be entertainment, how come so many people were *entertained?* It's a fair question; after all, there's not a single film in the series that made less than $200 million at the box office (and those are in 1980 dollars). I'm happy to allow it's entirely possible to be entertained by Episodes IV, V and VI, due to their novelty and the intervention of hired guns who aimed for entertainment even as Lucas was on his holy quest for mythology. Even then, however, *Return of the Jedi* was pushing it. I defy you to find any person who was genuinely entertained by Episodes I, II and III. Episode I in particular is an airless, joyless slog; in the theater you could actually hear people's expectations *deflate*—a whooshing groan—the moment Jar-Jar showed up. After the first weekend of Episode I, people went to the prequel trilogy films for the same reason so many people go to church on Sunday: It's habit, they know when to stand and when to sit, and they want to see how the preacher will screw up the sermon *this* week. You know what I felt when Episode III was done? *Relief.* I was *done* with the *Star Wars* films. I was *free.* I'm not the only one.

But even accounting for the fact that the IV, V and VI could be entertaining, they were still not meant as entertainment. In the final analysis they were means to an end, and an end that only one person—George Lucas—desired. This is *not* entertainment, save for Lucas, and it's wrong to say it is. And it's why saying we should have more entertainment like *Star Wars* is folly. Do we really need more entertainment that's designed only to make *one person* happy? Look, I write books that I'd want to read, but I don't pretend I'm not writing for *others* as well. George Lucas managed to con billions into thinking that he was entertaining them (or alternately, they so desperately needed to believe they were being entertained that they denied they weren't), but honestly. Once is enough. Fool me once, etc.

Look, here's a test for you. I want you to go out and find this movie: *Battle Beyond the Stars.* It's a piece of crap 1980 B-movie, produced by Roger Corman, that's clearly cashing in on the *Star Wars* phenomenon.

Hell, it's even a pastiche of the same things *Star Wars* is a pastiche of (it even has a planet Akir, named for Akira Kurosawa), and it was made for $2 million, which is nothing money, even back in 1980. Thing is, its screenplay was written by John Sayles (later twice nominated for the Best Screenplay Academy Award), and it's funny and smart, and the whole movie, rather incredibly, keeps pace. Watch it and then tell me, honestly, that it's *not* more entertaining than *Star Wars* Episodes I, II, III and VI. Unless you're so distracted by the cheesy special effects and the fact that John Boy Walton is the star that you simply can't go on, I expect you'll admit you were more entertained by this little flick than all that *Star Wars* mythology.

The reason: It *wants* to entertain you. Corman and Sayles, bless their little hearts, probably didn't give a crap about mythology, except to the extent that it served to help them entertain you, the viewer. They cared about giving you 90 minutes of fun so they could make their money back, and that would let them do it *again*. I'm not suggesting that there should be more SF like *Battle Beyond the Stars* (though I can think of worse things). I *am* suggesting that if we're going to talk about the *Star Wars* series as entertainment, we should note that as *entertainment*, it gets its ass resolutely kicked by a $2 million piece of crap Roger Corman flick. So let's not *pretend* that the *Star Wars* series is this great piece of entertainment.

Instead, let's call it what it is: A monument to George Lucas pleasuring himself. Which, you know, is fine. I'm happy for Lucas; it's nice that he was able to do that for himself. We all like to make ourselves happy. But since he did it all in public, I just wish he'd been a little more *entertaining* about it.

LOATHSOME DOT-COM WHINERS

Jul
11
2001

It's not every day that you read an article and hope that the people writing it have willfully made up the quotes and people in it, but, honestly, I'm hoping to God that Ruth Shalit and Robin Danielson Hafitz completely fabricated today's lead story in *Salon*. It's about how certain consumers feel personally victimized about the collapse of dotcom retailers, and is entitled, with typical *Salon* high drama, "The Day The Brands Died."

In the article, Shalit and Hafitz quote people who express self-loathing for taking advantage of the dotcoms' increasingly insane loss-leader brand awareness tactics ("There was a looting mentality going on," said one respondent. "Now we all feel shame") and are now dealing with the soul-crushing reality that they may have to do their own shopping again, just like common trolls ("After sitting at home in my bathrobe, and having some nice man hand me my movie, how can I ever go back to Blockbusters?" asked one woman. "It's like living in a Third World country.")

Who *are* these people? And more to the point, presuming they actually exist, why do Shalit, Hafitz or *Salon* think they're worth even the least bit of sympathy or interest from the rest of us? I don't feel at all sorry for the chick who's confused her own sloth for genuine deprivation, although I *do* suggest we take up a collection to kidnap her and ship her down to Guatemala, where she can pick coffee beans for sixteen cents an hour until her fingers bleed, the better to contrast her new living situation with the need to *actually leave the fucking house* to rent a video. Look, I'm waving a dollar here. Who wants to join me? At least she'd be out of our country for a while.

It's embarrassing to think that one shares a planet with people whose priorities are as screwed up as those in this article, an entire class of human that apparently believes that whole point of technology is to allow one never to leave one's own home. These aren't like the people who lived on the virgin prairie and relied on the Sears Roebuck catalogue for their staple needs, after all. In order to take advantage of a dotcom delivery service, you have to live in a big metropolitan area, i.e., somewhere you can walk down to the corner and buy your own goddamned beef jerky.

To feel an inexplicable sense of loss because now you have to go out onto the street and walk several yards for groceries indicates a disconnect from reality that borders on genuine psychosis, not to mention egomania. Webvan, one of the dotcoms featured in the article, managed to suck through a billion dollars in investor capital and put hundreds of workers on the streets, and all these jerks can think about is the idea that no one's going to arrive at the door with their Cherry Garcia anymore (note: that's what significant others are for, you dumbasses).

Articles like this reinforce in me the idea that what we really need in this country is good, long, severe depression. Not for everyone, of course. Certainly not for *me* (I did my stint of being poor growing up, thank you very much. I'm *done* with it now). But the laid-off goatee-and-cell-phone set, for whom having to sacrifice is having to settle for $70,000 a year doing IT at a bank instead of the $85,000 and options they had at their dotcom, well, a good solid dose of honest, stomach-clenching poverty is just what they need to get their priorities reset to a less complacently smug level. After a year or two having choose between the gas bill and food whose protein component doesn't come in a "flavor packet," they'll be happy to walk to Blockbuster under their own power and rent that video. And maybe they'll even say "thank you" to the clerk.

It's not likely. But one can dream—and dream that once these people leave their apartments to go shopping in the big scary world, the first thing they do is go to buy a clue. That is, if they actually exist. Let's hope they don't.

WHAT AUTHORS KNOW ABOUT THEIR CHARACTERS

Oct

29

2007

I n a *New York Times* piece on Dumbledore's homosexuality, critic Edward Rothstein suggests that J.K. Rowling, Dumbledore's creator, might not know what she's talking about:

> But it is possible that Ms. Rowling may be mistaken about her own character. She may have invented Hogwarts and all the wizards within it, she may have created the most influential fantasy books since J. R. R. Tolkien, and she may have woven her spell over thousands of pages and seven novels, but there seems to be no compelling reason within the books for her after-the-fact assertion. Of course it would not be inconsistent for Dumbledore to be gay, but the books' accounts certainly don't make it necessary. The question is distracting, which is why it never really emerges in the books themselves. Ms. Rowling may think of Dumbledore as gay, but there is no reason why anyone else should.

Sure there is: Because he *is*. Because the author made him that way. Whether or not anyone but the author knew about it up to last week simply doesn't matter. The author, in her formulation of the character, has this as part of his background, and that background informs how the character was written. Rothstein is under the impression that because Dumbledore's sexuality is not explicitly in the text it's irrelevant or not necessary. But it's not true; if Rowling had as part of Dumbledore's background that he was straight, or entirely asexual, his character would be different and his actions and responses and backstory would be different. *He* would be different. He wouldn't be the Dumbledore he is today (or was, because he's dead, but even so).

Rothstein seems to be falling into the trap of assuming that everything that goes into a character shows up on the page. This is entirely wrong. What shows up on the page is the *public life* of the character, so to speak: The things about a character that a writer chooses to let you know about them. The *private life* of a character exists off the page, and takes place between the writer and the character. You don't see that unless the author discusses it later, in interviews or commentary or whatever. Authors have privilege concerning our characters; we know more about them than the readers. Or as Neil Gaiman recently put it:

> *You always wind up knowing more about your characters than you can get onto the page. Pages are finite, and the story isn't about giving you all the information about everyone in it any more than life is. Things the author knows about characters (or at least, strongly suspects—it's never really real until it hits the page, because the process of writing is also a process of discovery) that don't make it onto the page could include the characters' backstory, what they like to eat, the toothpaste they use, what happens to them after the story is over or before it began, and what they do in bed. That something didn't turn up in the books just means it didn't make it onto the page or wasn't relevant to the story.*

Does the reader *need to know* Dumbledore is gay? Probably not. Does the reader have to *care* that he's gay? That's up to the reader. Do these facts mean that Dumbledore's sexuality is *unimportant* to who the character is? Absolutely not. The moment Rowling said (or discovered, however you want to put it) that Dumbledore was gay, it made a difference in how she perceived him and how she wrote him. The only way Rowling's statement of Dumbledore's sexuality would be *irrelevant* or should be *ignored* by the reader (should they hear of the fact at all) is if there were proof that Rowling was tacking on the sexuality of Dumbledore after the fact of the *writing*, i.e., that Rowling had no conception of Dumbledore's sexuality through all the books, and then is throwing the "dude, he's gay" statement out there now just for kicks. Given how much people have been saying "well, now such-and-such scene makes *perfect* sense," regarding the books, this doesn't seem like it's the case. She's got backup in the work.

Which is not to say such after-the-fact author revisionism doesn't happen. The reason that Ray Bradbury's recent declaration that *Fahrenheit 451* wasn't about censorship but was instead about television destroying literature is looked upon with such utter skepticism is because for the last 50 years it *has* been about censorship (Bradbury himself has explicitly noted this); while Bradbury takes a poke at TV in the book, the core of the story—what's in the text—is the effect of censorship on his primary character, who is himself a censor. Bradbury's free to say what he wants, but his own words and his own text speak against him, and on balance I'm going with the text, because it doesn't change its mind.

Now, if Rowling had lardered the Harry Potter books with tales of Dumbledore's heterosexual relationships, and had done numerous interviews about how in his younger years he cut a swath through witches and mugglettes alike, leaving a trail of women raving about his wandwork, then we would have reason to discard a latter-day revelation of his gayness; it would be patent nonsense. She did neither. Rowling's outing of Dumbledore might be surprising, but it's not inconsistent with what we know of the text or the character.

Rowling is getting some whacks because she never explicitly stated Dumbledore's sexuality within the books themselves, which is fair enough, although I think it's a little silly. Authors are not obliged to outline every detail about a character, and from what I know of Dumbledore (I haven't read the books themselves because the little I've read of Rowling's prose style doesn't set me aflame; I stick to the movies) it would be entirely in character for him to be circumspect about the topic of his sexuality, both in dealing with Harry and his pals, and in the clearly rather conservative world of magic. Rowling's made it pretty obvious that in her Potterverse it's hard to be "out" when you have an alternate lifestyle (cf. that Lupis dude), and there's no indication that the world of magic is any more gay-friendly than it is werewolf-friendly.

She built a world that has certain rules; characters in that world live by those rules. Those rules aren't necessarily the same rules as our world lives by.

Going back to Rothstein, the best you can say for his argument is that it notes that Dumbledore doesn't have to be gay for many of the influential events of his life to have had an effect on him. To which the correct response is to say, yes, well. And this would be different from the lives of *actual* gay people exactly how? We go through any number of events in our lives without our sexuality front and center—it would make sense an author would model a character similarly. But it doesn't mean that at the end of the day that sexuality doesn't matter to who the character *is*.

Dumbledore's gay: He was written that way. As a reader, you may not *need* to know it, or may even feel it's *essential* to what you see as his purpose, any more than in the real life you'd need to know if your mailman were gay, or your bank teller or your local librarian, or would see their sexuality as essential to how you relate to them even if you did. But what *you* know, and what these people know about *themselves*—and what an author knows about his or her characters, not to mention what the characters know about themselves—are separate things. And what they know matters to who they are.

So, no. Rowling's not mistaken about Dumbledore. Rothstein, however, is.

BEST CHEESE OF THE MILLENNIUM

Processed Cheese, or, as it's vulgarly called, American cheese. Hey, don't blame the messenger. I'm not the one who is forcing humanity to eat two billion pounds of the orange stuff annually. I'm just telling you that we do. Anyway, cheese is hardly the thing to get snooty about. Any product that is made intentionally to both smell like feet and be put in your mouth, well, honestly. How much respect should it *get*?

Cheese is in fact the first and best example that a great many of humanity's current culinary selections are based on bad judgment and/or someone drunkenly daring someone else to eat something entirely inappropriate. In the case of cheese, the going story (found on two entirely different cheese advisory sites, so you know it must be true) was that some 4,000 years ago, an Arab was crossing the desert with some milk in a pouch. What sort of idiot goes on a long journey across a desert with milk in a pouch? Well, see. This is the "bad judgment" part.

As the immortal song tells us, "in the desert, the heat was hot," so by the time the Arab fellow decided to have a pull off his udder squeezings, the stuff had fermented and became two separate and entirely smelly objects. The first was the runny, armpit-smelling liquid called "whey" (think of the ooze that floats on top of your sour cream before you stir it up—sour cream, incidentally, yet another dare food from the land of dairy), and the other, a lump of disgusting goo which was the first cheese on record.

Any sane person would have flung the pouch of curdled mommy juice as far from their person as it is possible to fling it. But we've already established the fact we're dealing with a fellow who's a few camels short of a full caravan. So this genius eats the goo and drinks the armpit liquid. The cheese flacks who convey the story would have us believe he was "delighted" with his discovery, which makes me want to sit these flacks down and see how "delighted" they'd be to ingest fermented mammal squirts that had been lying in the sun all day, breeding microorganisms in a largely anaerobic medium. The fellow was probably delighted that he didn't die the next day of food poisoning, and that's about the extent of anyone's delightment.

So why did he do it? I suspect the truth went something like this.

> Cheese-Eater: Damn it, my goat's milk's gone stinky and bad. Look at it (shows it to friend).
>
> Friend: Wow, that's truly vile. I'll give you a shekel to try some.
>
> Cheese-Eater: You're out of your freakin' mind. I'd rather tongue my camel.
>
> Friend: All right, two shekels.
>
> Cheese-Eater: There's no amount of money you can pay me to eat this stuff.
>
> Friend: Five shekels.
>
> Cheese-Eater: Okay.
>
> (Tries some; doesn't die.)
>
> Friend: How is it?
>
> Cheese-Eater: Not too bad. Want some?
>
> Friend: You're out of your freakin' mind.

When you think about it, cheese and the process you use to make it is still unspeakably vile. Take milk and let it go bad, either by exposing it to various forms of bacteria or by ladling on an enzyme called rennin, which is obtained from the fourth stomach of cows (this last one is why vegans will have nothing to do with cheese). After it's gone sufficiently bad, you dry it out and shove it in a corner for several months to let it go bad some more, only slower. You know it's done when allowing it get any more bad would actually, you know, cause you to *die* when you ate it. I imagine they lost quite a few cheese-making monks to this testing phase.

There are hundreds of types of cheese, from Abbaye de la Joie Notre Dame to Zamorano; the varied nature of cheese initially had less to do with anything humans were doing than to the fact that every place on the planet has its own sorts of bacteria, so milk goes bad in different ways in different places. Eventually people gained some sort of control over the cheese-making process and started intentionally making different kinds of cheese, although the high-volume commercial aspect of cheese making had to wait until 1851, when the first cheese factory was constructed in upstate New York. Wisconsin, cheese capital of the world, saw its first cheese factory open seventeen years later. It was a Limburger cheese factory. There's no punchline there, it's the truth.

Processed cheese, the cheese of the millennium, reared its bland orange head in 1911 in Switzerland. However, the cheese gods had already favored that land with its own sort of cheese, the one with all the holes in it, so it was left to the Americans to take the process and popularize it. And they did: James Kraft developed his cheese processing process in 1912, perfected it five years later, and unleashed the cheese food product on the world shortly thereafter.

The process of processed cheese is the secret to its blandness—the natural cheese ripening process is interrupted by heat (read: they fry the bacteria before it gets out of hand and gives the stuff actual taste), and what you get is a block of proto-cheese that has an indefinite shelf life. It's bland, but it lives forever: The Dick Clark of cheese.

Within the realm of processed cheese, there are gradations, relative to the amount of actual cheese in the cheese; the higher the number of qualifiers, the less cheese it has. To begin there's processed cheese, which is 100% cheese, just not a very dignified kind (usually some humiliated form of interrupted cheddar, labeled "American" so the other cheddars won't beat it up and steal its lunch money). Then there's processed cheese *food*, which features cheese by-products as filler. This is followed by cheese *food product*, which includes some entirely nondairy ingredients such as vegetable oils. Finally, of course, there's *cheez*, which may or may not feature plastics. The less said about that stuff, the better.

I certainly wouldn't argue that processed cheese is the best cheese of the millennium in terms of taste, texture, quality or snob appeal (I may be glib, but I ain't stupid), but I will suggest the utter ubiquity of processed cheese, *American* cheese, allows it to walk away with the title. Indeed, American cheese is to cheese as American culture is to culture: It's not necessarily *better*, it's just designed to travel, to be convenient to use, to be standard and unvaried and largely non-biodegradeable no matter where you find it.

We can even go so far as to say that American culture and American cheese will go hand in hand, right to the last. Thousands of years from now, after the inevitable apocalypse of some sort wipes out our civilization, future archaeologists will scour the land to make some sense of our times, and I think the process will go something like this.

Archeologist 1: Look, it's another temple of the ancestors' dominant faith. Note the golden arches.

Archeologist 2: And look what I've found in the storage crypt!

(pulls out a box of cheese slices)

Archeologist 1: Ah, the communion squares. For their ritual obescience to Ro-Nald, the demon destroyer of worlds. You can see his terrible visage bedecking the illuminated windows from behind the tithing altar.

Archeologist 2 (sniffing the cheese): These smell terrible. It must have been some sort of penance to ingest these.

Archeologist 1 (glancing over): You know, these samples have maintained their unholy orange taint. They may still be potent.

Archeologist 2: What are you saying?

Archeologist 1: I'll give you 10 glars if you eat one.

Archeologist 2: You're out of your freakin' mind.

Archeologist 1: All right, 20.

Archeologist 2: Okay.

ON THE
CREATION
MUSEUM

Here's how to understand the Creation Museum, which opened this year, just south of Cincinnati, across the border in Kentucky: Imagine, if you will, a load of horseshit. And we're not talking just your average load of horseshit; no, we're talking colossal load of horseshit. An epic load of horseshit. The kind of load of horseshit that has accreted over decades and has developed its own sort of ecosystem, from the flyblown chunks at the perimeter, down into the heated and decomposing center, generating explosive levels of methane as bacteria feast merrily on vintage, liquefied crap. This is a *Herculean* load of horseshit, friends, the likes of which has not been seen since the days of Augeas.

And you look at it and you say, "Wow, what a load of horseshit."

But then there's this guy. And this guy loves this load of horseshit. Why? Well, really, who knows? What possesses someone to love a load of horseshit? It's beyond your understanding and possibly you don't actually want to know, even if you *could* know; maybe it's one of those "on that path lies madness" things. But love it he does, and he's not the only one; the admiration for this particular load of horseshit exists, unaccountably, far and wide. There are *advocates* for this load of horseshit.

And so this guy who loves this load of horseshit decides that he's going to do something; he's going to give it a home. And not just any home, because as this is no ordinary load of horseshit, so must its home be no ordinary repository for horseshit. And so the fellow builds a temple for his load of horseshit. The finest architects scope this temple's dimensions; the most excellent builders hoist columns around the load of horseshit and cap them with a cunning and elegant dome; and every surface of the temple is clad in fine-grained Italian marble by the most competent masons in a three-state radius. The load of horseshit is surrounded by comfortable seats, the better for people to gaze upon it; docents are hired to expertly describe its history and features; multimedia events are designed to explain its superior nature, relative not only to other loads of horseshit which may compete in loadosity or horseshittery, but to other, completely unrelated things which may or may not be loads of anything, much less loads of horseshit.

The guy who built the temple, satisfied that it truly represents his beloved load of horseshit in the best possible light, then opens the temple to the public, to attract not only the already-established horseshit enthusiasts, but possibly to entice new people to come and gaze on the horseshit, and to, well, who knows, admire its *moundyness,* or the way it piles just so, to nod in appreciation of the rationalizations for its excellence or to clap in delight and take pictures when an escaping swell of methane causes the load of horseshit to sigh a moist and pungent sigh.

When all of this is done, the fellow turns to you and asks you what you think of it all *now,* now that this gorgeous edifice has been raised in glory and the masses cluster in celebration.

And you say, "Well, that's all very nice. But it's still just an enormous load of horseshit."

And this is, in sum, the Creation Museum. $27 million has purchased the very best monument to an enormous load of horseshit that you could possibly ever hope to see. I enjoyed my visit, admired the craft with which the whole thing was put together, and was never once convinced that what I was seeing celebrated was anything more or less than horseshit. Popular horseshit? Undoubtedly. Horseshit hallowed by tradition and consecrated by time? Just so. Horseshit of the finest possible quality? I would not argue the point. And yet, even so: Horseshit. Complete horseshit. Utter horseshit. Total horseshit. Horseshit, horseshit, horseshit, horseshit. I pity the people who swallow it whole.

So that is the key to understanding the Creation Museum. But what *is* the enormous load of horseshit that sits, squat yet moundy, at its very center? It's simple: That the Bible is the literal and inerrant Word of God. If the Creation Museum doesn't have that, it doesn't have anything. So what it does—and very cleverly—is to position the Word of God as a non-threatening and accommodating given right from the start.

In the first room of the Creation Museum tour there's a display of two paleontologists unearthing a raptor skeleton. One of them, a rather avuncular fellow, explains that he and the other paleontologist are both doing the same work, but that they start off from different premises: He starts off from the Bible and the other fellow (who does not get to comment, naturally) starts off from "man's reason," and really, that's the only difference between them: "different starting points, same facts," is the mantra for the first portion of the museum.

The rhetoricians in the crowd will already see how a card has been palmed here. The Museum is casually trying to establish an equivalence between science and creationism by accrediting them both as legitimate "starting points" for any discussion of biology, geology and cosmology. This would cause any scientist worth his or her salt to have a positively cinematic spit take, because it's horseshit, but if you don't know any better (say, if you've been fed a line of crap your whole life along the lines of "science is just another religion") it sounds perfectly reasonable. And so if you buy that, then the next room, filled with large posters that offer on equal footing the creationist and scientific takes on the creation of the universe and evolution, seems perfectly reasonable, too: Heck, we can both have our theories! They're *both* okay.

The problem with this is that creationism isn't a theory, it's an *assertion*, to wit: The entire universe was created in six days, the days are 24-hour days, the layout for the creation and for the early history of the planet and humanity is in the first chapter of Genesis and it is *exactly right*. Everything has to be made to conform to these assertions, which is why creationist attempts at science are generally so damn comical and refutable. This is also why the "different starting points, same facts" mantra is laughably false on its face—creationism *has* to have different facts to explain the world. It's a little idiotic to establish as a "fact" that both science and creationism acknowledge, say, that apes *exist,* but to paper over the difference in the set of "facts" that explain how the apes got here, or to imply that a creationist assertion (apes created on the fifth day) is logically or systematically equivalent to decades of rigorous scientific process in the exploration of evolution.

But none of this is immediately obvious stuff and certainly the Creation Museum isn't going to go out of its way to point it out; quite the opposite, in fact, since everything relies on the audience swallowing that whopping load of horseshit right up front. Thus the avuncular fake paleontologist at the start of the tour, looking all squinty and trustworthy and setting forth his load of utter horseshit in a tone of calm sincerity. Why *wouldn't* you believe him? He's a *scientist,* after all. Once you buy the initial premise, the rest comes easy, or, well, *easier,* anyway.

Let me say this much: I have to admit admiration for the pure balls-out, high-octane creationism that's on offer here. Not for the Creation Museum that mamby-pamby weak sauce known as "Intelligent Design," which tries to slip God by as some random designer, who just sort of got the ball rolling by accident. Screw *that,* pal: The Creation Museum's God is *hands on!* He made every one of those animals from the *damn mud* and he did it no earlier than 4004 BC, or thereabouts. It's all there in the *book,* son, all you have to do is look. Indeed, every single thing on display in the Creation Museum is either caused by or a consequence of exactly three things:

1. The six-day creation;
2. Adam eating from the tree of life;
3. Noah's flood.

Really, that's it. That's the Holy Trinity of explanations and rationalizations. And thus we learn fascinating things. Did you know, for example, that Adam is responsible not only for the fall of man, but also for the creation of venom? It didn't exist in the Garden of Eden, because, well. Why would it? Weeds? Adam's fault. Carnivorous animals (and, one assumes, the occasional carnivorous plant)? Adam again. Entropy? You guessed it: Adam. Think about *that*, won't you; eat one piece of fruit and suddenly you're responsible for the inevitable heat death of the universe. God's kind of mean.

The interplay of this Holy Trinity of explanations comes to its full realization when the Creation Museum considers what really are its main draw: Dinosaurs. Are dinosaurs 65 million years old? As if—the Earth is just six thousand years old, pal! Dinosaurs were in the garden of Eden—and vegetarians, at least until the fall, so thanks there, Adam. They were still around as late as the mid-third millenium BC; they were hanging with the Sumerians and the Egyptians (or, well, could have). All those fossils? Laid down by Noah's Flood, my friends. Which is not to say there weren't dinosaurs on the Ark. No, the Bible says all kinds of land animals were on the boat, and dinosaurs are a subset of "all kinds." They were there, scaring the crap out of the mammals, probably. Why did they die off after the flood? Well, who can say. Once the flood's done, the Creation Museum doesn't seem to care too much about what comes next; we're in historical times then, you see, and that's all Exodus through Deuteronomy, ie., someone else's problem.

But seriously, the ability to just come out and put on a placard that the Jurassic era is temporally contiguous with the Fifth Dynasty of the Old Kingdom of Egypt—well, there's a word for that, and that word is *chutzpah*. Because, look, that's something you really have to *sell* if you want anyone to buy it. It's one thing to say to people that God directly created the dinosaurs and that they lived in the Garden of Eden. It's another thing to suggest they lived long enough to harass the Minoans, and do it with a straight face. It's horseshit, pure and simple, but that's not to suggest I can't admire the hucksterism.

W

I'm quite clearly immune to the ideological charms of the Creation

Museum, but then, I never was the prime audience for the place. How were other people grokking the museum the day I was there? Honestly, it's hard to say. The place was certainly crowded; I and the friends I went with had to wait in line an hour and a half to get into the place (there's a bottleneck in the middle of the museum in the form of a short film about the six days of creation). No one I could see was getting sloppy over the place; people just more or less shuffled through each room, looked at the displays, read the placards and moved on. My friends occasionally heard someone say "oh, come *on*," when one of the placards tested their credulity (there's apparently only so much of "T-Rexes were vegetarian" propaganda any one person should be obliged to take), but for my part I just noticed people looking, reading and moving on.

There have to be people who believe this horseshit unreservedly, but I suspect that perhaps the majority of the visitors I saw were Christians who may not buy into the whole "six days" thing, but are curious to see how it's being presented. To be clear, the "horseshit" I've been speaking of is not Christianity, it's creationism, which to my mind is a teleological quirk substantially unrelated to the grace one can achieve through Jesus Christ. Now, the Creation Museum rather emphatically argues that a literal reading of the Bible is essential for true Christianity—it's got a whole red-lit section that suggests the ills of society are directly related to folks deciding that maybe some parts of the Bible are, you know, *metaphorical*—but that's just more horseshit, of a slightly different flavor. There are lots of Christians who clearly don't need to twist their brain like a pretzel to get around the idea that the universe is billions of years old and that we've evolved from earlier forms. For those folks, the Creation Museum is probably about culture, to the extent any installation largely created by someone who previously worked for Universal Studios can be about culture.

At the very least, this is high-quality stuff on the level of production. There are lots of things here that are cheesy, but there's not much that's chintzy; you can see where the $27 million went. Whether this will all age well will be an interesting question, although I don't plan on returning in five years to find out. Here and now, it's all pretty damn slick, and I think that in itself may be a draw for mainstream Christians. Christian culture has only recently ramped itself up into being something other than a wan and denatured version of pop culture (this is evidenced in part by the fact that many evangelical Christian teens now dress as badly as the rest of their peers), and this is another high-production-value offering for this particular lifestyle choice.

Will these folks find the arguments they find at the Creation Museum convincing? Again, you got me. I certainly *hope* not, but more to the point I would hope that these folks don't come away feeling that their love of Christ obliges them to swallow heaping mounds of horse-shit from people who are phobic about metaphor. I really don't think Jesus would care if you think that you and a monkey have a common ancestor; I think he would care more that you think you and your neighbor have a common weal.

What about non-Christians? I can't imagine that anyone who wasn't strongly religious or already inclined to agree with creationist ideas would be converted by this place. Between blaming Adam for everything from poisons to sweating and T-Rexes eating coconuts and a particularly memorable placard explaining why in early Biblical times it was perfectly fine to have sex with your close relatives, it's just way too over the top.

Indeed, it's over the top *enough* that I never could actually get angry with the place. Not that I was planning to; I admit to dreading coming to the place, but that's primarily because I thought it would bore and annoy me, not make me angry. In fact, I was never bored, and was genuinely annoyed only by the "paleontologist" at the start of the walk-through. The rest of the time I enjoyed it as I suspect anyone who is not some stripe of creationist could enjoy it: As camp. At some point—specifically the part where the Scopes Monkey Trial was presented as the end of decent Christian civilization as we know it—I just started chuckling my way through. By the time I got to the Dinosaur Den, with its placards full of patent misinformation about how soft tissue fossilization strongly suggested a massive, worldwide flood, I was a little loopy. It was just so ridiculous.

And I'm *happy* about that. In the end, the Creation Museum is one of those things that I suspect will comfort those who absolutely believe in creationism, amuse those who absolutely don't, and be a interesting way to spend a day to lots of people somewhere in the middle. It's not a front in the culture war, as much as I think it would like to be; it's designed too much like an amusement for that.

It is what it is: An attractive and diverting repository for a massive load of horseshit. And, well, let's be realists: That load of horseshit's not going away anytime soon. Might as put it somewhere that it's out of everyone else's way. The Creation Museum manages that well enough.

OH MY GOD!
THEY LOOK
JUST LIKE US!

The *New York Times*, which recently tried to homo-fy two guys socializing by call it a "man date," continues on its vein of mild heterosexual panic with an article that frets that thanks to heterosexual men deciding it'd be okay not to be a slob every once in a while, and gay men occasionally not giving a crap if their stubble is exquisitely sculptured, it's getting harder to tell the gays from the straights. The horror! The sheer, unadulterated, sexually-ambiguous horror! And if we can't tell the gays from the straights, then the bisexuals are *really* up the creek, aren't they? Simultaneously wearing a too-tight ribbed tank top *and* relaxed fit Wranglers won't *mean* anything anymore.

These sort of articles make me want to smack the *Times* upside the head and yell at it to try its hand at actual news again, you know, for a refreshing *change*. I hear there's a war on. Secondly: This is a bad thing? We live in an era in which an active quorum of religious bigots would quarantine gays into concentration camps if they could ("It's just like Guantanamo—only *fabulous!*"), and the *Times* is snarkily concerned that we can't simply visually identify the gay guys anymore? Hell. I'll happily wear a leather armband if it'll flummox a hateful Bible-wielder. And I'll let a gay man borrow my Wal-Mart purchased t-shirt, just to *really* throw them off. *He can't be gay—that shirt is 40% polyester!* Yes, the gay can *blend*. Just like *polycotton*.

You know, when I was younger, a lot of people, including members of my own family, vaguely suspected I was gay. Why? Well, all the cultural indicators were there. During high school, I had an overly-dramatic crush on a particular girl which kept me from dating other absolutely wonderful girls even when (on occasion) they were standing right in front of me, waving their hands about and saying "Hey, look over here." Professing to have a long-standing crush on an unapproachable girl, is, of course, *very* teen gay. So is being verbally clever, slight of build, an active participant in singing and theater groups and enjoying Depeche Mode on a regular basis.

And I took dance. Modern *and* Jazz. Oh, yeah.

Add it all up and I was queer to the friggin' *core*. The only thing that really pegged me as possibly being in the heterosexual camp was that I was a freakin' slob and that in addition to enjoying Depeche Mode I was also a big fan of Journey. But as anyone can tell you, gay teens compensate for their queerness by doing things like, you know, picking a random corporate rock band to obsess over, hopefully one with a moderately cute lead singer. In my era it would be Journey. 10 years later: Creed (Today: Well, hell. All those new rock bands seem pretty sexually all over the map, don't they? Have you gotten a gander at, say, Franz Ferdinand?).

So: On paper, as a teen, pretty *darn* gay. And yet, right through to the monogamous institution of marriage, heterosexual right down the line (it's a short line, I'll admit). Also, I'm not afraid to say it: As a general rule, I like me the women. In theory I accept the possibility that some guy out there could get me emotionally quivery and physically all winged-out, and I wouldn't be all angsty about it if happened. But you know what? Hasn't. Whereas women distract me *all the damn time*. I'm good with this; for one thing, simply as a practical matter, it's caused me far fewer headaches than the alternative. I am appropriately thankful that I and my life partner have our relationship recognized by everyone as being a marriage, and that there are no exclusionary dickheads hiding their pissy fears behind a Bible and telling us we're going to burn in eternal Hellfire for loving each other and defining ourselves, with our child, as a family. It's one less thing for me to deal with personally. Would every couple were as fortunate as we.

(It doesn't seem likely people would confuse me for being gay anymore, what with the wife and child and rural red-state lifestyle and the

Wal-Mart clothes, but if they did, you know what I would think? *Good.* Here in the US, gay is the new British, which is to say that if people think you're gay, they also think you are smarter, wittier, and more fun to be around than the average guy. Sure, you sodomize other men on occasion, but that's your business, and we Americans always suspected British men had sodomy as a required subject at Eton. So it's all the *same,* really. And in the meantime you always say the perfect thing at the perfect moment. You're more entertaining than cable! And what could possibly be wrong with that? If people know you're a straight guy, on the other hand, they automatically think you're a beef-witted social dullard in a Linux shirt hoping to delude some poor woman into accepting a sperm packet or two. In a word: *Eeeeeeew.* I blame *Queer Eye for the Straight Guy* for propagating this "befuddled pathetic straight guy" meme, but since *the New York Times* tells us it's getting harder to tell the queers and straights apart, at least it's on its way way out.)

Point is: the gay/straight cultural checklist utterly failed to predict my overt and flagrant heterosexual proclivities. And I don't doubt that even now, somewhere in my sleepy Midwestern burg, there's a guy flying a NASCAR flag, wearing a John Deere cap and owning a pickup with a "W '04" bumper sticker who is trying to decide if he should go see *Mr. and Mrs. Smith* yet again to enjoy his recommended daily allowance of Brad Pitt, or if he should just stick *Troy* into the DVD player and catch Brad in his buff, half-naked, remote-control-pausable Achaean glory. In the *real* world the dividing line between gay and straight doesn't exist anywhere but in the mind and in the bedroom. It's vaguely appalling that the writers and editors of the *New York Times* don't actually get this.

Actually, I'm sure they do. But they have newshole to fill. Well, like I said: Rumor is, there's a war on.

WHY WE GRIEVE

Oct
10
2001

nteresting article in *Slate* today, describing the fact that even though 3,000 or so people were killed on 9/11, most of them American citizens, relatively few of us (meaning the rest of us Americans) actually directly know anyone who was killed—even in New York. I can stand testament to that, since I know several people who live in New York, and as far as I know, none of my friends in NYC know anyone who has died, and like the *Slate*-sters, we come from the same pool of "elite college, financially oriented" people who largely populated the World Trade Center during the work day.

Personally, I myself know no one who has died; I live in Ohio, which narrows the possibility, but on the other hand several of my clients are in NYC, and much of my work is directly financially related. In fact, as I've mentioned before, one of the firms that I write financial brochures for was located in the WTC—in Tower 2, to be precise. But I don't know any of those people personally since I don't work for the firm directly; I work as a subcontractor for a marketing firm. I do know a few people in my professional sphere who know people who have died—one client of mine had four friends who worked at Cantor Fitzgerald, who as you probably know lost several hundred employees in the attack. But again, that's one step removed. The *Slate* article, interestingly, notes that 80 percent of Americans are like me and know someone who knows someone who died—"we are all mourners at the second degree," the article says.

The existence of the story is due to the dissonance that so many of us have felt between how we've reacted to the attacks and how, rationally, we feel it is appropriate to feel. Basically, the gist of the article, so far as I got it, was: "If I don't know anyone who died, why do I feel so bad?" (there is also a more egotistical, self-aggrandizing subtext to the article that asks "I went to good schools and make a good amount of money, so how could *I* not have known someone who died?" But let's ignore that one for now). Many people feel uncomfortable with grief if there's no personal connection; it feels inappropriate, and also, it feels unfocused. If someone you know has died, you have someone to focus your emotions on. If you don't, you just walk around in a crappy mood for days.

Generally speaking, I wholeheartedly agree with the philosophy that grief is best reserved for those you know and care about personally. I never mourn the death of celebrities, even those I admire, because I don't *know* them, and while I have been sad in several cases that this means there is no more output from that particular person, and that a singular mind that I know of has been lost, mourning the death as a personal tragedy is not my purview. I felt a mild twinge at Kurt Cobain, but that was a *zeitgeist* thing. I got over it in about ten seconds. It sounds callous to put it that way, of course, but remember: I didn't *know* Kurt Cobain. Really, it shouldn't have taken me *more* than ten seconds to move on.

But the 9/11 attacks are a singular event. 3,000 men and women died in the WTC and Pentagon attacks (not to mention the several dozen in Pennsylvania) which is an enormous number of people to have died at one time for any reason at all. That's going to be a shocker, to be sure—but it's not enough for grief. Let's hypothesize that 3,000 people died because of a terrible hurricane scouring across Florida and the gulf states. Americans would be horrified, of course. And we would be generous in helping those in need. But as a nation, we wouldn't be grieving. If one plane had somehow hit a World Trade Center tower by accident, causing a collapse of one or possibly both of the towers, again, we'd be shocked first and generous second. But we wouldn't be walking around with heavy hearts for weeks.

I think we grieve *because* we don't know those who died—because we know that those who performed the attacks didn't know them either, and wouldn't have cared if they had. I think we grieve because we know the attackers would have been happy to replace any of the thousands who died and thousands more who were wounded with any of us. We are interchangeable to them; they don't care which Americans they killed, they just wanted to kill Americans. And to that extent, they did the job: The casualty list of the attacks cut a demographic swath through our land. White, black, Hispanic, Jews, Muslims, Christians, atheist, gay, straight, rich, poor, middle class, Democrat, Republican, new immigrant, old money, war-monger and pacifist. It just didn't matter. More Americans to kill. I don't think it takes anything away from those who died to say that on a fundamental level who they were made no difference to their killers—they were meant to represent any of us, to *be* any of us. And they were.

This is why it's right and appropriate to grieve their passing, to feel the pain of their absence, even if you didn't know a single one of those people yourself. Look at the next person you see: But for time, location and personal circumstance, that person could be under the rubble. Look at your co-workers. Look at your family. Look at your child. Look at yourself. But most of all, look at *anyone*. That's who the target was. They just happened not to be in the buildings or on the airplanes. We grieve because we're all Americans, and in a real sense, it is a personal loss.

I watched Osama bin Laden and his odious lackey yesterday talk about how wonderful it was the towers went down and the Pentagon was hit, and all I wanted was a good five minutes in a room with either one of them and a lead pipe with a little heft to it. A lot of us have been going around and around about the root causes of the sort of terrorism that lead to these attacks, with not a few suggesting that America bears some responsibility for the chain of circumstances that brought planes and buildings together. I may be willfully obtuse, but just right now I can't see how or why that should matter, as regards hunting down these people. These people want *me* dead. They want my wife dead, my daughter dead, my family and all my friends dead too. If we'd been in the towers, they'd be happy we were buried beneath them.

Regardless of how these people came to believe these things, it's time for them to be stopped. I don't know anyone who died on September 11, but I know who was attacked. I was, and so were you. This is personal.

I Hate WE

Jun

22

2001

Here are all the reasons I hate the ad for WE, the new Women's Entertainment channel, that appears to be showing constantly at all times no matter which cable channel I am watching:

First off, it features the nine billionth use of Sister Sledge's "We Are Family" to telegraph funky female togetherness. Don't get me wrong. I'm thrilled that the song allows the members of Sister Sledge (who are, incidentally, actually sisters) to dine out and pay the occasional gas bill twenty-one years after the song hit the charts. But if I have to hear it one more time—*ever*—I may have to jab a sharpened Popsicle stick directly into an eardrum, and possibly not one of my own. That goes for Gloria Gaynor's "I Will Survive," too. I mean, enough. You've survived, already. Now shut up.

And anyway, it's a lie. Women, as a class, aren't a family. Just like men, some women like some other women, while absolutely hating the stinkin' guts of others. I mean, good Lord, doesn't anyone remember the gym shower scene in *Carrie*? (Playing "We are Family" in the background of that scene, now, that would have been a master stroke.) Demanding that all women fall into solidarity at the drop of an R&B hit is a little smug and cheap on WE's part, particularly as what they're supposed to fall in line for here is a cable channel.

(But that's the way it's always done in advertising, in case you haven't noticed. Women are always joyously banding to celebrate some damned thing or another, whether it's women's cable programming or zit creams or feminine napkins. One of the commercials that ranks high up there on my all-time Hate List is a recent pantyliner commercial in which a carefully multi-ethnic quartet of attractive young women hug each other enthusiastically while simultaneously shouting the name of the pantyliner brand. Forgive me, but I doubt that the natural expulsion of reproductive detritus into winged cotton batting has ever brought any group of women together, and if it has, well, those women are *icky*.)

Moreover, if I were woman, I'd be sick and tired of the assumption that what I *really* wanted to do all the time was watch other women sit around on a pastel couch with throw pillows, drinking coffee from oversized mugs and talking to other women about women's issues. I mean, hell. I'm a man, and just about the last thing I'd ever be doing is looking at some guys hanging out in a rumpus room, sitting on bar stools with their beers and talking about hot chicks and auto engines. Really, I'd rather *die*. Not just because it's boring as Hell, but also because as much as I *am* a man (harumph, harumph), it's not something that's really worth thinking an awful lot about on a minute-to-minute basis. Yes, yes, I have a penis. Fine. Be that as it may, I have other stuff to do. I can't imagine ever wanting to watch a *show* about men's issues, much less an entire freakin' network. This is why, not entirely coincidentally, I've never seen a single edition of ESPN SportsCenter.

Back to the WE ad. Once we get past the soul-jangling tones of "We Are Family," we get a montage of female celebrities—Victoria Williams, Cindy Crawford, and Faye Dunaway (carefully multi-ethnic!)—all declaring some of their various attributes. "I'm an actress. I'm an athlete. I'm a friend," one of them modestly declares, as the camera zooms in to examine her perfect pores. Then another comes in to announce her curriculum vitae. Then another. After two or three of these, what I really wanted was to see Steve Miller show up and declare "I'm a joker. I'm a smoker. I'm a midnight toker." Purely as a matter of gender, it would be inappropriate, but it would sure feel right.

As I've previously alluded, I'm not a woman, but even as a man, there's something condescending about these litanies of ability. The undertone behind the *I'm all these things* bullet points is that women still have to prove that they can do a whole bunch of things even though they're women. While I'm not foolish enough to argue that women have achieved equality in all or even most things—women are still earning 80 cents to a man's dollar simply because they don't have testicles—I also don't believe that women should feel compelled to qualify their successes through the prism of their gender. Any time you have to qualify your success, you implicitly diminish it.

(I just mentioned this point to my wife, who thinks I'm reading a little much into the litanies. But I'll stick to my guns here. Any time you see someone listing off accomplishments in an ad, it's because they've done so despite adversity—medical ads do this sort of thing all the time. I just don't think being a woman should be the equivalent of a chronic malady.)

Also, it bugs me that all the women in the ad are strikingly attractive. It's more proof that those who market to women consciously or unconsciously believe that women are swayed more by attractiveness than competence—which further calls into question the whole "I am..." thing. In her recital, Faye Dunaway declares "I'm a director." After I was done rolling my eyes (she's directed one cable movie in her whole life, and that for WE), I couldn't help but wonder: What's wrong with Betty Thomas? Or Penny Marshall? Or Mimi Leder? Each of these women are *real* directors, with $100 million grossing movies to their credit. I bet you one of them would have been happy to sign on as a spokesperson. They're just not as good looking as Faye.

I've nothing against good-looking women. Some of my best friends are good-looking women. But they ought to mix things up. I'll say it: I want to see an ugly woman as a spokeswoman for a women's network. Ugly men are out there all the time—look at Larry King, for God's sake. He looks like someone's talking underwear. Why not give America a spokeswoman who ain't much to look at but is competent as Hell? If accomplishments actually count for women, this ought to be a no-brainer.

In fact, I even have a suggestion: CNN's Candy Crowley. Crowley is without a doubt the lumpiest newsperson on TV, and every time I see her, I give a little mental cheer. You don't doubt she's a damn fine reporter, because as stupidly obsessed with looks at TV reporting is, particularly with female correspondents, Crowley nevertheless gets airtime.

Lots of of airtime (she's CNN's senior political correspondent). She's got journalism awards up the wazoo, too. Give her her own hour on WE (or Lifetime, or Oxygen, or wherever), and I bet she'd do a hell of a job.

So why not make her—or someone like her—a spokesperson? Does anyone doubt she's got the skills and accomplishments? Does WE's braintrust actually believe that women—their merry band of sisters— are so hopelessly shallow that they couldn't or wouldn't accept a physically unattractive but otherwise qualified woman as a public face for their network?

Well, I know where I stand on that question. The whole problem with the WE ad is that from the music to the words out of the attractive spokeswomen's mouths, it assumes far too little out of its audience. It panders rather than inspires. The individual components bug me personally, but the overall statement is one I find truly depressing for women. Think about it, women: This is supposed to be a network *for* you, and it can't appeal to you any better than this. Isn't that sad?

MULTIPLE
IDENTICAL
NEPHEWS

Watching children's commercials also made me aware that Froot Loop spokescreature Toucan Sam has joined the legions of single male animated characters who have multiple identical nephews with whom they share adventures. In the commercial in question, Sam and his multiple identical nephews are in a jungle, plundering massive fruit, when Sam accidentally drains the body of water on which they travel, causing the fruit to swirl together.

I'm sure someone more Marxist than I could make some sort of allusion to this commercial and how the colonial ambitions of the Europeans in Africa caused wholesale destruction of habitat and tribal identity (represented by the draining of the water and the swirling together of the "fruit"), but I'm more of the opinion they're just trying to sell those new Swirled Together Froot Loops. What can I say, the capitalist stooges got to me.

The phenomenon of multiple identical nephews (henceforth to be known as "MIN") in the animated medium has always astounded me, because these MIN always seem to arrive out of nowhere, with no verifiable provenance. Were you aware that Toucan Sam had siblings? Who are they, and what do they do? Is "Toucan Bob" selling radial tires outside Columbus? Perhaps "Toucan Fran" has a job as the saucy mascot of a tropical-themed strip bar in Georgia. Obviously they can't make ends meet, otherwise they'd never have sent off their children to stay with Sam, whose peripatetic life philosophy ("Follow Your Nose") doesn't seem to encourage the sort of stability and routine small children need and crave.

Of course, there's always the supposition that these "nephews" aren't actually nephews at all, but the bastard children of the animated characters in question, whose linage has been muddied for the sake of the wayward parent's career. This probably isn't the case with Toucan Sam himself, whose mannerisms and rainbow flag beak prove him to be clearly and serenely gay in that veddy-British, I-was-buggered-by-my-sixth-form-chums-at-Eton-and-it-was-the-best-time-of-my-life sort of way. But it's pretty obviously a viable theory for Donald Duck and for Popeye, both of whose MINs are spitting images of the adults themselves. Particularly Popeye's, whose MINs come complete with the sailor's trademark corncob pipe (Popeye also has the mysterious Sweet-pea to explain away; perhaps this is the real-life consequence of having a girl in every port).

Now, this sort of deception may have been necessary during the days of the Hayes Code, when these characters got their start. But as we're now approaching the millennium, I say it's time to let these beloved animated characters claim their children as their own. No doubt Huey, Dewey and Louie are already screwed up by the fact that they never see their "real" parents, because those "real" parents don't exist. Why not let Donald start the healing process by declaring they they are, in fact, his sons—his Multiple Identical Illegitimate Sons?

Aren't we a big enough country to accept the fact that even animated characters need love too, and that those needs sometimes lead to multiple identical issue? Haven't Donald and Popeye and all the rest already *been* fathers to these kids, supporting them, loving them, and taking them on all sorts of wacky, six-minute long adventures? I say, let the charade end. Write your local congressmen and animation producers now. The sooner Huey, Dewie and Louie call Donald Duck "dad," the better off we'll *all* be.

On
Carl Sagan

When I was eleven, I thought Carl Sagan was the coolest guy in the world. And that was because he was speaking right at me. At the age of 11, in 1980, I was a kid utterly convinced that he was going to grow up to be an astronomer—I loved the stars, I loved the science, I loved the toys—and here on my TV came Sagan, suave in his red turtleneck and buff jacket, surrounded by special effects and Vangelis music and telling everyone (but especially *me*) about how the cosmos is everything that ever was, everything that is, and everything that ever will be.

I fell for Carl with the sort of blissful rapture that I strongly suspect is only available to pre-pubescent geeks, a sort of nerd crush that, to be clear, had no sexual component, but had that same sort of swoony intensity. This was the guy I wanted to be when I was age eleven. Sagan sits as a member of my triumvirate of cultural heroes, the other two being John Lennon and H.L. Mencken. It's a odd trio of personal heroes, I admit, but then I'm *still* a little odd. But even among John and Henry, Carl came in first. Maybe it was the turtlenecks.

I'm a quarter century older than the eleven-year-old boy whose mother held a weekly viewing of *Cosmos* over his head as a bargaining chip for good behavior, and I'm still a great admirer of Carl Sagan, primarily because he did something I see as immensely important: he popularized science and with patience and good humor brought it into people's homes. He did it through *Cosmos*, most obviously, but he also did it every time he popped up on *The Tonight Show* and talked with celebrity fluidity about what was going on in the universe. He was the people's scientist. This is not to say that you'd look at Sagan and see him down at the NASCAR race; it is to say that he could easily use a NASCAR race to explain, say, relativistic speeds and what it means for traveling through the universe.

This is important stuff. Getting science in front of people in a way they can understand—without speaking down to them—is the way to get people to support science, and to understand that science is neither beyond their comprehension nor hostile to their beliefs. There *need* to be scientists and popularizers of good science who are of good will, who have patience and humor, and who are willing to sit with those who are skeptical or unknowing of science and show how science is *already* speaking their language. Sagan knew how to do this; he was uncommonly good at it.

I find that inspirational. As it happens, I am not a scientist—the flesh was willing, but the math skills were, alas, weak—but I write about science with some frequency; I've even fulfilled a life goal of writing an astronomy book, *The Rough Guide to the Universe*, of which I am about to compile a second edition. In my writing and presentation of science, I look to Sagan for guidance. Nearly all of what happens in the universe can be explained in the way that nearly any person can understand; all it requires is the desire to explain it and the right language. Sagan had the desire and language. I like to think I do too, in part because I learned my lessons from him.

I am aware of the need to avoid hagiography. I have an idealized version of Carl Sagan in my head, one that is notably absent any number of flaws that the real Carl Sagan had to have had simply because he was human. My connection to Sagan comes from some limited number of hours of television and a finite number of books, and in both cases the man was edited for my consumption. This is one of the reasons why, unlike the 11-year-old version of me, I don't want to *be* Carl Sagan, and I'm not even entirely sure I want to be much like him as a person, if only because, at the end of it, I don't know him as a person.

What I do know is that I like his ideas. I like his love of science. I like his faith in humanity. I like how he saw us reaching for things greater than ourselves, because it was in our nature and because it was a fulfillment of our nature. I like how he shared his enthusiasm for the entire universe with everyone and believed that everyone could share in that enthusiasm. These are things that, in giving them to everyone, he also gave to me, first as an 11-year-old and then continuing on. I've accepted them with thanks and made them part of who *I* am. If I use them well, I may be fortunate enough to share them with you as they were shared with me.

THINGS ONE
SHOULD NOT
FORGET

<table>
<tr><td>Jan</td></tr>
<tr><td>14</td></tr>
<tr><td>2008</td></tr>
</table>

Jonah Goldberg, who has never once used someone else's verbal flubs for mocking purposes, ever, gets annoyed that people are amused that during a talk at the Heritage Foundation (update, 2:13pm: actually, in this *Salon* interview; he apparently himself forgot where he said it, and this is what I get for following his memory on the subject; editing now to reflect provenance) he momentarily forgot why Mussolini was called a fascist, i.e., because he was the founder of the Fascist Party:

> *Any fair minded person would agree that I simply misspoke. Instead these bandersnatches ignore the rest of the entire speech and focus on this unfortunate but entirely innocuous flub as "proof" of my total and complete ignorance and dishonesty.*
>
> *My apologies for giving these buffoons the ammo, but anyone persuaded by this and this alone is beyond reasoning with anyway.*

Jonah, dude, I don't *doubt* that you misspoke. That's pretty obvious. But, really. How does one—particularly one purporting to write a book on fascism—*forget*, even for a minute, that Mussolini was called a fascist because he *was a Fascist*? And not just a Fascist, he was *the* Fascist; indeed, the Platonic Ideal of a Fascist. Maybe you were nervous about being interviewed—you do it so infrequently, after all—but it's kind of a big goof. We Americans may not know much about Mussolini, but we know three things: He made trains run on time, he bore an unsettling resemblance to George C. Scott, and that *he was a goddamn Fascist*. It's not something one easily forgets, nor should forget, especially when one is, say, talking *about* fascism to the press. Try to do better next time, Mr. Goldberg. You'll look less of an ass.

So that's taken care of. Now I want to make the point that, aside from the fact that Goldberg had a mental burp when he forgot Mussolini was called a fascist because he was a fascist, OG style, *yo*, he was also way off with the rest of the statement in question. Which is:

Mussolini was born a socialist, he died a socialist, he never abandoned his love of socialism, he was one of the most important socialist intellectuals in Europe and was one of the most important socialist activists in Italy, and the only reason he got dubbed a fascist and therefore a right-winger is because he supported World War I.

Well, out here beyond the conservative event horizon, we're pretty sure Mussolini, at the top of his authoritarian game, was happily right-wing and not a socialist. We know this because Benito—old school Fascist, fascist before fascist was cool—tells us so in the document in which he lays out the doctrine of Fascism:

> *Granted that the 19th century was the century of socialism, liberalism, democracy, this does not mean that the 20th century must also be the century of socialism, liberalism, democracy. Political doctrines pass; nations remain. We are free to believe that this is the century of authority, a century tending to the "right", a Fascist century.*

Now, I know it's not the fashion to prefer the original sources to current, revisionist views of history, but what can I say, I went to the University of Chicago, and we're old fashioned that way. So when Benito Mussolini—Fascist before Fascism became so popular no one went there any more—describes the "Fascist negation of socialism, democracy, liberalism" as a doctrine of the right, I tend to give credence to the man's word.

Which is to say: not only was Mussolini dubbed a fascist because he formed the Fascists, Fascism is a right wing doctrine because Mussolini, who founded the movement, *designed it to be*. Therefore, Mussolini:

right-wing *and* fascist! And self-admitted to both. You can read it for yourself.

I know, I know. Why should I believe anything Mussolini said? Dude was a *fascist*. We all know how *they* are. He probably called himself right-wing just to mess with the liberals and socialists. But when you remember that he dealt with liberals and socialists by actually killing them and then bragging about it on the floor of the Italian Parliament, you figure pulling literary pranks of this sort might have been a little *subtle* for him. Mussolini—fascist back when being fascist *meant* something, damn it—was all about the action. He'd tell you that himself, were he not eventually whacked by firing squad while trying to sneak out of the country and then hung upside down by meat hooks in the Piazzale Loreto for the general populace to abuse.

(To be fair to Goldberg, Mussolini did indeed do time, and prominently so, as a socialist. But eventually he stopped being one. You know why? Because he went and created the Fascist Party. Which was anti-socialist and right wing. Just ask the founder of it. I've not read Goldberg's book so I'm not entirely sure what alchemy he uses to argue that a right-wing, anti-socialist political movement is and always was actually a left-wing socialist political movement, but I do suspect whatever argument it is, Mussolini himself would have found it less than satisfying, and being as much the political journalist as Goldberg is, would likely have offered him fair argument on the point, if he didn't just have him, oh, *shot*.)

So. What have we learned today?

1. Fascism: Right wing authoritarian movement. Says so right there on the label.
2. When speaking in public about fascism, try not to forget why Mussolini, founder of Fascism, arguably a fascist movement, was called a fascist. Even for just a minute or two.
3. When declaring someone is a lifelong socialist and not right-wing, it helps not to have that person's own words and writings (and actions, really) actively contradict you.

4. Original sources are jazzy and fun, and everybody should read them!

5. If you're going to complain about people snarking without substance, don't give them something substantive to snark about, too.

Done for now.

Breastfeeding God

Mar

27

2002

PETA wants to promote breastfeeding in Mississippi with billboards showing the Baby Jesus suckling at the Virgin Mary's nipple. This is a bit like the Beef Advisory Council promoting their product by placing a burger in each of the many hands of Shiva. You could chalk it up to miscalculation and ignorance, but it's PETA, whose grand plan to promote their cause in the United States seems to boil down to "enrage meat eaters to such a degree that they choke on their steaks." Miscalculation isn't part of the plan.

Were I a meat-bearing animal (and unless I'm schlepping groceries, I'm not), the folks at PETA are just about the last people on Earth I'd want promoting my cause, since the short-term result of this sort of intentionally antagonistic marketing approach is that someone's likely to have protest grill-a-thon right under the billboard. You can see it now: *Eat a sausage for Jesus.* Clearly, this wouldn't help. Someone needs to do a study to see whether meat sales go up after every PETA stunt; I think we all might be surprised at the results. I don't think PETAs cause is unjust in the least, I just think the end result of their tactics is likely to be higher bacon consumption.

However, PETA is correct on two points. The first is that human breast milk is far better for infants than cow's milk (which is the point of the billboard) and in fact cow's milk can be bad for very young babies: Far too much sodium, for one thing (you can do a number on a baby's kidneys). There are also too many nutrients at too many different levels relative to the mix a newborn needs. I remember that while Athena was being born, a very good (childless) friend of ours who was feeding our pets also bought us two gallons of whole milk so we could be prepared. I certainly appreciated the thought (and still do), but I'd have been about as likely to pop open a can of Sprite and put that in our newborn's bottle as I would be to give her milk from the store.

PETA's billboard is fatuous to the extent that any pediatrician or ob/gyn who did not get a medical degree from a box of Trix already knows all this and will have communicated this information to their expectant mothers (as will have the instructors of their birthing classes, who comprise a veritable La Leche League mafia). So its only true value is to piss off religious conservatives, which is entirely why PETA did it anyway. But *technically*, it's not wrong.

The second point where PETA is correct is that the baby Jesus did breastfeed off the Virgin Mary. It was 2000 years ago, baby formula had not yet made inroads into the parenting market, and while there almost certainly was a cow around (Jesus was camping out in the animal's food bin, after all), chances are very good Mary guided Jesus to her breast instead. That's what breasts are *for*. Mary may have been a virgin, but she wasn't stupid.

The real question is why religious conservatives are so incensed by the portrayal. I don't mean this in the entirely fake way PETA officials are pretending to be shocked, shocked that anyone could see something as *natural* as a *mother* suckling her *child* as offensive, since if it hadn't have been offensive, PETA simply wouldn't have done it. They would picked some other outrageous image; this being the South, I imagine a billboard of General Sherman torching Atlanta, with the tagline underneath: *Haven't You Had Enough of Barbeque?* That'd get them going down in Dixie (Note to PETA: Steal this, and you'll get a call from my lawyers. They're carnivores).

PETA counted on it being offensive, but, fundamentally, why *should* it be offensive? Jesus was divine, but also human. He was a baby, he had to eat. Mary was the Mother of God but also a mother; she gave birth, her body pumped out milk so she could feed her baby. Mary suckled the Baby Jesus. Deal with it.

The response: We know she *did* it, we just don't want to *see* it or *think* about it. And of course, the answer here is: Why on Earth not? Well, for one thing, it's a *breast*—and we all know that looking at boobs arouses thoughts of sex. Sex leads to sin, sin leads to fear, fear leads to hate, hate leads to suffering. So we just can't have the Virgin Mary going topless. The kids will riot.

As you can imagine, this line of reasoning makes me giggle. For one thing, there's undoubtedly a special seating area in Hell for people who have lustful thoughts about the Virgin Mary (excluding, possibly, Joseph). Everybody knows this, so anyone who glances at the picture and thinks "Huh huh huh—the Virgin Mary is totally *hot*" is already feeling Satan's tines sticking his ass and has other problems to worry about.

For another thing, breasts being used for breastfeeding are unsexy in almost exactly the same way a vagina being used for birth is unsexy—indeed, it's a vivid reminder that God, in His wisdom, evolved dual uses for just about every fun-providing part of the human anatomy, and that second use is definitely not about having a good time. So I think we can shelve the "Boobs = sex" line of reasoning here. The Virgin Mary suckling the Baby Jesus is about as far from sex as we're likely to get, even without throwing in the nature of Mary's impregnation.

The other issue may simply be that Christians don't like dwelling on the human aspect of Jesus and Mary—just as any person prefers not to dwell on the grosser (in every meaning of the word) aspects of the humanity of their idols. But I have to say this doesn't make much sense to me. Christian theology is built on Jesus' dual nature as divine and human: Toss out one half, and the other half doesn't work. Jesus' suffering was rooted in his divinity—he was called on to redeem the sins of the world—but the actual *suffering* part was predicated upon his human nature. Being nailed to a cross to die doesn't work if He Who is Nailed doesn't have the humanity required to suffer.

Aside from Jesus, other major Christian figures relied on their humanity to confirm their divinity as well. You can't throw a rock in a room full of early Christian saints without hitting one martyred for his faith (depending on who you hit, in fact, the rock throwing bit is nothing new to him). Martyrdom is physical and painful, a reflection of Jesus' human pain on the cross. And of course there's Mary herself, chosen to carry Jesus for her essential humanity.

Dwelling on the humanity of Jesus and Mary doesn't weaken their divinity, it strengthens it. Showing a picture of the Blessed Mother and Child as the latter is breastfeeding off the former shouldn't been seen as sacrilege or blasphemy, but an acknowledgment of part of what makes them special, loved and revered. I think that people who are enraged by the picture should take a few moments and reflect on that fact. Jesus was human as much as divine, and it's simply wrong to deny His humanity, and the things that come with it.

It doesn't mean you have to walk around with a picture in your wallet of Jesus suckling from the Virgin Mary, mind you (or of Jesus performing any other human functions you might not care to think about on an everyday basis, because, you know, Jesus did those things *too*). But this way, when someone shoves a picture like this in your face as a cheap way to piss you off, you can laugh it away. And then you can have a nice slab of pork round. See who's more pissed off then.

Fun With the GMH

One of the things that really chaps my ass about the people who oppose gay marriage is that so many of them seem to believe that allowing guys to marry guys or gals to marry gals will tumble the entire nation into a festering cesspool of carnal inequity, in which everyone suddenly turns into lustful raveners who engage in group marriages with dogs and close relatives, like recursively genetic unfortunates or characters from a late-era Robert Heinlein novel. Aside from being patently irrational, it also points to a certain worldview that is simultaneously fearful, smug and insulting:

1. It suggests that the gay marriage-haters (henceforth referred to as "GMH") believe that the vast majority of people in the country are sexual degenerates who can only be kept from pets and the consanguineous purely by hard rule of law.

2. Or, should we wish to be charitable, it suggests that the GMH seriously believe that the rest of us cannot see or reasonably formulate a moral or legal difference between allowing a man to marry another man, and allowing a man to marry a bichon frise. This suggests the GMH think we're all stupid and unreasoning and therefore need to be guided by our intellectual and moral superiors, i.e., them.

3. It clearly suggests that the GMH believe that gay men and women are morally and legally equivalent to dogporkers

and uncleboinkers, despite so many of the GMH who suggest they're perfectly *fine* with gay people, it's just those dirty
nasty unfathomably evil gay *acts* they do that are so darn
bad. Actually, they *do* hate and/or fear and/or feel disgust
over gay people specifically, it's just that with the exception
of Fred Phelps and a few drunken frat boys cruising the
streets outside gay bars with pickups and bats, they realize
that announcing that fact to the rest of us marks them as un-
savory and intolerant, which should be a hint but is not.
4. It likewise clearly suggests that the GMH live in constant
and overweening fear for their own personal morality in the
face of differences in others; i.e., that should they encounter
a legally married gay couple, their personal moral compass
might swing so wildly askew that the next thing they know
it's 3 am and they're being bent over an interstate rest stop
picnic table by a leather bear named Chuck while a fetching
chocolate lab is licking their heroin-dusted nipples. They
didn't *want* it to happen. But they just couldn't *help* it.

Now, naturally, I entirely expect the GMH to violently object to this,
and maintain that they *don't* think the rest of us are brain-damaged per-
verts or that they're morally weak fag haters. But if you *don't* and if you
aren't, well, then, what is the problem? Really. What is the big deal, here?
If *we're* not all glory-hole-seeking morons, how will the prospect of hap-
pily-married gay people change us? And if *you're* not all prejudiced and
on the verge of a lapse of sexual ethics, how does possibly getting an
invitation to the marriage of Sue and Jill threaten you?

(Please don't come at me with the arguments that marriage is about
the possibility of procreation or that God says it's between men and
women. There are a number of religious denominations, Christian and
otherwise, which offer religious blessing on same-sex unions, and unless you're willing to ban the infertile from marriage, the second goes
out the window as well.)

Allow me to make a radical suggestion here, which quite obviously
I don't think is radical at all. I submit that I believe that gay marriages,

on average, are likely to be more stable and happy than straight marriages—that is to say, more likely to be "model" marriages in which the two partners are committed to each other in a loving fashion. And the reason for this, naturally enough, comes down to sex, as in, sex is not why gays and lesbians will get hitched.

Come on, you abstinence types. You *know* sex plays a significant role in marriage among the conservatively religious, who trend toward marrying younger than other groups. Indeed, it's one of the selling points: You can have all the sex you want! And God approves! But I submit that someone who marries for access to sex—or has it in his or her unspoken top three reasons, as I strongly suspect any heterosexual human who reaches his or her early 20s as a virgin *might*—will find he or she has a weak pillar in the marriage after the first bloom of sexual activity wears off. And you know how humans are when it comes to sex. They're all screwy for it. It makes them do things like have affairs and try to serve divorce papers on their wives in hospital recovery rooms and whatnot.

Now, take your gay couple. He and he (or she and she) don't have the same hangups about sex and marriage, for the simple reason that gay people have never had the need or expectations regarding marriage and access to sex. They have ever had their sex independent of the marriage institution. So it would seem reasonable to suggest that if a gay couple decided to marry, the fevered idea of *finally* getting to have sex (and the irrationality such a desire can bring) would not be one of the major motivating factors. Instead the decision would be based on other more, shall we say, considered factors, like basic compatibility, shared life goals and expectations, and a genuine and well-regarded appreciation for the other, in the relationship and out of it.

Let's be clear that I am *not* suggesting marriages between the religiously conservative are doomed once the rush of newlywed sex wears off (they're not) or that every gay person who marries will do so in a sober, well-considered manner (they won't). But I am suggesting that those gays who do decide to marry have one less distorting pressure on the marriage vow than many straights do.

For now, at least. Because here's the really interesting blind spot the GMH have on the matter of gay marriages—they have the potential to make people rather *more* "moral" than less. After all, if gays and lesbians have the right to marry, the GMH, who we may reasonably assume have a large overlap with the religiously conservative and those who wish to promote abstinence before marriage, may then do just that—promote sexual abstinence to gays and lesbians in a reasonable manner.

Let's grant that in their heart of hearts, most GMH wish gays and lesbians didn't have sex at all, and would go through their entire lives miserable and sexually thwarted (see point number three above). But realistically, that's just *not* gonna happen. So allowing gays and lesbians to marry is the next best thing, since it creates a structure that allows the abstinence-loving not only to limit gay and lesbian sexual activity on an individual basis but also on a larger scale. After all, the gay teenager who commits to abstinence before marriage is one less gay teenager having sex with other gay teenagers, and wallowing in the ancillary gay culture. It also quickly and efficiently stuffs the gay person into a monogamous relationship, thereby trimming away the promiscuity that (to the religiously conservative) defines the whole "gay lifestyle."

True, these people are *still* gay. But at least they'd be gay like the rest of the religiously conservative is straight. Honestly, for a religious conservative, that's as good as it's ever going to get.

But of course, I don't expect the GMH to see it that way (I also don't imagine gay men and women will go for the abstinence thing in any higher numbers than straight men or women, but that's another matter entirely). What I expect is for the GMH to continue to declaim that gay marriages will bring on zoophilia, incest and polygamy (or polyandry— I mean, why not?), and to continue to hate and fear and hate and fear and hate and fear some more long after the rest of us have welcomed the new gay married couple down the block to the next neighborhood cookout and traded wedding and proposal stories and have then gone on to other reassuringly mundane topics of conversation.

And to the GMH I say: Knock yourself out, kids. Just don't do it near me. Also, when your moral compass gets whacked off course because you just couldn't fight off the decadence, stay away from my dog.

Mr. Nice Guy

Mar

7

2003

There's no pleasing some people. I spent yesterday's Whatever slagging Dubya, and the mail I get pounds on me for a throwaway comment I make about Dubya probably being a nice man (I specifically wrote: "I don't doubt Dubya's a nice man and not traditionally what one describes as stupid, but his thought processes are shallow and stagnant, like week-old water in a unused kiddie pool.") Apparently calling the sitting President the most incompetent resident of the White House since Warren Harding, and doing so in an interesting and creative way, isn't enough. One has to maintain he's soul-warpingly evil as well, just the sort of guy who takes welfare babies, strangles them with wire, runs their tiny corpses through a deli slicer, pan fries the cold cuts and then feeds them to his Rottweilers, which he's kicked for three hours a day since they were puppies in order to make them extra vicious when he sics them on poor, wrinkled Helen Thomas at the next White House press conference.

Sorry. Can't do it, because I don't think Dubya is that guy. I would suspect that on a day-to-day basis and in his personal encounters the man is normal enough, which makes him, like most people, a generally nice person to be around. I'm also sure that, like most people, he has his moments of irritability, neuroses, and supreme dickheadedness, which unfortunately for him are played out on the world stage and make for good news, while the rest of us get to have our moments of incivil stupidity in relative obscurity. One correspondent, in listing Dubya's not-nice crimes against humanity, noted to me that the man is reportedly given to irrational bouts of rage. Well, maybe he is. On the other hand, yesterday I beat a malfunctioning phone to death with a hammer. So maybe I'm not the best person to judge someone for their irrational bouts of rage. And anyway, hammering my phone to death does not make me any less nice (except, in a very narrow sense, to malfunctioning phones). Yes, yes, where I hammer a phone in a fit of pique, Dubya can bomb a country. But I'm reasonably sure they'd bring in Colin Powell to hose him down first.

Dubya's nice. Bill Clinton was nice, too. All of our recent Presidents have been nice enough people, in the generally accepted sense of the term; you have to go back 30 years to Nixon before you find a genuinely unpleasant occupant of the Oval Office (Johnson was apparently no prize, either, but at least he was a principled son of a bitch rather than fetidly paranoid, as Nixon was). Our Presidents are at least superficially pleasant people because as a nation we are at least superficially pleasant as well; people who are actively unpleasant generally make us uncomfortable. While unpleasantness may work on a small scale (note the number of truly feculent members of the House of Representatives), at a national level, gross non-niceness is a serious liability.

Dubya-haters want him to be evil because they perceive his policies to be evil: A *nice* guy wouldn't invade Iraq or deprive children of school lunch money or take a weed-whacker to the Constitution and so on. The problem with that formulation is that it's totally wrong; nice people do these sorts of things *all the time*. On the extreme end of it, you have Arendt's banality of evil or Milgram's zappers: Otherwise normal, nice people doing horrific things to other people because they either don't see or choose to ignore the far-reaching consequences—or they don't see the consequences as being wrong.

Most of us don't take things that far, but the principle is the same: Fundamentally, there's no connection between whether someone is personally nice and whether they pursue an agenda inimical to what you perceive as desirable. On a day-to-day basis, evangelical Christians are some of the nicest people you'll ever meet, and yet the bland, theocratic, prayer-at-Friday-football-games and stadium-church-on-Sunday America many of them want to foist on the rest of us is something I know I'll wearily spend the rest of life fighting against. By the same token,

I'm sure that most evangelicals would find me genuinely pleasant to be around, since like most people I'm friendly enough, and I prefer people to be comfortable in my presence. But that's not to say they won't recoil in horror against my position that gay people should be able to marry, evolution is scientific fact while creationism is a fairy tale and both should be taught as such, and that a woman should get to evict an unwanted occupant of her womb if that's what she wants. We're all nice people. We just disagree vehemently about details.

Fact is, I have very little tolerance for the "If you disagree with me, you're evil/sick/just not nice" line of thinking. Rhetorically, it's boring. There simply aren't that many people walking around the US being evil on a daily basis, evilly buying groceries, evilly watching *Friends*, evilly having routine but pleasant married sex, and evilly putting their head on a pillow to dream of evil, evil, evil. As a society, we're not nearly that dysfunctional. But more importantly, it dehumanizes those whom you disagree with, and that's a dangerous thing. The process of dehumanization is subject to Newton's Third Law—you can't dehumanize someone else without dehumanizing yourself in the bargain.

I'm not in that much of a rush to dehumanize myself, thank you all the same. Anyway I'm perfectly capable of holding the thoughts of "You believe things I don't" and "You're not a bad guy" in my head without the fear of doublethink because they're not in fact automatically mutually opposing statements. I would suggest that if you believe otherwise you're probably rather intellectually lazy and you prefer to idealize those who oppose you as flat, uninteresting cardboard representations of evil rather than as interesting, capable, nice human beings who must be considered as such if you wish to overcome their positions or find some sort agreeable accommodation so you can both keep living your life with some reasonable measure of felicity. Which means you'll always be at the disadvantage. And that's just kind of stupid.

You're free to disagree with me, of course. I'm sure you're otherwise very nice.

THEY SHOOT
PEOPLE,
DON'T THEY?

Apr

3

2003

*"'They don't really advertise that they kill people,' Funk said. 'I
didn't really realize the full implications of what I was doing.'"*

—Marine Reservist Stephen Funk, on why he refused to
report for active duty, "Marine: 'I refuse to kill'," Seattle Post-
Intelligencer, 4/2/03

You have to be a really interesting sort of ignorant not to know that
the Marines kill people from time to time. Your first hint: The big
rifle so many of those Marines carry around. Your second hint: All
those movies, books and television shows, widely available to the general
public, in which Marines are shown, you know, *killing* people. Your third
hint: The fact that the Marines are widely acknowledged to be a branch
of the military of the United States, and militaries are likewise widely
known, by most people who are smart enough to stand upright on two
legs, to kill other people on occasion (typically members of other nations'
militaries, though sometimes they're not so picky, depending on country
and context).

A rather goopy column on Stephen Funk in the Seattle P-I describes
a kid who got over 1400 on his SATs and got accepted to a number of
excellent colleges, including my own University of Chicago, which is
widely known (when it is widely known at all) for being the sort of
school that remarkably stupid people don't usually have high on their
wish list of collegiate destinations (Funk eventually landed at University of Southern California, which is not nearly as encouraging an

indication of intelligence, but never mind that right now). In short, Funk is portrayed as a very smart kid, not the sort of person who, for example, needs a reminder that coffee may be hot, so please don't place it near your genitals, or, as another example, that the Marines occasionally go to war and kill people, being that they are an arm of the military.

The column piece suggests that the Marine recruiter filled Funk's head so full of tales of wild adventure and technical training that our young hero couldn't even contemplate the idea that Marines *might* go to war, which I would expect is true as far as it goes. The armed forces of the US spend a lot of time and money in their recruiting commercials pushing things like skills training, money for college and seeing the world, and less time pushing things like no showers for weeks, endless Meals Ready to Eat and the possibility of having to put a bullet into the gut of someone who wants to do the same thing to you but is slightly less quick on the draw, and who will then go down screaming because you've just turned a large portion of his small intestine into a crimson mess with the consistency of Libby's potted meat food product.

But even then, there's always the indication that the military is not exactly a peaceable organization. Take the Marines recruiting site. On the front page are three pictures, one of which features Marines handling rifles. Put your mouse over the pictures, and Java script pops up text. "Those Who are Warriors. Those Who are Driven. Those Who Belong." Click on "About the Marines" and the text that pops up reads, right from the beginning: "Marines are warriors. Comprised of smart, highly adaptable men and women, the Marine Corps serves as the aggressive tip of the U.S. military spear." The picture on this page is a squad of Marines, rifles sighted and ready to shoot, stalking the photographer. To be strictly accurate on Funk's immediate point, there's nothing on the Marine recruiting site that I can see that specifically says anything about *killing* people. But on the other hand, all this talk of warriors and pictures of rifles doesn't give the indication one is signing up for day care training, either.

The part of Funk's quote above that rings true is the second part: "I didn't really realize the full implications of what I was doing." This, I believe. I think it's entirely possible to sign up, get into training and then

YOUR HATE MAIL WILL BE GRADED

realize, *holy crap, am I ever in the wrong place.* Moreover, I think there's absolutely no disgrace in realizing that—indeed, it's better for everyone if you do, because the last thing I would want if I were a Marine would be a squadmate who's not sure he's ready to kill if he absolutely has to. Moral quandaries are fine, just not when an Iraqi Fedayeen is shooting at you wildly from the back of a fast-moving technical. Out with him.

But Funk and others in his situation should place the responsibility for this where it belongs: Not with a fast-talking recruiter, who promises adventure and fun and sort mumbles the fine print about having to shoot people under his breath, but with himself. He may not have realized what he was made of, but he almost certainly knew what he was getting himself into.

I HATE YOUR POLITICS

Mar

22

2002

I hate your politics.

No, I don't know what they are. And no, I probably don't know who you are, either. Really, those two points are immaterial (no offense). As it turns out, about 46% of you are liberal, 46% of you are conservative, and the rest of you just want your guns, drugs and brothels (here in the US, we call them folks "libertarians").

Each of you carries baggage from your political affiliation, and all of that baggage has a punky smell to it, like one of your larger species of rodent crawled in and expired in your folded underwear. Listening to any of you yammer on about the geopolitical situation is enough to make one want to melt down one's dental fillings with a beeswax candle and then jam an ice pick into the freshly-exposed nerve, just to have something else to think about. It's not so much that politics brings out the worst in people as it is that the worst in people goes looking for something to do, and that usually ends up being politics. It's either that or setting fires in trashcans.

In the spirit of fairness, and of completeness, let me go down the list and tell you what I hate about each major branch of political thinking.

Liberals: The stupidest and weakest members of the political triumvirate, they allowed conservatives to turn their name into a slur against them, exposing them as the political equivalent of the kid who lets the school bully pummel him with his own fists (Stop hitting yourself. Stop hitting yourself. Stop *hitting* yourself). Liberals champion the poor and the weak but do it in such condescendingly bureaucratic ways that the po' illedumacated Cleti would rather eat their own shotguns than associate with the likes of them. Famously humorless and dour, probably because for a really good liberal, everything is political, and *you just can't joke about things like that.*

Defensive and peevish even when they're right. Under the impression that people in politics should play fair, which is probably why they get screwed as often as they do (nb: 2000 Presidential election). Feel guilty about the freedoms their political positions allow them, which is frankly idiotic. Liberals are politically able to have all sorts of freaky mammal sex but typically don't; good liberal foreplay is a permission slip and three layers of impermeable barriers. The only vaguely liberal person we know of who seemed to enjoy sex in the last 30 years is Clinton, and look what he got out of it.

Fractious and have no sense of loyalty; will publicly tear out the intestines of those closest to them at the most politically inopportune times. The attention spans of poultry; easily distracted from large, useful goals by pointless minutiae. Not only can't see the forest for the trees, can't see the trees for the pine needles. Deserve every bad thing that happens to them because they just can't get their act together. Too bad those they presume to stand for get royally screwed as well.

Conservatives: Self-hating moral relativists, unless you can convince me that an intellectual class that publicly praises family values but privately engages in sodomy, coke and trophy wives is more aptly described in some other way. Not every conservative is an old wealthy white man on his third wife, but nearly every conservative aspires to be so, which is a real waste of money, youth, race and women. Genuinely fear and hate those who are not "with" them—the sort of people who would rather shit on a freshly-baked cherry pie than share it with someone not of their own tribe.

Conservatives believe in a government by the oligarchy, for the oligarchy, which is why the conservative idea of an excellent leader is Ronald Reagan, i.e., genial, brain-damaged and amenable to manipulation by his more mentally composed underlings. Under the impression they own the copyright on Jesus and get testy when other political factions point out that technically Christ is in the public domain. Conservatives don't actually bother to spend time with people who are not conservative, and thus become confused and irritable when people disagree with them; fundamentally can't see how that's even *possible*, which shows an almost charming intellectual naiveté. Less interested in explaining their point of view than nuking you and everything you stand for into blackened cinders before your evil worldview catches on like a virus. Conservatives have no volume control on their hate and yet were shocked as Hell when Rush Limbaugh went deaf.

Conservatives clueless enough to think that having Condi Rice and Andrew Sullivan on the team somehow counts as diversity. Pen their "thinkers" like veal in think tanks rather than let them interact with people who might oppose their views. Loathe women who are not willing to have their opinions as safely shellacked as their hair. Let their sons get caught with a dime bag and see how many are really for "zero-tolerance." Let a swarthy day laborer impregnate their daughters and find out how many of them are really pro-life.

Libertarians: Never got over the fact they weren't the illegitimate children of Robert Heinlein and Ayn Rand; currently punishing the rest of us for it. Unusually smug for a political philosophy that's never gotten anyone elected for anything above the local water board. All for legalized drugs and prostitution but probably wouldn't want their kids blowing strangers for crack; all for slashing taxes for nearly every social service but don't seem to understand why most people aren't at all keen to trade in even the minimal safety net the US provides for 55-gallon barrels of beans and rice, a crossbow and a first-aid kit in the basement. Blissfully clueless that Libertarianism is just great as long as it doesn't actually involve real live humans.

Libertarians blog with a frequency that makes one wonder if they're actually employed somewhere or if they have loved ones that miss them. Libertarian blogs even more snide than conservative blogs, if that's possible. Socially slow—will assume other people actually *want* to talk about legalizing hemp and the benefits of a polyamorous ethos when all these other folks really want is to drink beer and play Grand Theft Auto 3. Libertarianism the official political system of science fiction authors, which explains why science fiction is in such a rut these days. Libertarians often polyamorous (and hope you are too) but also somewhat out of shape, which takes a lot of the fun out of it.

Easily offended; Libertarians most likely to respond to this column. The author will attempt to engage subtle wit but will actually come across as a geeky whiner (Conservatives, more schooled in the art of poisonous replies, may actually achieve wit; liberals will reply that they don't find any of this humorous at *all*). Libertarians secretly worried that ultimately someone will figure out the whole of their political philosophy boils down to "Get Off My Property." News flash: This is not really a big secret to the rest of us.

I'm guessing you thought I was *way* off on your political philosophy but right on the button about the other two. Just think about that for a while.

PARENTS ARE THE WORST THINGS TO HAPPEN TO KIDS

Apr

24

2001

Sometimes it seems that parents are the worst things to happen to kids. This week's *Time* cover story talks about the increasing urge parents have to breed super-duper kids, ones that are smart and athletic and good-looking and career-minded, all by the age of five or so. Somewhere lost in there is the desire for kids to actually be *kids*: Goofy and young and occasionally disgusting, such as when they discover the existence of boogers and then spend the next few days announcing their discovery to all within earshot.

I certainly have nothing against parents wanting smart, capable children. It beats having them stick 'em in a hole until kindergarten, and God knows I stuff enough educational crap down Athena's tender young intellectual gullet. She doesn't already know how to operate a computer at age two-and-a-half for nothing, you know. On the other hand, over the last couple of months, her desire to use her computer has decreased dramatically. About a year ago, when she first got the thing, she needed to play with it every day, for at least a couple of hours a day. These days, she wants to play with it maybe once or twice a week.

So, what do I do to encourage her to play with the computer more? Not a damned thing. Because, to reiterate: *She's two-and-a-half freakin' years old.* Any parent who would force a two-year-old to stare at a computer when the kid would rather do something else deserves the rough side of a moving chainsaw blade. These days, Athena wants to spend most of her time outside, and what's not to like about that? So we take her outside and she plays in the yard while Krissy works on the garden, or goes out on the swingset, puts her belly into the seat of the swing, and pretends to be a Powerpuff Girl. She's having fun, and that's more important than any concerns I might have that she's not developing essential computer skills.

(Of course, having just written that, Athena just wandered into my office and declared that she wanted to play with her computer. So we did, for about an hour. Athena seems particularly interested in the part of her Pooh Preschool software where she gets to paint pictures; what's especially interesting about this is that the color she wants to paint everything is black. That's my little goth girl!

However, my point here isn't really compromised—*she* came in and wanted to play with the computer; I didn't drag her in and make her do it. And when she wanted to stop playing with it, we did, playing another favorite game of hers instead—the one in which she stands on my stomach and then hops, saying "Up! Down!" as she does it. It's "Hop on Pop"—the live action version.)

The problem is that parents confuse the means with the ends. Cramming flash cards and French lessons into your kid doesn't do a thing for them in the long run, except possibly to give them a complex about flash cards and the French in a general sense. The goal shouldn't be to make your child eat an entire set of encyclopedias by the age of six. The goal should be to encourage your child to be *curious*—to want to learn about the world, and explore the things that are in it. If you make a child eat a set of encyclopedias, he or she will eventually resent you for it. But if you help them *want* to read through that same set, your child will always appreciate what you've done for them.

As an example, I present to you: My own mother. My mother, bless her heart, had her ups and downs as a parent, as any parent does. However, she did do one thing absolutely as she should have: Even when it became clear I was (how shall we say this) not *like* the other kids, she never tried to make a trained monkey out of me, sitting me down and attempting to shovel calculus into my skull at age three. Instead, she made sure that when I *did* show an interest in something, she would help me take my interest as far as I wanted to take it.

For example, when I was six and I showed an interest in the concept of centrifugal force, she gave me a cup and some string and let me whirl them around in the living room (it was the stopping that was the hard part). In the days when my mother would sometimes have to choose between paying the electricity bill or a car payment, she'd literally save pennies to buy me those Scholastic books on volcanoes or planets or whatever (I still remember the author: Patricia Lauber). She let me stay up to watch "Cosmos" with Carl Sagan. She always encouraged me to ask "why" and then find out the answer. She pressed, but she didn't push. In this respect, she was the model parent of a precocious child, and I give her full marks for getting that aspect of my childhood exactly right.

What my mother had in me, and what I have in my own child, is faith: Faith that the child will, at the right time, in the right fashion, develop into a person of intelligence, curiosity and capability. For one thing, I'm smart, my wife is smart, and we don't spend *all* our waking hours sucked into the TV—our habits will rub off on the kid, no matter what. Beyond that, however, faith dictates that we don't prod Athena onto paths she has absolutely no interest in treading. I think that a lot of the drive to have overachieving children is defensive—the idea of making sure your child is fully armed against all the *other* kids, whose parents are busy packing their little brains with facts so they can claw their way into the Ivy League over the broken bodies of their classmates.

While this defensive posture surely communicates to the child that parents want the "best" for their kids, it doesn't really communicate the idea that the parents feel their kid's own wishes or desires matter a whole hell of a lot in the grand scheme of things. Intentionally or not, parents send the signal that developing one's own personality takes a back seat to jumping through the hoops society deems are necessary to succeed. The problem with *this* is that sooner or later, even the most staid and unimaginative person wants to tell society to go screw itself. Normally this is called a "midlife crisis." I worry that a lot of today's kids are going to go through their "midlife crisis" at age 24 and never quite recover. That's not good for them, and not good for us (and, more selfishly, not good for *me*, since these kids will be presumably paying for my Social Security).

I'm not saying I'm doing the parenting thing right while everyone else is doing it wrong (*believe* me on this one, folks). And I'm not saying that I'm never going to impress on Athena the value of, say, the occasional good grade over doing one's thing all the time—structure has its uses, many of them good, even if it doesn't seem like it when one is 15. All I'm saying is that I doubt that I'm ever going to be the kind of parents who worries that his child is not doing the "right" extracurriculars, or is "wasting" her childhood when actually what she's doing is simply being a kid.

For the first of these, I doubt Athena will lack enthusiasms. I didn't, and her mother didn't—although in both cases, our parents are probably better off not knowing what some of these extracurricular enthusiasms *were* (and no doubt we will be, too).

For the second of these, now, really. Being a kid is what childhood is *for*. Life is long. There's lots of time to be a grownup later. And I like my kid as a kid. I'm going to miss it —going to miss *her*—when this time of her life is done. No need to rush things. No need at all.

I Am
Married

Feb

20

2004

I keep hearing how allowing gays to marry threatens marriage. Fine. Someone tell me how my marriage is *directly* threatened by two men marrying or two women marrying. Does their marriage make my marriage less legal? Does their love somehow compromise the love I feel for my wife, or she for me? Is the direct consequence of their marriage that my marriage and the commitment therein is manifestly lessened, compromised or broken? And if the answer to these questions is "no," as it is, exactly how is marriage threatened?

I am part of a normal married couple. My wife and I have been married almost nine years. We have a child. We own a home. We pay our taxes and we live our lives in the midst of friends and family. Every day we tell each other that we love each other before we go to work. Every day we come home (well, she comes home, I work here) and spend our evening together as a family. Our wedding picture hangs over the mantelpiece, where we see it every day. We are immersed in the fact that we are married to each other; it's unavoidable. But that's the wrong word to use because we *don't* avoid it, and wouldn't wish to. We embrace it. I don't think there's a day that goes by where I don't have cause to be reminded how much better my life is for being married. This is what being married *is*.

If this very-married state of matrimony is not in the slightest bit threatened by two men getting married or two women getting married, how can the "institution" of marriage be threatened? The institution of marriage lies in the union of souls; to discuss marriage in general without acknowledging that it exists because of *marriages* in particular is a pointless exercise. If no single marriage is directly affected by two men or two women getting married—if I and my neighbors and my family and friends and even my enemies are still well-ensconced in our individual marriages to our spouses—how is the institution of marriage harmed? No harm has come to its constituents, who *are* the institution.

Oh, some of those who are married are insulted, or upset, or shocked or saddened or just generally feel less special, burdened with the knowledge that somewhere a man may marry a man and a woman may marry a woman. But those are feelings. The *facts* of their marriage—the legal and social benefits that accrue—are unchanged for them if two men walk down the aisle, or if two women do the same.

I've been looking at the pictures of the men and women getting married at San Francisco's City Hall in the last week, and I think it's interesting that in so many of the pictures, the couples coming out the City Hall imbue their marriage certificates with a significance heterosexual couples hardly ever do. I have a California marriage certificate too, as it happens. I remember reading it, I remember signing it. I know we've got it filed away somewhere. These couples won't file their certificates away. They're going to hang them above the mantel, pretty much in the same place and in the same manner I have that picture above. These people want to be married with a hunger that you only get from being denied something others have to the point of it being commonplace. I feel like I need to go and find my marriage certificate and give it a good long look: Something so easily provided me, so precious to someone else. I suspect they are treating their certificates in a manner more appropriate.

On what grounds do I as a married person tell others who want to be married that they are undeserving of the joy and comfort I've found in the married state? What right do I have morally to say that I deserve something that they do not? If I believe that every American deserves equal rights, equal protections and equal responsibilities and obligations under the law, how may I with justification deny my fellow citizens this one thing? Why must I be required to denigrate people I know, people I love and people who share my life to sequester away a right of mine that is not threatened by its being shared? Gays and lesbians were at my wedding and celebrated that day with me and my wife and wished us nothing less than all the happiness we could stand for the very length of our lives. On what grounds do I refuse these people of good will the same happiness, the same celebration, the same courtesy?

I support gay marriage because I support marriage. I support gay marriage because I support equal rights under the law. I support gay marriage because I want to deny those who would wall off people I know and love as second-class citizens. I support gay marriage because I like for people to be happy, and happy with each other. I support gay marriage because I love to go to weddings, and this means more of them. I support gay marriage because *my* marriage is strengthened rather than lessened by it—in the knowledge that marriage is given to all those who ask for its blessings and obligations, large and small, until death do they part. I support gay marriage because I should. I support gay marriage because *I* am married.

I am married. I would not be anything else. I wish nothing less for anyone who wishes the same.

The Meaning of Life

Apr

20

2004

Today's reader request, from Karl:

> *I would like to know what you think about the question, "what is the meaning of life?"*
>
> *Is it a good question? Does it have an answer? Do you know it? Is it a stupid question for people that are too anal?*

Oh, goody! I finally get to use my philosophy degree.

It's not a stupid question. I'm not one of those people who subscribes to the theory of "there's no such thing as a stupid question," because there *is*, and I submit that in most cases you're doing a disservice to the person asking the question by not pointing it out. However, this is not one. This does not automatically make it a *good* question, of course. Like many questions, what makes it good (or not) is the intent behind the question and the willingness to actually consider the response to it. Whether it's a good question, in other words, depends on you.

The thing that gets me about the question "What is meaning of life?" is that generally the implication seems to be that there is just *one* meaning to it. That doesn't make sense to me. It's like pointing to a multi-hued striped shirt and asking "what color is that shirt?" You can answer by naming one of the colors of the shirt (thus ignoring the rest) or perhaps use technology to find a chromatic mean to all the colors of the shirt and describe that color through the use of Pantone strips or even angstrom units (which tells only what color the shirt would be if you mashed all the colors together—not the same question). If I were presented with a striped shirt and asked to name its color, I would say "You phrased your question poorly. Try again."

"What is the meaning of life?" is to my mind phrased poorly; it implies all life has the same meaning, which would imply, among other things, that you have the *same* meaning to your life as your cat or a mat of blue-green algae—and no *more* meaning to your life than either. Both of these propositions may actually be true—but as with describing a striped shirt by naming one color, that's not all there is to it.

Also, of course, it implicitly suggests there *is* meaning to life—which simply may not be the case. "Meaning" is the handmaiden of causality, and while the religiously-minded take comfort in the idea of an agent of universal causation (usually called "God"), as a matter of science, causation is a tricky thing. This is due in no small part to our current limits in understanding the universe. We can get to a near-infinitesimally small fraction of a second before the Big Bang to a point called Planck's Time, but beyond that point the door is shut; our physical models of the universe fail. Beyond Plank's Time lies god or randomness or some intriguing combination of the two or something else entirely. *But* it's not inconceivable that our universe exists without causation (go see Dr. Hawking for the details), in which case asking for "meaning" for the universe or anything in it (including life) is in the final analysis like asking why chocolate doesn't breathe avian sonnets. It's not only a question without an answer, but a question in itself without (heh) meaning.

But let's make the assumption that the universe has meaning, or at the very least that meaning can be approached in a Gödelistic sense: Fundamentally incomplete but workable within its own parameters. In that case, "What is the meaning of life" is *still* the wrong question. I would phrase the question: "What are the *meanings* of life?" *This* is an answerable question, because I believe there are several answers. And here are some of them, roughly in order of specification:

The Meaning of Life is to Observe the Universe. One of the spookier aspects of our universe is that it reacts to being observed;

indeed, some of the stronger flavors of the Anthropic Principle suggest the universe *requires* observation in order to exist (and if the universe needs life to exist, how could it have existed to create life within it? See, there you go again, getting all hung up on causality).

I'm personally not especially convinced the universe *needs* life—most versions of the anthropic principle don't suggest it does, merely that this universe is of a design that supports it—but this is not saying that as long as life's around, it's not doing a mitzvah by being observant of its surroundings. Any life will do; most anthropic principles don't require intelligence, just sense—you don't have to understand the universe, man, you've just got to *feel* it.

What end is gained by this observation, if not snapping the universe into place? Sorry, that's another question entirely.

The Meaning of Life is to Make More Life. This particular meaning of life is neutral to other aspects of the universe and considers only what's good for *life* as opposed to the rest of the universe. The advantage this particular answer has is that it's manifestly true: Life, by definition, has within it the capacity to make more of itself and also by definition is compelled by instinct to make more of itself (otherwise it doesn't remain life for long).

The drawback is that it's not very satisfying—making more life is *fun* and all, but at the end of it all you get is more life and none of your existential yearnings fulfilled. Also, you're still going to die. But, you know. Not every meaning of life is going to be *deep*. Some are just going to be obvious.

The Meaning of Life is to *Create* the Meaning of Life. After all, who says we *can't*? Look: When you're born you have no idea what you're going to be when you grow up, right? You decide over the course of time what you're going to do with yourself. Same thing here, applied on a much larger scale. It's not inconceivable that life was created *without* meaning, a senseless agglomeration of amino acids that just happened to fold themselves into self-replication. But that doesn't mean it can't *get* a meaning. Maybe that's our *job* in this universe: To figure it out. It doesn't matter whether we were given the job by some creator, or just looked around and decided the job needed doing.

The problem here is that there's no assurance from the universe (or any presumed creator) that we're giving life the "correct" meaning, or that this meaning won't turn out to be an ill fit for life—that just as one can hopefully declare one is going to become a ballerina when in fact one is as coordinated and graceful as a drunken tortoise. But, you know, so what. If there's anything we know about life it is that more often than not there are second chances. If life doesn't stumble upon a good meaning to its existence the first time around, maybe it will later.

The other problem with this answer is that unless "life" hits upon a meaning in the next 50 or 60 years, most of you reading this will be dead when it's all figured out. And then a fat lot of good it will do *you*. Personally speaking I'm not optimistic about life figuring out the meaning in that time frame: It's had (on earth at least) more than a billion years to get a clue and it's still grinding its gears. We like to think humans might be able to crack this nut, but look: We can't even agree about what the hell *The Matrix* was really about. I love humanity—it's my favorite intelligent species!—but let's just say I'm not holding my breath.

The Meaning of Life is to Do What We're Told. This is the religious answer, and no, it's not meant to be dismissive. Religions come with rules. Rules are meant to be obeyed. That's one of the attractions of religion; it offers structure. Not only religions offer the religious answer, of course: All sorts of secular philosophies, political platforms and self-help books do the the same. But the added bonus of religion is that usually a reward is offered as a sweetener for following the rules—and among those rewards is often an understanding of what it's all supposed to be about. If religion is true, it's quite a deal: Most religions are not so onerous as to be impossible to follow (especially here in the US, with its general tradition of religious toleration), so the risk-to-reward ratio is generally substantially in the favor of the practitioner. If it's not true, well, you're no worse off than everyone else who is dead.

I often don't like how religious people practice their religions (especially when they decide their religious beliefs should be imposed on me through public policy) and as I've noted before I don't subscribe to any religious philosophy. But as a theoretical matter I don't see any harm in creating a meaning of life through a religious impulse; the fact that religion is ubiquitous suggests it offers something most people want or need (rules and the idea of continuation beyond this universe), and who knows? That impluse may even be correct.

The Meaning of Life is What You Want it to Be. This is the final and most specific answer: It's not the meaning of life as in "all life everywhere," or "all humans," or even "all the people who live in your house," but the meaning of life as in "the meaning of *your* life." And once again, who is to say that creating a meaning of life for yourself isn't what you're supposed to be doing? This meaning is specific, involves only one person and will not outlast your own life. But last I checked, "meaning" doesn't imply permanence. And it doesn't make it any less true, for the time it lasts.

The meaning of *my* life is pretty simple: To live my life without regret. But like many simple ideas, the execution is difficult. It means being a good husband and being a good father. It means working hard to support my family. It means doing my best to give others the respect they deserve. It means being involved in the life of my community and country. It means developing a moral system and the backbone to stand for what I believe. It means being willing to admit I was wrong. It means being willing to forgive (but more often to be willing to ask for forgiveness). It means being a good friend. It means being aware of life and being part of life.

It's a lot of work, and the real kick in the ass about it is that in a very real sense it's all process—there's no reward. Except one, which is in the very last seconds of my life I get to have the knowledge that the life I lived was as good as I could make it. That knowledge, a lifetime in its creation, is likely to last a fraction of a second before I'm gone. It's the meaning of life as a sand mandala. Will it be worth it? Well, you know. I don't know. I guess I'll find out. Briefly.

But in the meantime it's a good way to live (or to *try* to live—I'm not as regretless as I want to be), and I can genuinely say my life has meaning. It's not THE Meaning of Life, true enough. But like I said, I doubt there is THE Meaning of Life. It is, however, *a* meaning of life, and that's good enough for me.

WHY CLINTON
WON'T RESIGN

Dec

18

1998

A. M. Rosenthal of the *New York Times* called upon Clinton today to resign. As if. Clinton would rather slide his most sensitive parts over a cheese grater than to give up the Oval Office. When Gore or Bush or whomever walks into the Oval Office in January, 2001, they're going to have to pry Bill off the desk with a barnacle scraper. He would rather have the government implode than to leave willingly, and he may just get his wish. Asking him to resign is like asking a poodle to recite the Tibetan Book of the Dead. If it actually happened, you just wouldn't know what to make of it.

It's a difficult thing. At the end of it, I think the conservative Republican hatred of the man is as venal and irrational as anything in politics this century. They've *always* hated him, for the same reason dweebs and wonks have always hated the most popular boy in school: Teachers love him, girls adore him, and everything comes to him all too easily. I can sympathize with their desire to bring Clinton down, but it also points out their sad, jealous pettiness.

There's actually a Simpson's episode that perfectly encapsulates the whole situation: It's the one where Frank Grimes, a hard-working, decent, honest guy who had to scrape to get everything he has (which ain't much), encounters Homer Simpson, who bumbles through everything but has (in Grimes' eyes) managed to do well for himself. Grimes' frustration eventually leads him to fool Homer into entering a child's contest, which he wins.

When Grimes points out Homer's competing against children, the response is "Yeah, and he kicked their butts!" Grimes then goes insane, and in attempt to flout the rules as Homer does, ends up electrocut-ing himself and dies. The GOP today is right about at the point where Grimes was reaching for the high power lines.

On the other hand: Come *on*, people, Clinton's a pig. Like the most popular kid in school, he assumes he can get away with everything; like the most popular kid in school, he gets awfully testy when someone stops him from doing what he wants. Everyone who defends Clinton does so knowing full well that what the man needs is fifteen minutes in a back room with a bunch of thugs who know how not to leave any incriminating marks. In a sick sort of way, I admire how he gets the GOP all wound up. But there's no denying he asks for at least as much trouble as he gets.

The optimum outcome for this whole mess would be to have every-one in the whole sordid proceeding experience, simultaneously, a severe and debilitating stroke. It's hard to see how anyone in America would complain, and, tangentially, it would certainly renew *my* faith in a good and just God. But I don't see it happening. We're stuck with this mess.

BUSH SNORTED COCAINE

Aug

20

1999

I believe that George W. Bush snorted cocaine. At one point in the 70s, the man was probably offered a line by an acquaintance, and George inhaled. Why shouldn't he? It was the 70s, and everyone was tooting back some blow. And George, bless his cocaine-stressed heart, probably had no idea he'd one day be running for President. Heck, his DAD probably had no idea he'd be running for President. If dad hadn't gotten around to it, any Presidential ambitions of Bush *fils* would be, shall we say, almost Oedipally premature. So, *toot!* went the coke, and George probably spent the next couple of hours simultaneously convivial and paranoid. Good training, actually, for the office he wants to hold.

I have no problems with Bush having tried the coke. The man is clearly not a coke fiend today. Were he to assume the highest office in our land, there's little worry that between meeting the Prime Minister of Israel and a state dinner, he'd retire to his private office and fire up a rock (and then, ranting that Sri Lanka has the bomb, fire a preemptive strike against the Indian subcontinent). I think that most people, were they to discover that George once sucked up a white line, would probably shrug and not think about it again. So he did coke. In the 70s, the only people who didn't do coke were Billy Graham and Richard Nixon (his paranoia did not need pharmaceutical amplification).

Bush is running around these days trying to avoid the "did you do coke" question by saying he refuses to answer it, and then saying, incidentally, that he hasn't done any illegal drug in 25 years (at first it was seven years, and then it got kicked back to 20, and now 25. By the time you read this, it may have gotten back to the early 60s, when coke was still illegal, but Bush could have dropped all the LSD he wanted). Which means he *has* done an illegal drug of some sort (almost certainly pot, and most likely coke as well), he just doesn't want to admit to the details. Because it would send the wrong message to the kids, you see: *Do coke, and you can be President one day!* And because he won't say what his drug of choice was, the question is going to hound him for the rest of his campaign.

I'm not planning to vote for George, but I'd respect him a hell of a lot more anyway if he'd just say "Why, yes, I *did* do coke. It wasn't the smartest thing I've ever done, and now I regret having done it." All of which would be true, and all of which most everyone could accept. Everyone's done dumb things they've later regretted. And additionally, having done drugs in the past does not make you a hypocrite if you're anti-drug now (doing drugs *now* would make you a hypocrite).

Now, many people feel that Bush shouldn't have answered the question at all, that he should be entitled to a certain zone of privacy. And actually, I have no problems with that, either, if Bush had in fact just said, "It's no one's damned business but my own," and left it at that. But of course that wouldn't do, and so we have this "admitting to something but not really anything" policy. I mean, really. Just admit it, George. You blew some blow. Really, we don't mind.

This "maybe I did cocaine, maybe I didn't" thing leads to an interesting question of what past behaviors these days would disqualify one for the Presidency. As I mentioned, I don't think Bush having done cocaine in the past would ultimately hurt him. And if he owned up to toking up some pot, people these days would hardly blink. And obviously President Clinton's infidelities have not dislodged his tenacious, barnacle-like hold on the White House.

So what gossipy nuggets from the past would put a dent in one's drive to the White House? Well, here's a list of the things I think would do it (and some that would not):

Would I Be Disqualified From Running For President If The Press Found Out I...

Did Pot? NO

Did Cocaine Once? NO

Did a LOT of Cocaine? NO

Did Crack? YES (it's a low-class drug, you see)

Did Acid Once? NO

Did a LOT of Acid? YES

Did Speed? NO

Did Downers? NO

Did Heroin? YES

Did PCP? YES

Did Viagra? YES

Am Currently A Practicing Alcoholic? NO

Spit Tobacco? YES (Really. You want a president with a spitoon? This ain't Andy Jackson days)

Cheated on my spouse? NO

Cheated on my spouse last night? YES

Cheated on my taxes? NO

Participated in a college heterosexual orgy? NO

Participated in a campaign trail heterosexual orgy? YES

Participated in a threesome? NO if the two other members were of the opposite sex; otherwise YES

Had homosexual sex? Ohmigod YES

Really? Even if it was just that one time in the high school gym shower, which if you think about it, wasn't really sex at ALL, just more sort of a fumbling thing? YES

Had a nervous breakdown once? YES

Beat my wife? YES

Was arrested for driving drunk? NO

Was arrested for driving drunk last night? NO

Was arrested for protesting in the 60s? NO

Burned a flag? YES

Kicked my dog? YES (if there are pictures)

Spanked my kid? NO

Slapped my kid? YES

Owned porn? YES

Used the word "Nigger"? YES

Used the word "Spic"? NO (Hispanics—low voter turnout)

Had and/or paid for an abortion? YES (yes, even for Democrats)

If I had to pick the three things that would be automatic presidency killers off that list, I'd have to pick homosexual sex, flag burning, and the abortion thing. The press unearths any of those in the past, you're dead meat in a red-hot flaming stick. Most of the others you could at least attempt to wiggle your way out of: You could tearfully admit to wife-beating way back when and bawl how wrong you were, and maybe pull it off. Mention you paid for her abortion and you might as well pack up and go home. I can't even imagine what would happen if some presidential candidate ever had to field questions about having gay sex ("Did you inhale?"). It would probably be followed either by a suicide or an assassination.

Mind you, I'm not discussing the relative "right" or "wrong" about each of these things, or how I personally feel about them. I'd happily vote for a man or woman who has had gay sex for President, for example, if they were an otherwise qualified candidate. But I am, shall we say, in an extreme minority here. And I wouldn't expect any Presidential candidates in the next, oh, 30 years, to go and prove me wrong.

THE WORLD IS LAUGHING

Nov
18
2000

About every seventh news article about the crap that's going down in Florida is about how everyone else in the world is laughing at us Americans because our Presidential election is so screwed up. *Ha ha ha*, says the rest of the world. *So much for your democratic ideals! You're no better than the rest of us! Ah ha ha ha ha!* At which point they go back to their 30-cent-a-day jobs injecting plastic into Barbie molds or whatever it is they do in whatever country they are from, unmindful that we've still got *plenty* of nuclear warheads loitering in the wheat fields of South Dakota, so it's really not a good idea to piss us off when we're as edgy as we are.

I say, let the rest of the world have their fun. Sure, it's a good little laugh, the richest and most powerful country in the history of the world, suddenly running around without a leader (ha ha ha ha....eh). But the rest of the world is forgetting three things. First, of course, is that this will get settled in fairly short order, and we're all real confident of that—despite all the lawsuits and name calling and whatever, there's not been a mad rush for toilet paper and ammunition at the Wal-Marts around this big fat nation of ours.

The second is that this little intramural squabble won't change America's *modus operandi* of blithely lecturing the rest of the world on how it should run itself. The very fact we can walk around for weeks without a clear idea of who our next president is *without* slaughtering our neighbors in an internecine killing spree attests to the strength of our political institutions (and thus, why they need to be exported at the earliest possible opportunity). Far from humbling us, this experience will only make us more smug and insufferable, if that is somehow possible (and you better believe that it is, pal).

The third, and probably most salient point, is simply this: Here in the States, we don't actually *care* what anyone else thinks of us. Aside from policy wonks and a few American UN bureaucrats that are desperately trying to get into the pants of that hot assistant to the Bulgarian attache, not one of us gives a fart in a bathtub what they're saying about us in Moscow or Mozambique. Because at the end of the day, we're still us (i.e., most powerful nation ever in the history of the world, blah blah blah), and they're still not. And to the minds of most Americans, that means we don't *have* to pay attention to what they think. If they were really so smart, wouldn't they have emigrated by now? Of course they would've!

(Not that we would let them in. Because, honestly, if you don't like the way we do things here in America, you can just go back to where you came from, even if you have not, in fact, left. Indifference and xenophobia: Two rank tastes that go rankly together.)

I'd like to be able to distance myself from the great mass of Americans and say that I'm not piggishly indifferent to the jibes of the world regarding our election mess. It really is a high holy clusterfuck and exactly the sort of thing that, were it to have happened in some other country where people are more likely to be barefoot than in business suits, would have the US solemnly intoning about the need for international vote observers.

But I'm afraid I can't. The hoots and catcalls of the world leave me curiously unmoved. Aside from the opinion of a select few Canadians who also actually happen to be my friends (and who I think are allowed to have valid opinions of the US, seeing as they share the other half of the Great North American Duplex with us), I just don't care about the international egg-throwing. I don't see it amounting to anything, and in any event, it's their perogative to crack a few jibes our way. Hell, if I had to think about the US all the time, I'd love to watch it fall on its ass, too. As a nation, the United States can take a ribbing. So I'm unconcerned. At least it's an unconcern not born out of ignorance. *My* indifference is fully informed, thank you very much.

CELEBRITIES: RUINING EVERYTHING

Jan

12

2008

Another day, another letter from someone who thinks that having work out there in the market means that I need to shut up about the political process here in the United States. This is not a wholly uncommon occurrence for me and usually plays out like this: Someone reads *Old Man's War*, assumes because it's military fiction that I am some stripe of conservative and/or Heinleinian libertarian, comes here, catches me on a day I'm writing about politics, has the veins in their neck pop, and then writes me a letter or makes a comment suggesting that I shouldn't write things they don't like because then they might not be able to buy any more of my books, hint, hint.

To which my response is always the same: Kiss my ass, hint, hint. Someone who thinks that buying my books entitles them to suggest I need to be silent about *anything* is someone whose money I don't need or want. It's always the righties who do this; I can't remember the lefties who disagree with my politics, and yes there are some, ever pulling this kind of stunt (on the other hand, the lefties who disagree with something I write often want me to write *differently* than I do, which is not something I get from the folks on the right. This may be indicative of larger political pathologies relating to the American right and left wings; I invite master's theses on this subject).

To be clear, the vast majority of my right(ish) fiction readers who are aware of my personal politics appear to be content to let me be an idiot on the subject and buy my books anyway; I thank them for their patronage, from the very bottom of my mortgage, and I also thank them for their (ahem) liberal attitude on the subject. I am always glad to see when someone, right or left or orthogonal, decides that as a general rule they don't have to filter every single aspect of their life through a screen of personal political orthodoxy. It speaks well of their higher cognitive functions, in my opinion.

That said, this particular letter was a new variation on the theme: rather than threatening not to buy future books *unless* I shut the hell up, which is the usual tactic, this one said that the decision not to buy future books was already made, because "I respect celebrities who are humble enough to keep their political views to themselves, and after visiting your website, it seems you do not fall into this category." Mind you, there's still an explicit "STFU" message here, which boils down to *oh, if only you followed the rules and been a silent little monkey from first you entered the marketplace, I could still give you my precious, precious coin.* But the "more in sorrow than in anger" tone here is a nice touch.

But the part that really got me was the implication that I am now a "celebrity," and that celebrities, by this gentleman's formulation, should be "humble enough to keep their political views to themselves," which is a formulation that is less about humility, I expect, and more about "I own your work and therefore I own you, so shut up, monkey." But let's take each of these points in turn.

Celebrity, me: Yeah, really, not so much. Yes, I'm a writer who is well known among people who read science fiction, and among people who read blogs. This is *not* the same thing as being a "celebrity" in the generally accepted sense of the term. I don't get recognized in public; hell, a lot of the times I don't even get recognized at science fiction conventions, which is the one place people might have some inkling of what I look like, and are sometimes even looking for me.

This is fine. I used to interview movie stars and musicians, you know, and have friends who work with and near the genuinely famous. I'm not unfamiliar with actual celebrity. It seems *tiring*. When I was younger, I thought it would be nice to be famous; at this point in time I'm content to be well known in my own field. It seems to give some of the nicer perks of fame (i.e., people seeming to be glad to meet you, once they know who you are), without some of the more annoying aspects (i.e., absolutely no privacy whatsoever about any aspect of your life). True, this means I miss out on groupies, but I suspect after the first several hundred they lose their luster as well. I could be wrong. I might be willing to find out.

I don't want to be disingenuous or artificially humble about my notability, but at the same time, let's have some perspective. Let's say I am a celebrity among science fiction writers. Fine. You know who is more famous than me? My cat. Who is more famous than her? Wil Wheaton. Who is more famous than him? Neil Gaiman. Who is more famous than Neil? Tila Tequila. And thus, we learn the value of celebrity. And more to the point, if I'm going to be required to shut up because I'm a celebrity, I want to be at least more famous than my cat. Although to be fair, my cat rarely gives her political opinion on anything. Maybe this guy should buy books from her. Soon to come from Ghlaghghee the Cat: *Everything I Ever Really Needed to Know About Disembowling Defenseless Rodents I Learned from Karl Rove*. Brilliant!

As for respecting celebrities humble enough to keep their political opinions to themselves, allow me to suggest, humbly, even, that this fellow really ought to grow up a little. What he's really saying is that he doesn't want his fantasy image of celebrities messed with through the inconvenient fact of a celebrity being an actual person. But, alas, celebrities are not merely poseable action figures for our enjoyment and control; they regrettably come with thoughts and brains and opinions and such, which they may wish from time to time to use and express. Possibly some of these celebrities will be not particularly astute in their opinions; you could say the same about real estate agents, plumbers, doctors, bloggers or any other group of people, including, alas, politicians. I wonder if this fellow also only patronizes real estate agents, doctors, plumbers, etc, who never express a political opinion outside the confines of their own brain, and if he does, if as a consequence he's become quite the handyman.

(Also, you know: What about political celebrities? They *are* celebrities, after all. And clearly caught in a bind by this man's strictures, for the moment they speak or write, they make it impossible for him to give them campaign contributions! Or buy their books! Oh, the conundrum.)

But at the end of the day, of course, it's this man's choice, and his money. I would not have him do other than stick to his guns; indeed, I celebrate his choice and wish to help him achieve it. This fellow offered a list of representiative celebrities—aside from me—who he thinks ruin his fun with their persistence in talking about politics: Tim Robbins, Susan Sarandon, Ben Affleck and Sarah Jessica Parker. I'm sure there's something that connects all four of those actors, but I'm not quite sure what it is. Nevertheless, to aid this fellow in his quest to purge from his entertainment dollar all entertainers who just can't keep their mudflaps shut about politics, there's a list of conservative celebrities at BoycottLiberalism.com. I'm sure he will get right on not supporting any of their projects with his money. Likewise, I'm sure that in science fiction, this fellow will henceforth avoid any books by John Ringo, Orson Scott Card or Jerry Pournelle, to name just three gentlemen who unnecessarily sully the air with public announcements of their own political thoughts.

I wish this fellow the best of luck in his purge of all entertainment by people who have ever publicly expressed a political thought, and hope that he finds his resulting entertainment choices—nutrition information panels and car owner manuals, mostly—keep him gripped and on the edge of his seat, waiting to find out what happens next (**SPOILER:** Riboflavin did it! In the B Complex!)

For my part, I think restricting one's entertainment only to those people who don't ever speak about politics is pretty damn stupid, even when those entertainers have the temerity to have opinions that aren't exactly like mine. But I suppose that's because, silly me, I think that a multiplicity of political views is actually a good thing for the health of the country, as is the willingness of all Americans to speak their mind on the subject, even famous people, even when they disagree with me. I also think there's more to life than just politics, and pity those who apparently don't. But, hey, I'm a celebrity. What do I know?

10 Things Teenage Writers Should Know About Writing

Apr

27

2006

Dear Teenage Writers:

Hi there. I was once a teenage writer like you, although that was so long ago that between now and then, I could have been a teenager all over again. Nevertheless, recently I've been thinking about offering some thoughts and advice on being a teenage writer, based on my own experiences of being one, and on my experiences of being a teenage writer who kept being a writer when he grew up. So here are some of those thoughts for your consideration.

I'm going to talk to you about writing as straight as I can; there's a possibility that some of what I say to you might come off as abrupt and condescending. I apologize in advance for that, but you should know that I sometimes come off as abrupt and condescending toward everyone, i.e., it's not just *you*. Also, I hope you don't mind if I don't go out of my way to use current slang and such; there's very little more pathetic than a 36-year-old man dropping slang to prove he's hip to the kids. I own a minivan and the complete works of Journey; honestly, from the point of view of being cool, I might as well be dead. You might find what I have to say useful anyway. Here we go.

1. The Bad News: Right Now, Your Writing Sucks.

It's nothing personal. When I was a teenager, my writing sucked, too. If you don't believe me, check out my Web site to find a short story I wrote in high school, and (God help us all) the lyrics to a prog-rock concept album I wrote in my first year of college. Yeah, they suck pretty bad. But at the time, I thought they were pretty good. More to the point, at the time they were also the best I could do. No doubt you are also pounding out stories and songs to the best of your ability... and chances are pretty good that your best, objectively speaking, isn't all that good.

There are reasons for this.

a) You're *really* young. Being young is good for many things, like being flexible, staying up for days with no ill effects, not having saggy bits, and having hair. For writing deathless, original prose, not so much. Most teenagers lack the experiential vocabulary and grammar for writing well; you lack a certain amount of perspective and wisdom, which is gained through time. In short: You haven't yet developed your true writing voice.

Now, if you're really good, you can *fake* perspective and wisdom, and with it a voice, which is almost as good as having the real thing. But usually, sooner or later, it'll catch up to you and your lack of experience will show in your writing. This will particularly be the case when you have a compelling, emotional story, which would require the sort of control and delivery of your writing that you only get through time. You may simply not have the wherewithal to express your very important story well. Yes, having a great story you're not equipped to tell pretty much bites. Normally, this is when teens look for help from the writers they admire, which brings us to the *next* reason your writing sucks:

b) You're besotted by your influences. If you look at those two early pieces of mine, they rather heavily bear the mark of people like whom I wanted to write—humorist James Thurber in the case of the short story, and Pink Floyd lyricist Roger Waters in the case of the would-be concept album. If I were to subject you to other writing of mine from the time (and I *won't*), you'd see the rather heavy influence of other favorite authors and lyricists, including Robert Heinlein, Dorothy Parker,

H.L. Mencken, P.J. O'Rourke, Bono, Martin Gore and Robert Smith. Why? Because I thought these people wrote really, really well, and I wanted to write like them.

You are not likely to have *my* influences, but you almost certainly have influences of some sort who you love and to whom you look as models and teachers. But since you're young and haven't gotten your own voice worked out, you're likely to get swamped by your influences. My concept album lyrics aren't just bad because they're the work of an immature writer, but also because it's clear to anyone who cares to look that I was listening to whole hell of a lot of Pink Floyd when I was writing them. Extracting Roger Waters out of those lyrics would require radical surgery. The patient would not likely survive. That's bad.

c) When you're young, it's easier to be clever than to be good. Now, when you're *older*, it's easier to be clever than to be good *too*, and you'll see a lot of writers doing just that, even the good ones. This is because "clever" gets laughs and attention and possibly sex (or at least flirting) with that hot little thing over there who thinks you're so damn amusing. And none of that *ever* gets old. So this is not just a teenage problem. Where teenage writers are at a disadvantage is that you're not always aware when you're genuinely being good, or merely being clever. It's that whole lack of experience thing. Yes, the lack of experience thing crops up a whole lot. What are you going to do.

There's nothing *wrong* with being clever, and it's possible to be clever and good at the same time. But you need to know when clever is not always the best solution. Even older writers find this a tough nut to crack, and you'll find it even more so.

So those are some of the reasons your writing sucks right now. There may be others. But, now having told you that your writing sucks and why, you're ready to hear the next point:

2. The Good News: It's *Okay* That Your Writing Sucks Right Now.

Because, look. *Everyone's* writing sucked when they were teenagers. Why? Simple: Because they were just starting out. Just like you are now.

Writing is tricky thing, because everyone assumes that the act of writing to move and amuse people with words is somehow only slightly more difficult than the act of writing to place words into vaguely coherent sentences. This is like saying that playing professional baseball is only slightly more difficult than hitting a beach ball with a stick. Most everyone can hit a beach ball with a stick, but very few people would think that means they're ready to play in the World Series. Given that, it's funny that people think that they're going to be really excellent writers from the first time they try to tell a story with the written word.

Excepting the freaks of nature, which very few of us are, anything we decide to do takes us time to get good at. It's just that simple. The figure I hear a lot—and which I agree with, mostly—is that it takes about a decade for people to get truly good at and creative with their craft. The prime example of this is the Beatles; at 17 John Lennon and Paul McCartney were beginning their musical collaboration together, and ten years later they were writing *Sgt. Pepper's Lonely Hearts Club Band*. The "ten years" thing is a guideline, not a rule—some people hit their stride earlier, some later, but the point is that there was work involved. This is even true of the people you've never heard of before—scratch most "overnight sensations" in whatever field and you'll find they did their time outside the spotlight.

Understandably, no one wants to hear that you've got to wait the better part of a decade to hit your stride—who doesn't want to be brilliant *now?*—but I think that's looking at it the wrong way. Knowing you've got years to grow and learn means you've got the time to take risks and explore and figure out what works for you and what doesn't. It's permission to *play* with your muse, not stress out if every single thing you bang out is not flat dead brilliant. It's time to gain the life experience that will feed your writing. It's time you need to write—and time you need to *not* write and to give your brain a break. It's the time you need to learn from your literary influences, and then to tell them to piss off because you've got your own voice and it's not theirs. And it's the time you need to screw up, make mistakes, learn from them and move on.

The fact that your writing sucks now only means that your writing sucks *right now*. If you keep working on it it'll very likely get better...and then comes the day that you write something that really *doesn't* suck. You'll know it when it happens and then you'll get why all that time banging out stuff that sucked was worth it: because it's made you a writer who *doesn't suck anymore*.

So don't worry that your writing sucks right now. "Suck" is a correctible phenomenon.

3. You Need to Write Every Day.

I'm sure you've got this wired, and I'll note that for teenagers today, it's easier to write every day, because there's an entire social structure revolving around writing that didn't used to exist: Blogs and blog-like things like MySpace, or whatever thing has replaced MySpace by the time you read this. Writing isn't the isolating experience it (mostly) was before.

Now, be aware that writing in your blog or journal isn't the *same* as writing stories or songs or whatever your writing aspirations might be. Blogging very often takes the form of what writers call "cat vacuuming," which is to say it's an activity you do to avoid *actual* writing. You want to avoid doing too much of that (yes, there's some irony in me writing this in a blog entry—particularly a blog entry being written when I could be writing part of a book I have due to a publisher).

"Cat vacuuming" though writing in a blog may be, any sort of daily writing will help build the mental muscle memory of sitting down to put your thoughts into words, and that's not a bad thing. So write something today. Now is good.

4. I'm Not Going to Tell You to Get Good Grades, But, You Know, *Try* To Pay Attention.

High school is often asinine and lame—I'm not telling you anything you don't know here—but on the other hand it's a place where you're actually encouraged to do two things that are a writer's bread and butter: to observe and to comment. Provided your teachers are not entirely defeated drones who have bought into the idea that their sole purpose is to detain you in soul-numbing classes so you and your fellow students won't set fire to the school with them in it, they will actually be *pleased* if you ask a few pointed questions now and then, and as a result, you might *learn* something, which is always a nice bonus for your day. School is a resource; use it.

(Also, for the love of all that is holy, please please *please* pay attention in your English composition class. You should know English language grammar for roughly the same reason you should know road rules before you go driving: It avoids nasty pile-ups later.)

Being writers, I don't need to tell you that observing your fellow students is also hours and hours of fun, but don't just look for the purposes of wry mockery. Any jerk can do that. Work on your *empathy*—try to understand why people are the way they are. This will achieve two things. One, it's a good exercise for you to help you one day create characters in your writing who are not merely slightly warped versions of *you*. Two, it'll make you realize there's more to life than wry mockery.

5. Read Everything You Can Get Your Hands On—Even the Crap That Bores You.

And here's why the crap that bores you is worth reading: Because someone *sold* it, which means the writer did *something* right. Your job is to figure out what it was and what that means for your own writing. It should also give you hope: If this bad writer can sell a book or magazine article, then *you* should have no problem, right? *Excellent*.

This suggestion is actually more difficult to follow than you might think. People like to read what they like, and don't like to read what they don't like. That's fine if all you want to be is a reader, but if you want to be a writer, you don't have the luxury of just sticking to the stuff that merely *entertains* you. Writing that's not working for you is still working for *someone*; take a look and see if you can find out why. Alternately, pinpoint why it *doesn't* work. Fact is, you can learn as much from writers you *don't* like as you can from writers you do—and possibly more, because you're not cutting them slack, like you would your favorite writers.

A corollary to this is: Read writers who are new to you. Don't just stick to the few writers you know you like. Take a few chances. You don't have to spend money to do this: Most towns have this wonderful thing called a library. We're talking free reading here, and the publishing industry won't crack down on you for it. Heck, we *like* it when you visit the library.

6. You Should Do Something Else With Your Life Than Just Write.

There are practical and philosophical reasons for this. The practical reason: Dude, writers make almost *nothing* most of the time. Chances are, you're going to have a day job to support your writing habit, at least at first. So you want to be able to get a day job that doesn't involve asking people if they want fries with that. Just something to keep in mind.

The philosophical reason: the writer who *only* writes isn't actually experiencing much of life; his or her writing is going to feel inauthentic because it won't reflect reality. You want to get actual life experience outside of being a writer, otherwise your first novel will be like every *other* first novel out there, which revolves around a young writer trying to figure out his life, and then sitting down to write about it. People who write books where the main character is a young, questioning writer should be shot out of a cannon into a pit filled with leeches. Don't make us do that to you.

"Doing something else with your life," incidentally, also includes your college major. There are people who would advise you to be English majors and then go after an MFA, but I'm not one of them (I'm a philosophy major myself—useless but interesting). The more things you know about, the more you're able to incorporate your wide range of knowledge into your work, which means you'll be at a competitive advantage to other writers (this will matter). You might worry that all those English majors and MFAs are learning something you really need to know, but you know what? As long as you're writing (and reading) regularly and seriously, you'll be fine. Writing is a *practical* skill as much as or even more than it is an area of study.

Now, I'm sure many of those English majors and MFAs might disagree with me, but I've got ten books and fifteen years of being a professional writer backing me up, so I feel pretty comfortable with my position on this.

7. Try to Learn a Little About the Publishing Industry.

If you're going to be a writer for a living (or, if not for a living, at least to make a little money here or there), you're going to have to sell your work, and if you're going to sell your work, you should learn a little how the business of writing works. The more you know how the publishing industry works, the more you'll realize how and why particular books sell and others don't, and also what you need to do to sell your work to the right people.

This is *not* to say that at this point you should let this information guide you in what you write—at this point you should write what interests you, not what you think is going to make you money one day, if for no other reason that the publishing industry, like any industry, has its fads and trends. What's going on now isn't going to be what's going on when you're ready to publish. But there's nothing wrong about knowing a little bit about the business fundamentals of the industry, if you can stomach them.

If you think you're going to write in a specific genre (science fiction or mystery or whatever) why not learn a little about that field, too? A good place to start is by checking out author blogs, because authors are always blathering on about crap like that. *Trust* me. Also (quite obviously), authors are prone to offer unsolicited advice to new writers on their sites, because it makes us feel all mature and established to bloviate on the subject. And sometimes our advice is even useful.

There's no reason to be obsessive about acquiring knowledge of the industry at this early age, but it doesn't hurt to know; it'll be one less thing you have to ramp up on when you're ready to start putting stuff out there. Which reminds me:

8. Be Ready For Rejection.

It's *very* likely the first few years that you submit material to publishers and editors, or query them for articles, your work and queries are going to come back to you unbought. Why? Because that's just how it is. I'll give you an example: Recently I edited a science fiction magazine. For the issue of the magazine I edited, I had between 400 and 500 submissions. From those, there were about 40 I thought were good enough to buy. And of those, I bought 18. That's a 95.5% rejection rate, and an over 50% rejection rate of stuff I *wanted* to buy, but couldn't because I didn't have the space (or the money, because I had a budget, too). Now, as it happens, for this magazine I also managed to give first sales to four writers because I wanted to make a point of finding new writers—but I imagine if you asked them how long they'd been submitting work before that sale, you'd find most of them had been doing it for a while.

There are things to know about rejection, the first of which is that it's not about *you*, it's about the work. The second is that there are any number of reasons why something gets rejected, not all of them having to do with the piece being bad—remember that I rejected a bunch of pieces I *wanted* to buy but couldn't. The third is that just because a piece was rejected one place doesn't mean it won't get accepted somewhere else. I know that at least a couple of pieces that I rejected have since been bought at other places.

Rejection sucks, and there's no way to get around that fact. But if you're smart, when you start submitting you'll consider pieces that are rejected simply as ready to go on to the *next* place. Keep writing and submitting.

(Which brings up the question: If you have pieces *now* that you want to submit, should you? Well, I'm sure submissions editors everywhere will hate me for saying this, but, sure, why not? If nothing else it'll get you used to the rejection process, and there's always a chance that if it *is* good, someone might buy it. But, on behalf of the submissions editors, I *implore* you not to submit unless you really think the work in question is the best you can do.)

9. Start Getting Published Now—Yes, That Means the School Newspaper.

I know, I know. But, look, you're going to have to deal with editors sooner or later. And you know how many editors in the real world were editors of their school newspapers? A whole lot of them. Lots of writers were, too (I was editor-in-chief of both my high school *and* college newspaper, so that makes me a two-time loser). Basically, as a writer you'll never be rid of these guys, so you might as well learn how they work. But also, and to be blunt, school newspapers may be piddly, but they give you clips—examples of your writing you can show to others. You can take those clips to your tiny local newspaper and maybe get a few small writing assignments there—and then you're professionally published. And then you can take *those* and use them to get more serious gigs over time, and just keep trading up.

You can also also use those high school clips to help you get on your college paper, and when you're in college, working at the college newspaper can be *very* useful. I used my college newspaper clips to freelance with the local indie papers in town and also with one of the major metropolitan newspapers...and *those* clips help me get my first job out of college, as a movie critic at a pretty large newspaper. And *all* of that started doing little articles for my high school newspaper, the *Blue & Gold*.

What does this teach us? First, that it can be worth it to deal with the high school newspaper editor, even if he or she is an insufferable dweeb, and second, that all the writing you do *can* matter and help you to continue on your writing career.

10. Work on Your Zen.

Being a writer isn't easy; it's a lot of mental effort for often not a lot of financial reward. It takes a lot of time to get good at it—and even when you *are* good at it, you'll find there's still more you have to learn, and things you have to deal with, in order to keep going in the field. It takes a measure of patience and serenity to keep from completely losing it much of the time, and, alas, "patience" and "serenity" are two things teenagers are not known to have in great quantities (to be fair, adults aren't much better with this). Despite that, you'll find as a writer that there is a great advantage in keeping your head, being smart and being practical, even when everyone around you is entirely losing their minds. It helps you see things others don't, which is an advantage in your writing, and also in the workaday aspect of *being* a writer.

So: Relax. Spend your time learning, observing, writing, and preparing. Don't worry about writing the Great American Novel by age 25; don't worry about being the Greatest Writer Ever; don't worry about winning the Pulitzer. Focus on your writing and getting better at it. As they say, luck favors the prepared. When the moment comes, if your skills are there, you'll be ready to take advantage of it and to become the writer you've been hoping you would be. Your job now is to get yourself ready for the moment.

You've got the time to do it. Take it.

THINKING ABOUT
THE GOD
DELUSION

Sep
17
2006

One of the nice things about doing a signing at a bookseller's trade show is that afterward you get to wander through the tradeshow floor and admire all the marvelous books that publishers are giving away to booksellers, and maybe snag one or two for yourself. I had to be careful to limit myself to just a few, on account I brought only my backpack with me, not a packing box; even so I walked out of there with five books. One of them is Richard Dawkin's latest book *The God Delusion*, in which the eminent public scientist enthusiastically takes a cudgel to the very notion of God, representing Him as unneccesary, something of a bother and a definite public health hazard.

And by "Him," we're specifically talking about Yahweh, the god who is the God of half the people on the planet. Indeed, Dawkins is cheerfully rude about Yahweh—he calls Him psychotic, in point of fact—and appears to relish the idea of getting the religious host entirely bunched up about it. One portion of his book has him airing some e-mail he gets from some of the more idiotic and intolerant religious folk; as I was reading it I wondered if he was merely excerpting a blog entry he did somewhere along the way. Much of the book has the informal "whacking the idjits" feel of a blog entry, just in printed form. Perhaps this is an intellectual atlas of stature: When you're a student, grad student or associate professor, you vent in your blog; when you get tenure, you get to vent in a book.

I think *The God Delusion* is a very good and interesting book, but I have an ambivalence regarding Dawkins' delight in trashing God and religion. As far as things go, I suspect Dawkins and I are in the same boat regarding the existence of God, which is to say we're agnostic about it, roughly to the same amount we're agnostic regarding invisible pink unicorns. On the other hand, unlike Dawkins, I don't tend to believe the concept of religion itself rises to such levels of risibility that those who follow one must be apprehended largely as credulous dolts. Even if I believed they were, as long as they kept their credulous doltery out of my way, I would be fine with it. My quarrel with religion, when I have one, is when those who practice it wish to impose it on *me*, often in ways counter to the expressed beliefs and goals of the religion they espouse, or counter to the Constitution of the United States, the wisdom of the freedoms and rights granted therein I find myself progressively astounded by as the years go on. Enjoy your religion, folks. Just keep it to yourself, if you please.

Also, there's the nagging question in my mind of how much, on a purely *practical* level, the human condition would change if our species were somehow magically innoculated against the idea of God. In the book, Dawkins posits the idea that religion is a byproduct of some useful human evolutionary adaptation—a byproduct that has gone awry, much as a moth spiraling in toward a flame is an unfortunate byproduct of the evolutionary adaptation that allows the moth to navigate by starlight. In this particular case, Dawkins speculates religion might be a byproduct of an evolutionarily advantageous adaptation that makes children susceptible to guidance by parental (or elder) authority.

(Dawkins is careful to say that he's just throwing out that particular possible explanation as an example, and that his real allegience is to the idea of religious belief as a less-than-advantageous offshoot of a more useful evolutionary adaptation, but I have to say that I find that particular idea intriguing—I'm projecting onto Dawkins here, but when I read this hypothesis of his I couldn't help think about the idea that mentally speaking, dogs are child-like wolves; that is, as adults they have activities (wagging tales and barking being the obvious ones) that wolves outgrow. Grey wolves and dogs are the same species—taxonomically dogs are a subspecies. Would Dawkins suggest that religiously-minded humans are to agnostic humans as dogs are to wolves, i.e., mentally suspended at a pre-adult stage in some critical way? Again, to be clear, this is *my* supposition of Dawkins' possible implicit argument; don't go blaming him for my trying to model his thinking process. But this is what *my* brain leapt to, and I wonder if Dawkins had left that there for the biologically-adept to pick up.)

If Dawkins posits that religion and religious belief are merely an evolutionary byproduct, then the problem is obvious: Even if we flush God down the toilet and send the religions of the world swirling down with Him, the *biological root cause* of the God delusion is still extant, and will inevitably be filled by some other process, just as getting rid of all man-made open flames won't keep a moth from circling another sort of artificial light source, be it a lightbulb or a glowstick or whatever. God knows (sorry) that entirely atheistic authoritarian schemes have exploited the same human tendency toward obedience, and Lysenkoism, for one, shows that you don't need a religious doctrine to pervert science. Getting rid of God intellectually doesn't change the human condition biologically. It will simply create an ideological vacuum to be filled by something else. Which it will; nature abhors a vacuum.

Perhaps Dawkins is an optimist about humans and their ability to plug up the God hole with a more pleasant and useful alternate scheme; I regret I would not share such optimism. Indeed, if an agnostic wanted to make an argument *for* the continuance of religion, it would be the (no offense) "devil you know" argument: Most religions give at least lip service to the idea of love and peace, so clearing that out of the way is not necessarily a good thing from a practical point of view. Say what you will about Jesus, for whom I have nothing but admiration even without the "son of God" thing, but one of the things *I* find him useful for is reminding people who allege to be following His teaching just how spectacularly they're failing Him, in point of fact. The Book of Matthew is particularly good for this, I've found.

I don't doubt Dawkins could make a perfectly good rebuttal for this (possibly along the lines of if we're going to look at it practically, the cost-benefit analysis suggests that religions do more damage than the thin line of agnostics/atheists berating religionists to live up to their role models could possibly ever hope to repair through public shaming), but for the rest of us it's worth thinking about: one may argue that a belief in god or the practice of a religion is bad, but what suggestion do we have that what follows after God and religion will be any better? This may or may not be an argument against eradicating God, or at least attempting to do so, depending on one's taste; it still ought to be considered.

Moving away from this particular aspect of the book, one thing Dawkins notes is that here in the US, being an atheist is the worst possible thing you can be; people would apparently prefer you to be gay than godless (which means, of course, pity the poor atheist homosexual, particularly if he wants to marry his same-sex partner). Dawkins notes that the Atheist-American community (which would apparently include agnostics in the same manner that the gay community accepts bisexuals) is a pretty large community (22.5 million strong, according to the American Atheists), but that it's politically pretty weak, in part because atheists and agnostics in the United States don't have the same sort of strong lobby that, say, the Jewish community has.

I find this an interesting point. Personally speaking I have yet to feel marginalized or discriminated against because I am an agnostic. Part of this, I'm sure, is because I also happen to be a white, educated, heterosexually-bonded non-handicapped male of above average financial means, and those facts matter more in this society. Another part, I'm sure, is that I simply don't *care* what other people think about my agnosticism, and I also know my rights, so in general an attempt to marginalize me probably wouldn't really work. Another part is that, in fact, I *haven't* been marginalized or discriminated against for my unwillingness to adhere to a religion. I'm not suggesting it doesn't happen; I'm saying it hasn't happened to me. It may be possible that if I were to run for public office, my agnosticism would become a campaign issue; what I think would be more of a campaign issue is that I'm neither a Republican nor a Democrat. Which is to say I would have an uphill climb even before my agnosticism were an issue.

I'm an open agnostic—ask me, I'll tell you—but I don't spend a lot of time defining myself through my agnosticism, and I pick and choose my battles. Teaching creationism (disguised as "intelligent design" or otherwise) in classrooms? Fight worth having. Getting worked up about

"In God We Trust" on the coinage? Someone else can shoulder that load. I suppose this triage might upset some certain segment of folks who self-identify as agnostics and atheists, but honestly, if I'm not going to get worked up about God's vengeance, I'm not going to get worked up about their pique.

Also, as previously suggested, I worry more about the religious when they want to impinge on my rights from the point of view of a *US citizen* than the point of view of an agnostic, because my rights as the latter are predicated on my rights as the former. This is an important distinction to make, because there are more US citizens than US agnostics/atheists, and because as it happens, when the religious-minded wish to impinge on *my* constitutional rights, they *also* usually end up impinging on the rights of others who are not the same religion as them, or if they are of the same religion, have beliefs that do not require that they try to shove them on others. Therefore, I have common cause with religious people who, like me, do not wish their rights abridged by some noxious group of enthusiastic God-thumpers who believe their religious fervor outweighs the US Constitution. And I'm happy to make that cause with them, and I'm not going to go out of my way to say to them "thanks for your help, even if you are a complete idiot to believe in that God thing." I'll just say thanks.

I think that should be sufficient for anyone, including Richard Dawkins.

BEST EMOTION OF
THE MILLENNIUM

Dec
14
1999

Angst. And I'm pretty bummed out about that.

Let us stipulate that "angst" is one of those words that people use a lot but which they don't really understand; in today's nomenclature, it is a trendy synonym for fear or even annoyance (e.g., "I went to Starbucks and my latte was mostly foam. I was filled with angst." Aw, poor baby). This dreadful misuse of the word is problematic, but in one way it's indicative of the fundamental nature of the concept of "angst," which is, like diet-related obesity or supermodels, a leisure society's affliction. Poor, ill-educated serfs didn't know from angst. They didn't have the time, or the inclination.

Which is not to say that didn't have fears, of course. To a poor, illeducated serf, the world is full of fear: Fear of one's feudal lord. Fear of the Plague. Fear of that witch down the lane, you know, the one with all the cats. Above all, a fear of God, He who could squash you in this life and the life everlasting, thank you very much. The point here is: Fear had direction. It was like a sentence; there was an subject (you) and an object (the thing that was gonna get you), and the verb "fear" was adequate to describe what your typical serf had going on in his brain, such as it was.

Angst is something else entirely. If fear is hard working and has a goal, angst is like fear's directionless cousin, the one that has a trust fund and no freakin' clue what he wants to do. Angst by definition has no definite object; it is formless and ubiquitous, and it just sits on your head and freaks you out. Søren Kierkegaard, who wrote the book on angst ("The Concept of Dread," 1844), believed that dread was a desire for that which you fear. This led to sin; sin leads to guilt, and guilt leads to redemption, preferably (at least from Kierkegaard's point of view) through the good graces of Christianity. God always gets you, sooner or later.

Martin Heidegger took angst even further, suggesting that dread is fundamental for a human being to discover freedom, as dread can lead to a man to "choose himself" and thus discover his true potential. When you're full of angst, you see, you tend to concentrate on yourself and not to sweat the little stuff—say, everything else in the entire universe (to say this is a massive simplification of Heidegger's work is to say you can get a cup of water out of the Hoover Dam). Embracing oneself brings one closer to embracing nothingness, and thus full potentiality of authentic being.

Confused? Join the club. Heidegger's writings are so famously impenetrable they could be used by SWAT teams in place of Kevlar; to the uninitiated, he sounds a little like the self-help counselor from the third circle of Hell ("Love your Dread! Embrace the Nothingness!"). Left unsaid is what happens after one has in fact embraced the nothingness; one has the unsettling feeling that it's difficult to get cable TV. Also, there's the question of what happens when one has reached a state of authentic being, only to discover one is authentically an ass. Heidegger is unhelpfully silent on these matters; he himself embraced the nothingness in 1976 and will have nothing more to do with us inauthentic beings.

Angst is probably best described not through words but through pictures, and fortunately we have a fine illustrator of angst in Edvard Munch. Munch knew all about dread; first off, he was Norwegian. Second, he was a sickly boy whose family had an unfortunate tendency of dying on him: His mother when he was five, his sister when he was 14, then his father and brother while he was still young. His other sister? Mentally ill. Munch would write, quite accurately, "Illness, insanity and death were the black angels that kept watch over my cradle and accompanied me all my life." They weren't no bluebirds of happiness, that's for sure.

Munch's art vividly showed the nameless anxiety that Munch felt all around him. The most famous example of this, of course, is "The Scream," in which a fetal-looking person of indiscriminate sex clutches its head and emits a wordless cry. The weird little dude is Munch himself:

"I was walking along the road with two friends," he wrote, "Watching the sunset—the sky suddenly turned red as blood—I stopped, leant against the fence, deadly tired—above the blue-black fjord and the town lay blood and tongues of fire—my friends walked on and I was left, trembling with fire—and I could feel an infinite scream passing through the landscape."

Perhaps the infinite scream was the knowledge that one day his painting of the event would become such a smarmily iconic shorthand for angst that it would lose its power; it's hard to feel dread when the screaming dude is on some VP of Advertising's tie. More's the pity.

Fortunately, there is other, less exploited, Munch work which still packs a punch. "The Scream" is just one element in Munch's epic "Frieze of Life," a collection of 20-odd canvases jam-packed with angst: One of the four major themes of the work, in fact, is "Anxiety." But even the more supposedly cheerful theme of "Love," features paintings swaddled in depression and dread: check out "Ashes" or "Separation," and angst leaps up and hits you like a jagged rock. Don't even view the "Death" pictures if you've skipped your Xanax for the day. Viewing any of the pictures, you immediately grasp the concept of angst; it sits on your chest like a weight, pressing the air out of you. Edvard Munch himself suffered a nervous breakdown, a fact which anyone who has spent any time with his work would find entirely unsurprising.

The irony about naming angst as the emotion of the Millennium is that at the moment, most everyone who can read this is living in almost entirely angst-free world. The economy is booming, people are well-fed and cheerful, most of us are safe and content. This is surely a switch from most of the 20th Century, the Century of Angst, which opened up with the perhaps the most dreadful war of all time, World War I, and then hunkered down under two decades of global depression, followed by a genocidal holocaust, a cold war, the cultural malaise of the 70s and the unvarnished capitalist ugliness of the 80s. Ask anyone then what the 90s would be like, they would have suggested more of the same, but without trash service.

Instead we have Britney Spears, SUVs and 28-year-old stock millionaires; our most difficult decision is whether to buy a DVD, or just stick with the VCR until we go and get an HDTV. Oh, sure, we think we feel angst on occasion, but closer examination reveals it to be irritation, pique or annoyance. I wouldn't suggest that this is a bad thing—nameless dread can really crap on your whole day—but I might suggest that the absence left by angst ought to be filled by something more than the luxurious malaise of sated comfort. What that something might be, I'll leave to you. Hint: It's not a "Scream" coffee mug.

PURITY BALLS

Apr
19
2006

Q uestion in e-mail today asking me what I thought of "Purity Balls," the odd fundamentalist Christian ritual in which daddies take their young daughters to a sort of mini-prom and at the end of it the daughters pledge to remain sexually pure and the daddies pledge to defend that purity. Basically, the reason for the dance is the pledging, which strikes me similarly to Mark Twain's definition of golf: "A long walk, spoiled."

My own thought about these purity balls is that they're really icky—we could go on all day about what's wrong about dads making their very small daughters think about sex, or indoctrinating them into thinking their sexuality should be contingent on the dictates of the men in their lives—but given the high holy terror with which fundamentalists regard human sexuality in general and female sexuality in particular, I don't find these mechanisms of control and indoctrination particularly surprising. I feel sorry for the little girls that their quality time with daddy comes at the price of pledging to submit their will to daddy's whims until such time as they equally surrender to their husband's will, but I guess that since they get to wear *such* pretty dresses, it's a fair trade. So *that's* all right.

Speaking as a father—and one of a girl just about the right age to take to a "purity ball" at that—I'm not going to criticize one of the underlying desires of the purity ball, which is a father's desire to express his commitment to care for and protect his child. I happen to have the same desire. I will note, however, that the expression of that desire can take on rather substantially different forms. These "Purity Ball" fathers think it's best expressed through control; I think it's best expressed through knowledge. I don't want my daughter to pledge her "purity" to me, as if having a sexual experience is some sort of karmic besmirching; I want to *inform* my daughter so that when she has sex, she knows what she's doing and she has it on her terms, and she comes away from the experience satisfied (as much as anyone comes away from their first experience in such a state) and able to integrate it into her life in a positive way.

Which is not to say I *want* her having sex, oh, anytime before she can *vote;* indeed, you can believe me when I say to you that among the discussions we'll have will be the ones where I suggest that abstinence really *is* the best policy through high school, for many very good and practical reasons (hey, it worked for me). I mean, I suppose I *could* just say "You shouldn't have sex because I've told you not to, and that's the end of it," and demand she respect my authority. However, if Athena is anything like me as a kid (and it's becoming rather abundantly clear that she *is*), any attempt at parental rule by fiat is likely to be politely but deeply ignored, and she's going to do what's she going to do.

That being the case, rationally outlining the consequences is going to work rather better than trying to ram a pledge down her adorable little throat. Indeed, I doubt I *could* do that, even now—she's already remarkably resistant to me pulling the "because I said so" act, because she's already internalized the idea that things should happen for a reason. And of course, I feel *immensely proud* about that, even if it does make getting her to clean up her room a real pain in the ass sometimes.

Also, not to put too fine a point on it, I think *not* having pre-marital sex is pretty idiotic. This is a separate issue from promiscuity—I'm not a big fan of totally indiscriminate appendage insertion or acceptance—but if you're serious enough about someone that you're contemplating marriage, you damn well better know what your own sexual playing field is, and you damn well better know if you're sexually compatible with your presumed marital partner. Waiting until you're married to find out if you're sexually compatible with your spouse is like waiting until you're married to find out if you actually speak the same language as your spouse. Yes, you probably could make a marriage work without actually being able to *speak* to your spouse, but that's not really a *good* marriage, is it. I wouldn't suggest it for anyone I know.

All of which signals to you that I have a rather different view of sexuality in general than your average "Purity Ball" father. Which is, of course, all right by me. As I said, I can't fault what I see as the root impulse for the purity balls, but I'm glad that my expression of the desire to keep my daughter safe is not that one. Because if you really want to fetishize sex for a little girl, I really can't think of a more effective way to do it than something like a purity ball. And you know what? Fetishizing sex for little girls is *so very much not* what I want to be doing with my time.

BEST GAY MAN
OF THE
MILLENNIUM

Richard I of England, otherwise known as Richard the Lionhearted. He's here, he's queer, he's the King of England.

Although, certainly, not the *only* gay King of England: William II Rufus, Edward II, and King James I (yes, the Bible dude) are reputed to have indulged in the love that dare not speak its name (On the other hand, rumors pertaining to the gayness of King William III have been greatly exaggerated). Women, don't feel left out: Anne, queen from 1702 to 1714, had a very interesting "friendship" with Sarah Churchill, Duchess of Marlborough, who was her "lady of the bedchamber." Which was apparently an actual job, and not just some winking euphemism.

The difference between Richard and the rest of the reputedly gay monarchs of England is that people seemed to think fondly of Richard, whereas the rest of the lot were met with more than their share of hostility—though that hostility has less to do with their sexuality than it did with other aspects of their character. William II Rufus, son of William the Conqueror, was known as a brutal tyrant who smote the weak and raised their taxes; he took an arrow in the back in 1100, in what was very likely an assassination masterminded by his brother, Henry. James I, who had been King of Scotland before he was also made King of England, spent a lot of money and lectured Parliament about his royal prerogatives; they thought he was a big drooling jerk. Queen Anne had a weak will which made her susceptible to suggestion, a point that Sarah Churchill, for one, exploited to its fullest extent.

(However, then there's Edward II. Not a very good king to begin with, Edward further annoyed his barons by procuring the earldom of Cornwall for Piers Gaveston, Edward's lifelong very good friend, and the sort of fellow who wasn't a bit shy about rubbing your nose in that fact. The barons continually had him exiled, but Edward continually brought him back; finally the barons had enough, collared Gaveston, and in 1312, lopped off his head. Edward himself met a truly bad end in 1327; having been overthrown by his wife Isabella and her lover Roger Mortimer, he was killed by torture that included a red-hot poker as a suppository. You can't tell me *that* wasn't an editorial comment.)

On the surface of things, there's no reason that Richard, as a king, should be looked upon any more favorably than these folks; in fact, as a king, Richard was something of a bust. During his decade-long reign, he was in England for a total of six months, and most of that was given over to slapping around his brother John and the barons, rather than, say, handing out Christmas hams to the populace. Richard wasn't even very much interested in being King of England. His possessions as the Duke of Aquitaine were substantially more important to him, enough so that he went to war against his father Henry II over them. Seems that after Henry had made Richard the heir to the throne, Henry wanted him to give the Aquitaine to John, who had no lands of his own. Richard said no and went to arms; this aggravated Henry so much, he *died*.

What Richard really wanted to do, and what is the thing that won him the hearts of the subjects he didn't even know, was to lead the Third Crusade against Saladin, the great Muslim hero who had conquered Jerusalem in 1187. Saladin had taken Jerusalem from the Christians, who had nabbed it 88 years before, and who, it must be said, acted like animals doing it. When Saladin's troops regained the city, it was remarked how much nicer they were than the Christians had been (why, the Muslims hardly slaughtered *any* innocent bystanders!).

In one of those great historical coincidences, Saladin is also rumored to be gay, which would be thrilling if it were true. The idea that both sides of one of the greatest of all religious wars were commanded—and brilliantly, might I add—by homosexuals is probably something neither today's religious or military leaders would prefer to think about. Put that in your "Don't Ask, Don't Tell" pipe, guys: The Third Crusade was won by a pansy!

(Which pansy, of course, is a matter of debate. Richard's exploits and military brilliance during the Third Crusade are the stuff of legend, and he did manage to wrest a three-year truce out of Saladin, which, among other things, assured safe passage for Christians to holy places. On the other hand, Richard never *did* take back Jerusalem (which was the whole point of the Crusade), and if you check the scorecards of most judges, they'll tell you Saladin and Richard fought to a draw, so the title goes to the incumbent. However, Richard's crusade was not the unmitigated disaster that later crusades would be—ultimately the Christians were booted out of Palestine. So in retrospect, Richard's crusade looked pretty darn good. Way not to lose, Richard.)

Yes, yes, yes, you say, but I don't give a damn about the Crusades. I want to know who Richard was *gay* with. Man, you people disappoint me. But fine: How about Philip II Augustus, King of France concurrent to Richard's reign as King of England. You may have already known about this particular relationship, as it constituted a plot point in the popular play and movie "A Lion in Winter." However, even at the time, the relationship between the two was well-documented. Roger of Hoveden, a contemporary of Richard I and his biographer, has this to say:

> *"Richard, [then] duke of Aquitaine, the son of the king of England, remained with Philip, the King of France, who so honored him for so long that they ate every day at the same table and from the same dish, and at night their beds did not separate them. And the king of France loved him as his own soul; and they loved each other so much that the king of England was absolutely astonished at the passionate love between them and marveled at it."*

(Other translations—Hoveden wrote in Latin—replace "love" with "esteem," toning down the breathless m4m feel of the passage, thereby allowing the nervous to assume Richard and Philip were just really really *really* close buds. Whatever works, man.)

Richard and Phil's relationship, beyond any physical aspect, was tempestuous at best. On one hand, Richard appealed to Philip for help (and got it) when Henry tried to take the Aquitaine from him. On the other hand, once Richard became king, he fortified his holdings in France, on the off chance that Philip might, you know, try to stuff a province or two in his pocket while Richard was away at the Crusades.

As it happens, Philip went to the Third Crusade, where he had a falling out with Richard and eventually headed back to Paris in a huff; once there, he tried to slip some of Richard's lands in his pocket, just like Richard thought he would. The two eventually went to war over the whole thing. Richard was winning until he was shot in the chest by an archer and died. Legend has it that Richard actually congratulated the archer for the shot, which, frankly, strikes me as taking good manners just a little too far.

You may wonder what about any of this makes Richard the best *gay* man of the last 1000 years. Actually, nothing; when it comes right down to it, Richard's sexuality is one of the least interesting things about him. This is one facet he shares in common with other notable gay men of the last 1000 years, from Michelangelo to John Maynard Keynes.

It's also something he shares, of course, with the vast majority of heterosexual men through the years as well. Although since that's the sexual norm, we don't think about it that way. Rare is the moment in which we say "Albert Einstein discovered the theory of relativity. And, you know, he was *straight*." One day, if we're lucky, we'll think the same about gay men and women. In the meantime, we'll have Richard to remind us we're more than the sum of our sexualities. That's worth my vote.

WHY CHRISTMAS

Yesterday Athena and I were chatting about Christmas and I asked her if she knew why we had Christmas, and she explained to me that we had Christmas so that we could be with family and get presents and have food and be thankful. To which I said, yes, those are things we *do* on Christmas, but do you know why there's a Christmas in the first place? To which she confessed she did not. So I explained to her how it was Jesus' birthday, and how many people believe Jesus was the son of God, and that celebrating his birth was important to them. This then moved into a discussion of how old Jesus would be if he were alive today, and also how old God might be, and then we watched Tom & Jerry brutalize each other in cartoon fashion.

We had this conversation for a simple reason, which is the same reason I've explained to her why people vote or how the sun is out there in space or why she can't stick her finger in a wall socket just for fun: I want her to actually understand the world around her and why things are the way they are. As most of you know, I'm not in the slightest bit religious personally; at the same time I think it would be wrong if Athena's only understanding of Christmas was as a jolly and secular gift-giving event. That's not *why* Christmas exists; it exists because some 2000 years ago, someone was born who a couple billion people on the planet believe is the son of God, and those people want to commemorate the event. Athena, being five, might not understand all the implications of knowing that Christmas is Jesus' birthday, not the least because she's a little shaky on the theological implications of Jesus being Christ. And that's fine; people who are considerably older have a difficult time wrapping their brains about it as well. But putting that into her consciousness now means that at some future point in time we can expand on it and explore it more. I see it as a building block.

And what will I teach her about Christmas as she gets older? Everything I think is important, and also everything she wants to know (which may not always be the same things). I'll read to her the Biblical stories of the birth of Jesus; I'll also explain to her one of the reasons we celebrate Christmas when we do was a matter of the Church co-opting Solstice observances to accommodate previously pagan converts. We'll sing Christmas carols; I'll explain the history of the Christmas tree and Santa Claus. I'll answer the questions she asks, and help her find the answers for herself. I think over time she'll get a good understanding of Christmas as a religious holiday and as a secular gift-exchange extravaganza. And in the end, if all goes as planned, she'll make her own decisions about the importance of each of these aspects to her. But it's critically important she understand that at the root of it all is the birth of a child many consider divine. As they say, it's the reason of the season.

As I'm not personally religious, some of you may ask why I would make the effort to teach Athena the religious aspects of the holiday. The reasons are several. The first is that even if one doubts the Christhood of Jesus, one may still admire him as a man, a thinker, and an icon of peace. You don't have to be a Christian to want your child to know that Jesus is at the heart of Christmas. The second is that it's my job as a parent to teach my child these things; I don't want my child picking up theology on the proverbial street corner because we don't teach her about it at home. That seems a fine way for her to pick up some dubious knowledge from dubious people who might eventually get her in trouble. Better that we introduce her to that sort of thing. Third, it's not a bad thing to reinforce the idea that when Athena *does* have questions about any subject, she can come to us, and we're going to tell her as much of the truth of things as we can.

Also, unlike a fair number of the non-religious, I'm not antagonistic toward religion per se, or Christianity specifically. As I've said elsewhere, I think Christianity is a fine religion, and I wish more Christians practiced it. And, not entirely separately, of course one reads a story in the newspaper about Christians were who so incensed that a manger scene was taken out of a school play that they voted down much-needed funds for their school district, or that they've mandated teaching "intelligent design" in high school biology classes, and one wonders why so many Christians seem to believe that Jesus wants their children to be dumb as lard, as if there's some sort of natural opposition between accepting Christ as one's savior and increasing one's knowledge of the world to the limits of one's God-given abilities. But that's not about Christianity, or religion in general; that's about some people's thick-headed interpretation of it and the religious impulse. I don't blame Jesus for the stupidity of some of his followers; we don't get to choose our fans.

I am not religious, but I would not be disappointed if my daughter decided to become so, over the fullness of time and through a depth of knowledge, since it is not a failure of the either the human intellect or spirit to seek the divine. Where I would have failed her is if her religious impulse were to take on a close-minded, fearful and intolerant cast. I would have equally failed her if she were non-religious but also close-minded, fearful and intolerant of those who had such an impulse.

In the end, I want to teach my daughter about Jesus so she can understand him, understand those who see him as the son of God, and understand how he fits into her own view of the world. Making sure she understands why Christmas exists is a good starting point. It's early in her understanding of all of this, of course. But better early than too late.

Ayn Rand: Mom!

Mar

26

2002

Mail from Libertarians (more than one) discussing the crack I made in the "I Hate Your Politics" rant about them all being disappointed that they're not the illegitimate children of Ayn Rand and Robert Heinlein. Most are admitting this is true (The Libertarians as a group are being rather good-natured about the ribbing, much like a secure bald guy tolerates jokes about not having any hair), but a couple have expressed a horror contemplating at least one of these authors as a progenitor. The most recent e-mail along this line, solidly in Ayn's camp, noted: "I would have been satisfied to have Ayn Rand as a mother, [but] to have the author of numerous execrable Lazarus Long novels as my father would cause me to contemplate self-destruction."

Which of course caused *me* to contemplate: Given the choice between Heinlein and Rand, which would I want as a parent? Let's posit that one couldn't have both—beyond such a union causing the cracking of at least four of the seven seals, there's a pretty good chance that after about 15 minutes in each other's presence, either or both of them would have been thumbing their holsters. There can only be one Alpha Male in the room. In a shootout, incidentally, it'd be even money: Heinlein would probably be faster off the draw, but Rand would probably need a stake through the heart to go down. (Before you start: I know about Rand and her thoughts on force. But let's just see her try to reason with Angry Bob.)

Personally, I'm not so sure I'd want Heinlein for a dad (too much weapons-handling and gruff-but-fair cuffing around the ears), but I can say with absolute certainly that the idea of Rand as my mother fills me with an unholy terror. As, I'm sure, it would fill Rand to contemplate me as a child of hers, or, really, to have any children whatsoever. Some people want children, and some want acolytes, and Rand was well into that second camp. Children are unreasonable. Acolytes aren't (well, maybe they *are*, but they know to keep it away from you).

But why go on into detail about all the reasons I wouldn't want Ayn Rand for a mom when a cheap-and-simplistic Top Ten list will do? And so, without further ado:

The Top Ten Reasons You Don't Want Ayn Rand as Your Mom

10: Her not-so-secret disappointment that you weren't able to operate a speedboat the first time you saw one, even after watching the help do it for ten whole minutes.

9: Birthday gifts: Erector sets and a "Lil' Smelter" kit.

8: Pushing you to date her young male followers after she's "vetted" them is really kind of creepy.

7: At bedtime, reads you *The Giving Tree* as a cautionary tale.

6: Wouldn't speak to you for a week after you admitted that you kind of like useless ornamentation.

5: Her "Birds and Bees" chat to you sounds like a particularly seamy scene in a film by David Fincher.

4: Always ends arguments by throwing down a bunch of pictures of modern buildings; seems angry that you don't see the logic.

3: Dismisses your desire to visit Disneyland as "Anti-Life." She's right, of course, but you're still disappointed.

2: Tears down the house rather than let you choose the wallpaper for your room.

1: Your Babysitter: Alan Greenspan.

THINGS TO KNOW ABOUT CLONES

Oct

4

2005

Just some general notes on the care and feeding of clones.

1. They will always want to dress exactly the same. It's a group identity thing. Try to get one to wear a different shirt or maybe some pants while the others are wearing shorts, and they all start screaming in this weirdly-synchronized, air-siren-like way, which is damn annoying. Since you'll no doubt have tattooed the bottoms of their feet or the back of their neck or where ever with the usual identifying barcode, what do you care? Let the idiots all dress the same. The good news is that clones apparently have no fashion sense and will be happy to wear cheap T-Shirts and denim more or less on a constant basis. Wal-Mart fashions were made for clones.

2. Many of you will think that once you've created a clone, you can get it to do all your work for you while you lounge on the deck, drinking a frosty mug of brew. What is rather *more* likely to happen is that your clone will be just as lazy as you are and will tell you to mow your own damn lawn, and then grab the remote to watch Sports Center. Adding additional clones does not help the situation; what you end up with is a couch full of people who look just like you, mocking you about your work habits. You want someone to mow the lawn, hire a gardener.

3. Your clones will be under the impression that they are also married to your wife. You need to nip *that* shit in the bud, like, *pronto.*

4. Clones are naturally apprehensive about their purpose in life, so they are understandably somewhat humorless when you answer their "why am I here?" questions with answers like "why, to be harvested for organs, of course." Especially when that is, in fact, why they are here. Really, people. Don't *tell* them. It just makes them jumpy and liable to come after you with handy tools.

5. Tangentially related: Evil clone? Never happens. Bitter, sarcastic clone? Every freakin' time.

6. Clones eat like the proverbial horses. They will tell you that it's due to shortened telomeres, or body fatigue from being forced to grow into an adult body or whatever. It's all lies, despicable lies. Clones will go through a week's worth of food in two days, and then you'll just have a chunky version of yourself grazing in the pantry. Establish "you pay for what you eat" rules early and often or you will never hear the end of it.

7. If you have more than one clone, they will blame the other ones for whatever terrible things they did (i.e., "it wasn't *me* who ate the last donut/vivisected the cat/tried to asphyxiate you while you slept—It was Clone Two!"). Early on you will be able to counter this through the fact that even though clones have the same DNA, they have different fingerprints, but then they get wise and start wearing gloves. They're sneaky, you see. Simple solution: GPS chips embedded in the shoulder *before* you first wake them up, otherwise they'll dig them out with a screwdriver or butter knife or *something*, and then aside from having an unchipped clone on the loose and wreaking havoc, there's all that blood you have to clean up. And no, the other clones won't mop it up for you. See point number 2.

8. One good thing about clones: They are *endlessly* fascinated by the folks who come to the door wanting to talk to you about Jesus. Also telemarketers. Indulge them (it's harmless enough) but under no circumstances let them near your credit card numbers.

9. Games of "Rock Paper Scissors" with a clone always end in a tie. At first it's kind of cool. But then the clones just can't let it *go*.

10. Eventually your clone will get the idea of cloning itself. You might think it's a bad idea at first—everyone knows that a clone of clone is like a second generation photocopy, and it becomes slightly more smudged, and then next thing you know you've got a drooling idjit that

looks like a mashup between you and the late Marty Feldman—but on the other hand, by the time your clone gets this idea, you'll have realized that all your clone is good for is sitting on the couch and mocking you while it eats your food and tries to trick your wife into having sex with it. Doesn't your clone deserve to be similarly afflicted? Sure it does. Be warned, however: Your clone's clone will still want to sleep with your wife. They're just that way.

Unasked-For Advice to New Writers About Money

Feb

11

2008

I made $164,000 last year from my writing. I've averaged more than $100,000 in writing income for the last ten years, which means, for those of you who don't want to bother with the math, that I've made more than a million dollars from my writing in the last decade. In 2000, I wrote a book on finance, *The Rough Guide to Money Online*. For several years I wrote personal finance newsletters for America Online. When I do corporate consulting, it's very often been for financial services companies like Oppenheimer Funds, US Trust and Warburg Pincus. I mention this to you so that you know that when I offer you, the new, aspiring and dewey-eyed writer, the following entirely unsolicited advice about money, I'm not talking *entirely* out of my ass.

Why am I offering this entirely unsolicited advice about money to new writers? Because it very often appears to me that regardless of how smart and clever and interesting and fun my fellow writers are on every other imaginable subject, when it comes to money—and specifically their *own* money—writers have as much sense as chimps on crack. It's not just writers—all creative people seem to have the "incredibly stupid with money" gene set for *maximum expression*—but since most of creative people I know are writers, they're the nexus of money stupidity I have the most experience with. It makes me sad and also embarrasses the crap out of me; people as smart as writers are ought to *know better.*

The following advice is not complete; there's lots I won't be covering here. Some it is repeated from things I've written before but are so far down in the archives I know you'll never find them. Some of this advice may not apply to you; some of it may apply to you but you may be too delusional or arrogant to acknowledge it, or you may decide you don't like my tone and ignore it all because of that. Most of it is applicable to writers who are not new, too, but I don't know how many of them are interested in taking advice from *me*. This is US-centered although may be generally applicable elsewhere. It's meant for writers but may have application to you in other fields; decide for yourself.

I do not guarantee this advice will make you a more successful writer or a better human being. Follow this advice at your own peril. That said, know that it's generally worked for me. That's why I'm sharing it with you.

One more thing: This is long.

1. You're a writer. Prepare to be broke.

Writers make crap. Why do they make crap? For many reasons, beginning with forces outside their control (publishers pay as little as humanly possible; lots of would-be writers willing to work for pennies, keeping the pay rates low) and working up to forces entirely *within* their control (writers playing with their XBox 360s instead of writing; willingness to be to paid stupid low rates for their work). Most salaried writers in the US are lucky if they get above $50,000 a year; most freelance writers in the United States (which includes novelists, screenwriters, etc.) could make more money being assistant manager at the local Wal-Mart. It's not a joke.

(But, you say to me, *you're* a freelance writer and you've made at least $100,000 a year for the last decade. Yes I have. And I'm an *outlier*; I'm over there to the right of the writing income bell curve. I'm there for many reasons, luck, skill and business sense being the big three, and all three interact with each other. Skill and business sense you can work on; luck happens, or doesn't. There are lots of writers I know who have two out of the three. Many of them make less than I do. It's not necessarily fair. Funny how that works.)

(Also, and not coincidentally, *before* those last ten years were the seven in which I was making rather quite a bit *less*. Oh, my, yes. That income didn't come from nowhere; I did my time in the salt mines, trust me.)

It's *possible* to make a good amount of money as a writer. Most writers *don't*. You should assume, strictly for business purposes, that you won't, or at the very least, won't for a very long time. It's not all about you, it's also about the market. Don't get defensive. The median personal income in the US in 2005 was $28,500. You have a lot of company in the bottom half.

More to the point, coming to peace with the fact that writing is likely *not* to make you a lot of money means that you can realistically look at that money going forward, which will put you in a better financial position than someone who just blunders along assuming that any minute now people are going to start tossing money at them for their lovely, lovely writing. These people become bitter and intolerable soon enough. You don't want to be one of them.

Noting all the above, we come to point two:

2. Don't quit your day job.

Lots of wanna-be writers wax rhapsodic about how great it would be to ditch the day job and just spend all their time clickety-clack typing away. These folks are idiots. Look, people: someone is paying you money and giving you benefits, both of which can support your writing career, and all *you* have to do is show up, do work that an unsupervised monkey could do, and *pretend to care*. What a scam! You're sticking it to The *Man*, dude, because you're taking that paycheck and turning it into *art*. And you know how The Man hates that. You're supposed to be buying a big-screen TV with that paycheck! Instead, you're subverting the dominant paradigm better than an entire battalion of college socialists. Well done, you. Well done, *indeed*.

People who aren't full-time writers tend to have a hazy, romanticized view of the full-time writing life, in which writers wake up, clock four-to-six hours of writing *truth*, and then knock off for the rest of the day to be drunk and brilliant with all the rest of their writer friends. They tend to gloss over the little things like all the time you spend worrying about where the next writing gig is coming from, or all the e-mails and phone calls to publishers reminding them that, hey, they've owed you a check for nine months now, or (due to the previous) deciding which bill you can allow to go to a second or third notice, or the constant pressure to produce something you can sell, because you've heard of this crazy idea called "eating," and you think you might like to give it a whirl. The full-time writing life isn't about writing full-time; it's about a full-time quest to *get paid* for your writing, both in selling the work, and then (alas) in collecting what you are owed. It's not romantic; it's a pain in the ass.

Think of all the writers whose work you love. The vast majority of them have day jobs, or *had* them for a significant portion of their working lives, usually until it became quite clear that they were shooting themselves in the foot, economically speaking, by not writing full-time (this happens *rarely*). But even then, their having had a day job was a good thing, because it meant that they actually developed some life experience, not the least of which was consorting with real live human beings who *weren't* writers. Yes, they exist. Try the grocery store; they hang out there and *buy* things.

Yes, having a day job takes time away from your ability to write. So does watching TV or playing video games or sucking on your toes or posting angry screeds on the Internet. Unlike any of those things, however, a day job *gives you money*, which is something you as a writer will generally find hard to come by. Your day job is a friend to your writing career (not to mention to your family, to your mortage, and to your eventual retirement). Don't be in a rush to give it up. Instead, prioritize everything else you do, and see where you can find writing time in that.

3. Marry (or otherwise shack up with) someone sensible with money, who has a real job.

Hear me now, and note well what I say to you, because I am dead serious here: The single smartest thing I *ever* did for my writing career was to marry my wife. And this is why:

a) She is incredibly good with money by training and temperament and handles the domestic finances for us, leaving me free to focus on *making* money through my writing;

b) She has a real job with benefits, which gives us a month-to-month income (i.e., a secure economic baseline), shields us from the classic American financial disaster of the medical emergency, and has allowed me to take chances with my writing career I might not have been able to otherwise.

Also, you know. It's nice to have someone to listen to me whine, to cheer me on, and generally to go through life with. But *economically*, which is what we're concerned with here, a fiscally responsible spouse with a solid bennies-laden job is a pearl beyond price for writers.

Let me note *strongly* here that one thing I'm *not* saying here is that this sensible, fiscally-responsible spouse should expect to have to support you for years and years while you fiddle away on your Great American Novel (which is code for "playing Halo 3 from 9:30 to 4:30"). Letting your spouse support you while you tinker pointlessly makes you no better than all those heavy metal bassists who spend entire careers sponging off a series of girlfriends. You *better* be working, and contributing to the household income. For us, that meant using a fair amount of my writing time doing consulting work (not romantic writing but pays well) as well as writing books. It also meant being the at-home parent, which saved us a bundle on day care (which kept our costs down, which counts as "contributing").

Or to put it another way: Your spouse is giving you a gift by giving you security and flexibility. Make sure you're making it worth their while, too. And make sure they know *you* know how much they're doing for you. Don't be a heavy metal bassist.

Let me also note that this is the one piece of advice that I suspect writers will have the least control over. It's hard enough getting people to like you *anyway*; finding one who is fiscally responsible *and* willing to pitch in for you while you develop your writing career is a tall order. What I'm saying is that if such a person comes along, grab them with both hands, make snarly territorial noises at all the other writers hovering nearby, and then try *really hard* not to screw up the relationship. In addition to being likely to make you happy as a human, this person will also likely be an excellent economic complement as well. It's nice when that happens.

4. Your income is half of what you think it is.

When you work for someone, the employer withholds your income and Social Security taxes for the IRS, pays part of your Social Security, automatically deducts for your 401(k) and health insurance, and (if you're not an idjit) also kicks in a bit for the 401(k). When you're a free-lance writer, *none* of this happens. The problem is, lots of writers forget that and spend everything they get when they get it, so when taxes come due (which is quarterly, because per the earlier notation, the government quite sensibly doesn't trust freelancers to pay their taxes in one lump sum) lots of writers go "oh, *crap*" and have to suck change out of sofas and the few remaining pay phones to square the debt. This is also why many writers never get around to funding IRAs or other retirement vehicles, and spend their lives hoping they don't slip or catch cold or get hit by a taxi, because they have no health insurance.

Simple solution: Every time you get a check, divide it in two. One half is yours to pay for bills, rent and groceries, and if there's any-thing left over, to play with. The other half, which you deposit into an interest-bearing account of some sort, goes to federal, state and local taxes and your Social Security taxes, and anything that's left over goes to fund your IRA (do the Roth IRA, it'll pay off in the end) and, if you're not lucky enough to have either number two or three above, your health insurance (have a day job or a spouse with bennies? Save it anyway. Be one of the wacky single-digit percent of Americans who actually save something in the bank. Also, and more usefully, that money you're saving becomes a "buffer" for the times when you have bills but no income on the way. The buffer is your friend. Love the buffer. *Fund* the buffer).

Yes, it sucks to take half of your money and never see it again. But you know what else sucks? Owing the IRS a huge chunk of money sucks. Hospitals playing musical chairs with you because they don't want your uninsured ass cluttering up their emergency room sucks. Not ever being able to stop working because you didn't plan for it sucks. All of these things, in fact, suck *worse*. So suck it up and put that half of the check aside.

Related to this and extremely important: *The money you have in hand is all the money you have.* For the purposes of budgeting, do not allow yourself to think "oh, well, such-and-such publisher owes me this, and then I should get royalties for that, so that's more money coming in..."

That's a really fine way to spend money you don't have and maybe aren't going to get.

Is the money in your hands? Then it's yours (half of it, anyway). Is it not in your hands? Then it doesn't exist.

5. Pay off your credit cards NOW and then use them like cash later.

If you're anything like the average American, and economically speaking you probably are, at some point or another in your life you bought into the idea that the credit limit on your credit card was actually money you could spend—and should spend! On an iPod! And a big tv! And on pizza! In Italy!—and now you have close to $10,000 in consumer debt at 19% APR which you are making monthly minimum payments on, which means that you'll still be paying off that debt when you're 70. Congratulations, average economic American! You *rock*.

Okay: Remember when I told you to put aside half of your income for taxes, and then if there was anything left, to invest it an IRA and otherwise save it? Well, if you have more than a token amount of credit card debt, forget about saving it and apply it to your credit card payment instead. Why? Because it makes absolutely *no* sense to save or invest money if the return rate for that investment is less than the annual percentage rate of your credit card debt. Net, you'll lose money (especially if you're investing from scratch). You need to buy down that credit card debt as quickly as you sensibly can. It is your number one debt priority. Once you've paid down your debt you can begin saving and investing. But pay that debt *first*.

So, now it is some indeterminate amount of time later and you've paid off your credit card debt. Do you tear up all your credit cards and swear never to use them again? No, because as sensible as it would seem to be, there is some benefit to using credit cards. For example, I use a card for all my business-related purchases because at the end of the year I get an annual statement, which makes it a hell of a lot easier for me (or, actually, my accountant) to do my taxes. And like it or not, regular (and responsible) activity on credit cards is useful for your credit rating.

No, what you do is you get rid of all your credit cards but one, and when you use it, you only put on it what you can pay off at the end of the month—you don't carry a balance, since carrying a balance is the root of all credit card evil. You treat it as cash, and if you don't have the cash to pay off what you're charging, you don't buy it. Simple. Personally, I use American Express because it is technically a charge card, not a credit card—i.e., it *has* to paid off at the end of the month, and Amex looks askance at you if you try to carry anything over. This helps keep me from overspending, and as mentioned earlier also helps me keep track of my business-related purchases.

Just remember that credit cards are not your friends; their entire purpose, from the point of view of the bank that gives them to you, is to make you a consistent and eternal source of income, forever and ever, amen. If you want to be in economic thrall to a bank until the very moment you *die*, that's your business, but it's a pretty dumb way to go about things. Especially if you're a writer, who doesn't necessarily have a solid month-to-month income anyway.

Related to this *very* strongly:

6. Don't have the cash for it? You can't have it.

To reiterate, the reason that Americans are as generally economically screwed as they are at this moment in time is because they bought into the fundamentally *insane* idea that buying tons of shiny crap they didn't need on a high-interest installment plan made any sort of *rational* sense at all. And as completely idiotic as it is for the average American, it makes even *less* sense for a writer, who often doesn't know when or even *if* they're going to paid again. Committing to a non-essential monthly cost when you don't have to is *stupid*. You need somewhere to live, so a monthly rent or mortgage payment makes sense. You don't need a monthly charge for two years to pay for that 42-inch 1080p TV. Use your brain.

But you *want* that 42 inch 1080p TV! I understand; I want it too. What you do is *save* for it. When you save for something, it's like you're making a payment on it, except that you don't have an evil credit card company charging you 19% for the privilege. I realize it's condescending to put it that way, but, look: If people actually *knew* this, they wouldn't have thousands in credit card debt, now, would they? And yes, it's true that while you're saving for that HDTV (or whatever), you don't *have* it, and we as a nation are no longer used to the idea of not having what we want now now now now *now*. Well, *get* used to it, you insolvent jackass. Otherwise some bank owns your ass well into the next life. Really, that's all I have to say about that.

And in the meantime, there's always the local sports bar. Pay your $3 for a beer and watch the game on *their* massive HDTV. That's why they put the HDTV there in the first place. And while you're packing away the money to buy the 42-inch 1080p widescreen TV, there's likely to be a bonus, in that the cost of that TV is likely to come down a bit, because that's what happens with so many consumer goods over time. It's like getting cash back on your purchase.

The other advantage of having to save for things, incidentally, is it makes you ask yourself if you *really* need it (or, at least, want it so much that you're willing to part with your money for it). You are likely to be surprised at how many things it turns out you don't really need if you have to wait to get them, and can actually *see* the mass o' cash you're laying out for 'em. And that's all to the good for you.

7. When you do buy something, buy the best you can afford—and then run it into the ground.

I am not now, nor have I ever been, an advocate for cheap crap. Cheap crap sucks; it's badly made, it breaks, and then you have to go buy a replacement, so effectively the cost of whatever cheap piece of crap you bought is twice what your originally paid for it (or more, since having learned your lesson, you didn't buy cheap crap the second time).

I am an advocate for *thrift*, however, and in my life, being "thrifty" means that you buy well, and then you use what you buy until it no longer has value. You buy it for the long haul. This was something that came naturally to people of my grandparents' generation (the Great Depression kind of drummed it into them) but these days, when the marketing folks at Apple strive to make you feel a wave of intense, personal *shame* that you didn't pony up for the Mac Air the very *instant* it was released, this is a virtue we've lost track of. And it's true enough that if every single

American thought like this, the economy would collapse even faster than it is doing at the moment. But you know what? Let the rest of America worry about that. We're here to worry about *you*.

I practice what I preach, here. In 1991, when I was out of college and starting my first job, I bought the best car I could afford: an '89 Ford Escort, Pony edition (i.e., even more underpowered than the average Escort!). I paid $4800 for it and I drove it for 12 years until it could barely chug into the dealership to meet its replacement (not an Escort). In 1997, we bought Krissy a Suzuki Sidekick; she still has it 150,000 miles later. Going back to 1991, I bought a stereo system for $400; I used it until just this last Christmas, when it finally gave up the ghost as it spun a holiday CD. The TV I bought for myself in 1991 still chugs away in my bedroom; we're likely to replace it when the switchover to digital happens next year, but then again, we might not (it's hooked up to Dish Network, which will scale down the signal to 480p). Hell, our answering machine is seven years old; I think it may use a *tape*.

Point is, we're not afraid of spending money, but we don't spend money *just* to spend money; we look for something that we can live with for a long time. That usually requires spending a bit more upfront, in order to save a lot more on the back end. As long as you combine this with point six, and buy with money you've already saved, this shouldn't be a problem.

It *does* require, as writer Charles Stross would put it, the ability to make a saving throw against *the shiny*; i.e., internalizing the idea that you don't need every new thing just because it's nice and pretty and can do one thing that thing *you* have like it can't do. This is a tough one for me, I admit. I do so love *the shiny*, and sometimes I give in when I shouldn't (as long as I have the money for it). But most of the time, I buy well, and buy to last—and then use it until it begs me to let it die. And then I use it for a year after that! Grandpa would be proud.

8. Unless you have a truly compelling reason to be there, get the hell out of New York/LA/San Francisco.

Because they're friggin' expensive, that's why. Let me explain: Just for giggles, I went to Apartments.com and looked for apartments in

Manhattan that were renting for what I pay monthly on my mortgage for my four bedroom, 2,800 square foot house on a plot of land that is, quite literally, the size of a New York City block ($1750, if you must know, so I looked at the $1700 - $1800 range). I found two, and one was a studio. From $0 to $1800, there are thirteen apartments available. On the *entire island* of Manhattan. Where there are a million people. I *love* that, man.

Admittedly, mine is an extreme example; I don't think very many writers want to live where I live, which, as I like to say, is so far away from *everything* that the nearest McDonald's is eleven miles away. At the same time, between the bucolic splendor of the Scalzi Compound and the insanity that is the Manhattan real estate market is rather a lot of America, most of it quite tolerable to live in, and almost all of it vastly cheaper than the cities of NYC/LA/SF.

But, I hear you cry, I *need* to live in New York/LA/San Francisco because that's where all the *work* is. To which I say: *Meh*. I will tell you a story. From 1996 through early 2001, I lived outside Washington DC, which was a great place for writing work, because I had a lot of clients in the area for consulting work, and I could fly up to New York quickly for meetings and whatnot. But then my wife decided that we needed to move to Ohio so our daughter could be closer to my wife's family. I agreed, but I warned her that the move was likely to compromise my ability to get work. She understood and we moved. And two weeks after I moved, all my clients called and said, more or less "so, you're moved in now? You can get back to work now?" and started sending me work. *Nothing had changed.*

Now, maybe that's a testament to how *awesome* I am, but all ego aside, I think it's rather *more* to the point that thanks to the miracle of the Internet and such, it just doesn't matter where people are. Look, we live in an era where people working in adjoining cubicles IM each other rather than exercise their vocal cords. Leaving aside the interesting pathology of this fact, IMing someone half a continent away feels no different than IMing someone ten feet away. Distance hardly mattered when I was doing my consulting work, and now that I'm mostly writing books, it matters even less.

Don't get me wrong: I love LA, and San Francisco, and New York. They are some of my favorite places. I'm always excited to have an excuse to visit. But we're talking about money here. Your money—of which you will have little enough as it is—will go further almost every other place in the United States than these three cities. Your living space will be cheaper and more expansive. You will have more money for bills and to draw down debt. You will have more money to save. It will cost you less to do just about everything. People don't realize this when they are in thrall to NYC/LA/SF, but once they leave, as if people coming out of hypnotism, they shake their heads and wonder what they were thinking.

Think about it this way: once you're hugely successful, you can always go back. And now that the housing bubble is popping, it might even be cheaper then! Go, recession, go! But until then, find someplace nice that you like and feel you can do productive work in, and try living there instead.

9. Know the entire writing market and place value on your own work.

A few years ago I was at a science fiction convention, on a panel about making money as a writer, and one of the panelists said something I found absolutely appalling, which was: "I will write anything for three cents a word." This was followed up by something I found even *more* appalling, which was that most of the other panelists were nodding in agreement.

I was appalled not by the fellow's work ethic, which I heartily endorse (I, too, will write pretty much anything, although not for that quoted rate), but by the fact that he and most of the other folks on the panel seemed to think three cents a word was somehow an acceptable rate. It's really *not*; in a word, it is (yes) appalling. The problem was, this very talented writer, and the others on the panel, had largely confined themselves to the science fiction writing markets (and other related markets), in which the *major* outlets pay the grand sum of six to nine cents a word, and in which three cents a word is considered a "pro" rate.

Well, not to be an ass about this, but *this* pro doesn't consider it a pro rate; this pro won't even roll out of *bed* for less than twenty cents a word. Anything below that rate and it becomes distinctly not worth my time; if I do it, it's because it has some other value for me other than money (i.e., mostly because I find it amusing or interesting in some way). I can have this snooty attitude not because I'm *so damn good*, but because I know that out in the real world, I can get 20 cents a word (and usually more—20 cents a word is the lower bound for me) writing other sorts of things for other markets, and so can many other writers with anything approaching a competent work record. To be sure, this can often mean doing writing that's not typically described as "fun"—things like marketing pieces or Web site FAQ text or technical writing. But this sort of writing can pay well, expand your repertoire of work experience and (paradoxically) allow you the wherewithal to take on the sort of stuff that doesn't pay well but is fun to do or is otherwise interesting to you.

There is nothing wrong with writing as a sideline and not worrying overly much about payment. But, if writing is something you want to do full-time, it needs to be something you *can* do full-time; that means finding ways to make it pay and be worth the time and energy you put in it. Part of that is understanding the entire universe of writing opportunities available to you, not just the ones that appeal to you (a *Writer's Market* is a good place to start). Part of it is understanding that getting that writing gig that is dead boring but pays off the electric bill is in its way as valuable as selling that short story, or humor piece, or music review, all of which will pay crap but which you enjoy.

Be willing and ready to write anything—but make sure that you're making the attempt to make *more* than three cents a word off it. Because I will tell you this: If you only value your work to that amount, that's the amount you're going to find yourself getting paid. Over and over again.

This brings us to our final point today:

10. Writing is a business. Act like it.

Every writer who writes for pay is running a small business. You have to create product, track inventory, bid on work, negotiate contracts, pay creditors, make sure you get paid and deal with taxes. Work has to be done on time and to specification. Your business reputation will help you get work—or will make sure you don't get any more. This is your job. This is your business.

If you don't mind your own business then others will do it for you—and make no mistake that you *will* lose out, not because the people you are working with are evil or shifty, but simply because they are approaching their end like it is a business and will naturally take anything you leave on the table. That's business. That's how business works.

Lots of writers miss this, or ignore it, or try to pretend that it's different than this. Lots of writers assume or just want to believe that the only thing they have to do is *write*, and the rest of the stuff will take care of itself. It won't, and it doesn't. This is why so many writers find themselves in financial trouble: they don't have enough money because they valued their work too cheaply, or they weren't wise with the money they received, or they lost track of the money they were owed.

If you can't or won't approach writing as a business, then think about doing something else with your time. Stick with the day job as your main source of income and think about writing as a hobby or side gig. *There is nothing wrong with this.* Some of the best writers did their work "on the side"—as recreation away from their primary profession. Writing part-time does *not* lessen the work; the work is its own thing.

But if you *are* going to try to write as a serious profession, primary or otherwise, treat it seriously. As a writer, you're going to make little enough as is; why give any away through negligence or lack of focus? That's just *silly*. But it really is up to you. This is your work, your *money*, and your business. Respect the first two by paying attention to the third.

When Stupid People
Do Stupid Things,
And Then Do Even
Stupider Things

Aug
7
2007

Josh Marshall hauls up the story of Florida state legislator Bob Allen, who was recently arrested for soliciting sex in a public restroom; specifically it's alleged that he offered an undercover cop a Jackson if he'd let the legislator blow him. This was not a smart thing to do. But having been caught doing something stupid, Allen, who is a pudgy white fellow, has decided to double down on his stupidity by offering what is a truly, spectacularly—indeed, *magnificently*—dumb reason for soliciting another man for sex: Fear of a Black Planet!

"This was a pretty stocky black guy, and there was nothing but other black guys around in the park," said Allen, according to this article in the *Orlando Sentinel*. Allen went on to say he was afraid of becoming a "statistic."

Now, if you go to either Josh's site or the *Sentinel* article, you'll see that according to the officer (who, incidentally, was not there originally to entrap pudgy white state legislators in public restrooms, but was instead staking out a burglar at a nearby condo), it was Allen who initiated the contact. So let's think Allen's rationale through:

Allen, during the middle of the work day, was at the park, just minding his own business, enjoying the Florida sunshine or whatever, like you do, when he suddenly noticed that the park was *full of black men*. Fearing for his own personal safety, he decided that the best course of action was to go into the public restroom, peer over a stall—twice—to *locate* a black man, and offer that black man $20 and a blow job if he'd *just leave him alone*.

Which leads me to ask: What, is this like a *Florida* thing? For generations, have the white men of Florida pulled aside their sons and passed along the secret knowledge that the best way to avoid racial conflict with a black man is to offer him pizza money and a hummer? Is this part of a whole slate of intergenerational Floridian white man knowledge, up there with how to wrassle a gator and the best way to get James Baker to handle your recount? Clearly this all needs to be bound up in a book: *Everything I Ever Needed To Know About Being a White Man in Florida I Learned in a City Park Bathroom Stall.* I, for one, breathlessly await its publication.

What I find rather interesting is that Allen must believe, in some dim fashion, that people will actually *buy* this, and more than buy this, *agree* with it, which is to say that Allen believes that the average Floridan would think to himself or herself, "why, yes, when confronted with a park full of black men, a white man turning himself into some sort of ATM/suction device combo is *an entirely rational response.*" Now, I fully admit to not being an expert on Floridians, so maybe this *does* make sense to them. You hear so many strange things about Florida; Hell, it's got its own tag on Fark, for crying out loud.

Having said that, I would like to believe that the vast majority of Floridians see this for what it almost certainly is: idiotic nonsense. The only real bit of news out of all of this is that Allen would rather be seen as a terrified racist than as someone willing to solicit strangers in a public restroom to get some man-on-man action. Well, here's the thing, Mr. Allen: Clearly, you can be *both*. There's a statistic for you.

ADORABLE
LITTLE PUNKS

Mar
11
1999

Krissy and I went out last night and were surrounded for five hours by a variety of adorable little punks. We went to the Offspring concert, a band which we had assumed was enjoyed by folks near our own age. Boy, were *we* wrong. The average age was below that of a driver's permit; when we came out of the concert (before the encore—yep, *we're* adults), a line of idling minivans filled with parents went past the arena and stretched out the back. You would have thought we were at a Backstreet Boys concert, except for all the Offspring T-Shirts with the words "Stupid Dumbshit Goddamn Motherfucker" on them (it's a refrain from one of their most popular songs, in case you were wondering).

Which also brought home how young this crowd was: They were so young they didn't realize it was hopelessly uncool to wear the t-shirt of the band you were there to see. But what are you going to do. There's no Punk Etiquette Master at the door. *I'm sorry, sir, you can't come in here wearing that t-shirt. You can rent a TSOL t-shirt for the evening. Or perhaps something in a Hüsker Dü?*

The winsome little punks (what to call them? Punkettes? Mini-punks? Punkies? After much deliberation, Krissy and I decided on "Punklets") also made for both the largest and most polite punk mob I'd ever seen. The Offspring concert was general admission, and all the kids gravitated towards the floor, thus creating defined strata of age in the seats; the higher up you went, the older the crowd was (until you got to the highest seats, which were populated exclusively by pot smokers of all ages). The mass of youth on the floor was excited and bubbly. *Hey, guys, let's crowd surf!*

And up would go all these 14-year-old bodies, long before music would actually start playing. The crowd surfers would eventually get dumped into the Security line at the front of the stage; the Security dudes, confident in their ability to handle 85-pound 7th graders, would simply pluck the surfers from the crowd, right them on their feet, and send them on their merry way. It was cute. When mosh pits formed, the giggly teens just sort of lightly slammed into each others, a bumper car ride without the bumper cars. You can just see some English punk from 1977 viewing the pits, thinking, *Right then, time to show them how it's done,* and pinwheeling in there to do actual damage. No one was injured last night. Bruises would clash with their makeup in school the next day.

I'm not running down the punklets. It would be hypocritical for me to do so. It's not like *I* was a true punk in my teenage years (When I was 14, I was listening to Journey! And it *rocked!* Don't Stop Believin', man!). While I'd debate the wisdom of having Offspring be a concert for the training wheels set (the woman in front of us brought her four-year-old to the concert, though I don't know that she could be pictured as representative of parents in general, since she wore a t-shirt that said "Industrial Body Piercings" and had a hoop through her lip), certainly better the Offspring than, say, Matchbox 20 or 98 Degrees.

The kids were all right; in fact they were having a ball. There is a certain amount of irony in having all these dewey-eyed youngsters listening to the music of angst and alienation and then happily trundling back to mom's SUV for the ride home, though the irony would be lost on this crowd. But then, I suppose there's irony in the fact I was listening to music of angst and alienation, and I have a mortgage. So the kids and I are even. An ironic time was had by all.

THE PROBLEM
WITH PARENTS

<table>
<tr><td>Feb</td></tr>
<tr><td>**20**</td></tr>
<tr><td>2005</td></tr>
</table>

Those of you who come here often know that I'm no fan of the more obnoxious elements of the "childfree" community, and indeed positively delight in their snitty impotent rage at small children and the people who breed them. That being said, I will give the childfree folks credit for harping on one very important truth, which is that becoming a parent often turns people in assholes.

Which is to say: They weren't assholes before (or maybe they were and either they hid it well or were in such a way that they were generally indistinguishable from other non-child-bearing people), but later, in the performance of their child-raising duties, they somehow became sphincterfied. In other words, they're not assholes who happen to be parents, they are assholes *because* they are parents. Simply put, there are a lot of asshole parents out there, and if their numbers are not growing, then they at the very least drawing more attention to themselves.

I say this in the wake of reading the cover stories of last week's *Time* and *Newsweek* magazines: *Time's* cover story was on how obnoxious parents are making it difficult for teachers to teach, on account that they go ballistic every time junior comes home with a "B" instead of an "A"; *Newsweek's* piece was how today's mothers feel suffocated by "The Myth of the Perfect Mother"—the idea that they can be great moms and great at work and great spouses and, oh I don't know, great at origami, too. Naturally, living up to this expectation is no fun and a lot of women are running around ragged and irritable at the end of the day, and secretly (but not so secretly they they didn't confide it to the author of this

Newsweek article) enjoy childrearing about as much as they enjoy any other dreary household chore. And naturally they feel guilty about *that*. In the case of the *Time* parents, they really *are* assholes; in the case of the *Newsweek* mothers, they're worried they are assholes if they're not perfect, and making all the effort required to be perfect is likely to make them a bit of an asshole.

I'm an asshole, and I'm also parent, although I try not to be former because of the latter. Be that as it may, I feel I'm qualified to comment on both topics. So let me forward one theory of mine, which, while not the complete answer, is at least part of it.

This is the era of the Gen-X parent, and if we know anything about the Gen-X stereotype, it's that this cohort of Americans was shaped by Atari, Star Wars action figures, and divorce, divorce, divorce, divorce. Thereby, I suspect that many observers might say Gen-X parents are fueled by a desire to do a better job at parenting than their parents, and yet, given what a botched job their parents made of it, feel like they have no positive role models and/or ideas on how to go about being a good parent. So they overcompensate in their neurotically smothering way. If this essay were a Gen-X movie, this would be the part where a goateed Ethan Hawke would explain, between unfiltered cigarette puffs, how he and all his friends were raised by Bill Cosby and Meredith Baxter Birney on Thursday nights far more than their own fathers.

As attractive as this is as an excuse, it's a pretty crappy excuse, and I don't know if it's on point. For one thing, the majority of the Gen-X cohort is now on the far side of 30, and the unwritten rule is if you're over 30 and still blaming your parents for, well, *anything*, you need to be taken aside and told quietly to get a life (you get a pass if your parents are still actively trying to screw with your life, but honestly, that takes more effort than most senior citizens are going to make). Yes, yes, it's awful you were in the middle of that horrible divorce. Here's a hug. Now move on. And point of fact, most Gen-Xers *have* moved on, settled their issues with mom and dad, and I doubt are actively taking these dormant issues out on their kids thereby.

I don't think it's that Gen-Xers are asshole parents because they have issues with their own parents anymore, I think they're asshole parents because they have issues with *each other.* Allow me to posit a central truth regarding Gen-Xers: **We don't much like other Gen-Xers**. It should be obvious: We're all witty and smart, in that casual, pop culture-y way that makes for amusingly light banter at get-togethers that cleverly disguises the true purpose of Gen-X communication, which is to find that weak link in someone else's intellectual defenses that exposes them as a fraud, confirming that they're not *really* your equal no matter how much money, sex or prestige they have, relative to you. It's a generation of defensive egalitarians—it's not "we're all equal," it's "none of you is better than *me*." And that's no way to run a railroad. As Gen-Xers get older, this approach to their cohort has expanded to deal with people who are older than they (because we're all adults now), and adults younger as well (because they don't know much).

How does this liberal (and, coming as it does from a Gen-Xer, self-incriminating) beating on Gen-Xers relate to parenting? In relation to the parents having issues with the teachers, simply enough: When a teacher suggests your kid is something other than your own personal conception of your kid, it's an implicit criticism of *you*, and that's not to be borne, because what does the teacher know? If the teacher were actually someone important enough to be listened to, they wouldn't be a *teacher*, now would they? Fucking teachers, man. The problem lies not in you—it couldn't—therefore, the problem is the teacher, or the school, or the damn No Child Left Behind act that all those red state bastards rammed through Congress. And out come the knives and out comes the attack. Meanwhile, little Jimmy is over there eating his crayons and not actually learning much. But this is the point: It's not about the kid, it's about the parent. The poor kid, in this instance, is an extension of the parent's twitchiness in dealing with the world in general.

(This also goes back to the childfree folks' complain about parents in a general sense—they've got these children completely off the hook in a public space and when someone calls them on it, the parents get monstrously defensive. But they're *not* reacting to the criticism of their children's behavior—they're reacting to the criticism of them as a person. Again, the kid enters into the equation only as a tangential.)

With the "perfect mother" issue the "Gen-X self-dislike" factor is somewhat more muted simply because the expectations of mothers in general are rather more complicated, and I think that in this situation there's a lot more concern for the actual children involved. At the risk of sounding sexist, I think "motherhood" is more child-oriented than "parenthood"; "Parenthood" is a slightly more dispassionate state that acknowledges the rest of the world, whereas "motherhood" is *about* what happens between you and your kid ("fatherhood," ideally, has the same dynamic). But naturally we compare how we handle out relationship with our child with how others like us handle theirs, and in the Gen-X, with its implicit undercurrent of antagonism, this is fraught with issues.

What to do? Well, naturally, I think the first thing for Gen-X parents to do is to get over themselves and whatever festering defensiveness they have regarding other people. Gen-Xers *are* capable of liking people their own age, of course: We all have close friends. It'd be nice if we didn't automatically question the competence and/or worthiness of everyone else we meet. In other words, try to reset our defaults to actually *like* people until and unless they go out of their way to prove they are, in fact, generally unlikeable. It's a thought, anyway. The end result of this is that parents then might be able to listen to teachers and others without feeling like it's a referendum on them as a person. It's not (generally). It's about your kid, and what your kid needs.

Which is the second thing. Your kid: A little person who is probably like you in a lot of ways and yet is *not* you at all. Despite your best efforts, your kids will turn out as someone who is not you, and who has their own agenda in the world. In my opinion, the goal of parenthood is to teach your kid how to explore the world and find himself or herself in it; this naturally requires that the focus is on the kid, and not the parent. The parent who is leaping in and mud-wrestling a teacher over a "B" or bribing the local daycare center staff to get their kid in is probably not focused on what the kid needs so much as what the parent thinks he needs to prove. The parent who gets her hackles up about someone complaining her kid is acting like a hopped-up monkey in a public place isn't actually doing her kid a favor if the kid is, in fact, acting like a hopped-up monkey.

What it comes down to is that when parents act like assholes, it's usually because they're thinking about themselves more than they're thinking about their kids. As parents, it's time to get over ourselves. It's probably better for our kids, and it's certainly better for how the rest of the world sees us as parents.

THE ELECTION
AND KERRY'S
SHOES

Oct
8
2004

Iwant to be clear on this, so that there's no confusion. If John Kerry cannot beat George W. Bush in this election, he should be taken out and beaten to death with his own shoes. How can any major party candidate *not* beat a sitting president who is the first since Hoover to have the economy lose jobs on his watch? How can any candidate *not* beat a sitting president whose economic policies took the federal budget from massive surpluses to massive deficits in such an alarmingly short time? How can any candidate *not* beat a sitting president whose rationales for a war of choice have been shown over and over again to be false and reckless—and because of that 1000 members of the US armed forces have no better reason for their mortal sacrifice than "presidential misadventure"? How can any candidate *lose* to the most incompetent man in living memory to hold the office of president?

Don't talk to me about the Republican smear machine, or stupid voters, or a complicit media. This is a candidate's *job*, to make his case to the American voters. John Kerry has been blessed with an opponent who makes Warren Harding look like a sharp tack, whose major policies have uniformly been one fat disgusting disaster after another, and who by most polls has lead the country in what most Americans view to be in the wrong direction. And here it is, 25 days before election day, and Bush and Kerry are still more or less statistically tied; Kerry's up today, but not enough that he won't be behind tomorrow if he doesn't ace tonight's debate.

This is *appalling*. It is unfathomable to me that at this late date in the campaign that Kerry is not more than a percentage point or two—at best—beyond the statistical error of the polls. I am reasonably confident that Kerry will be a perfectly acceptable president, certainly by comparison to his predecessor if nothing else. But as a candidate, he gives me the smacky shakes. I understand that this is his *modus operandi* in campaigns: to come up fast in the final quarter, just like he did in his senate campaign against William Weld in 1996. But look, Dubya ain't no William Weld. Bush doesn't have the 70% approval ratings Weld had. Dubya doesn't have the successful executive track record Weld had. That race deserved to be close. This one *doesn't*.

And let's also be clear on this: Kerry needs to win *outside* the margin of error. Bush got into the White House in 2000 because Gore, that stupid, stupid man, let the race get close; he lost his own home state, for God's sake, and then it all came down to Florida, where Dubya's brother was governor, and then got kicked upstairs to the Supreme Court. If it all comes down to Florida again, there will be riots and Disney World will burn, baby, burn, but it'll go to Bush again. Or what if it comes down to Ohio, home of Diebold and a Republican Secretary of State who attempted to disallow voter registration cards because of *the weight of the paper* until he was shamed into backing up? Come *on*, people. Do you *really* think if it's close that the Republicans will let it get away? When it comes to elections, you don't let the GOP get close. Letting them get close just means you can't see where they're planning to jam in the knife.

And you know what—I totally respect that. In 2000, I enraged a rabidly liberal friend of mine by saying, basically, that the reason Bush was in the White House was quite simply that the GOP wanted it *more*. The Florida recount was a dirty business all the way around, and the GOP, rabid little powermongers that they were, were like the poor schmucks at a radio contest who were willing to dive headfirst into a vat of pig shit to get the sparkly prize, while the Democrats were only willing to get in to their knees ánd half-heartedly pick around, and complain that they shouldn't *have* to wallow in pork crap in the first place. Well, you know. That was the game at that point. If it comes to that again, you know the GOP has got the snorkels at ready.

This is why Kerry needs two have a two or three state margin (at least!) at the end of the day. This election needs to be incontestable; on election night, Dubya and the GOP have to look at the tally board and know that short of a military coup they've only got a few more weeks to enjoy the use of the Air Force One snack bar. Otherwise it will *never* end. I have entirely too much respect for the GOP's ability to pull an electoral rabbit out of the hat to be anything less than totally paranoid if Kerry continues to let Bush and his buddies keep it close.

And what if—as is *entirely* possible—Bush actually wins? Not by leaning on Jeb or his pals at Diebold, but definitively, by two or three states worth of electoral votes? Ach, the reckoning there will be *then*, my friends. Because then the only thing that Bush and the GOP will have learned from all of this is that competence simply doesn't matter, and if it doesn't matter, then why bother. As for the Democrats, the best they can hope for is that they manage to get 50 seats in the Senate and hold on for dear life until 2008, and I wouldn't count on either. And while the rest of us don't necessarily have to start stocking dry goods in the cellar, we should at the very least know where we can get our hands on a 55-gallon drum of beans when the time comes.

As for Kerry, I imagine he'll become one of the most reviled men in the country. He's already reviled by the folks on the right, simply as a reflex, so that much is taken care of. But the ones in the left and in the center will revile him too, because he couldn't close the deal against the manifestly worst sitting president in decades. And as I've said before, yes, George Bush is an utter incompetent. But think how much more incompetent you have to be to *lose* to him. Death by his own shoes would not be too fine a punishment for such an act.

CHRISTOPHER ROBIN IS OUT THERE IN THE WOODS

Dec
8
2005

As part of a barrel-full of Winnie the Pooh anniversary events, Disney is working on a new animated series that will replace Christopher Robin with a 6-year-old girl.

"We got raised eyebrows even in-house at first, but the feeling was these timeless characters really needed a breath of fresh air that only the introduction of someone new could provide," says Nancy Kanter of the Disney Channel.

"Christopher Robin is still out there in the woods, playing," she says.

"One thing I had never noticed before," said Christopher Robin, "is how very large the Hundred Acre Wood is for such a very small boy."

Christopher Robin had been walking in the woods for quite some time. On his way to visit Pooh, he had the idea to go a new way. The idea came into his head—*plop!*—and so with a left where there was usually a right, Christopher Robin walked into the woods he'd known all his life, stepping high like a military drummer on the march.

For a happy time he explored through the woods, climbing trees, meeting squirrels and kicking leaves, all the while walking, or so he thought, toward the House on Pooh Corner. But as the wind took on just a bit of a chill, Christopher Robin stopped.

"What an odd thing," he said, to no one in particular. "I've been walking all this time, but I don't seem to have gotten closer to Pooh at all!"

Christopher Robin wasn't worried, of course. The Hundred Acre Wood was big enough for many adventures, and here was another. He recalled many times where Pooh and Piglet would set out on a journey and lose their way, only to find their way home in time for tea and honey. If that silly old bear could find his way home, so could Christopher Robin find his way to his friends.

But as the day wore on, Christopher Robin found that every part of the Hundred Acre Wood looked like a new part he'd never seen before. He went left and found a new stream filled with frogs who croaked their unconcern for Christopher Robin's plight. He went right, back the way he came, but the trees seemed to have moved their places when he wasn't looking. So Christopher Robin went back again, to the stream with the croaking frogs, only to find he'd lost the way.

"This *is* a puzzle," Christopher Robin said. "And now I've become quite hungry and cold."

And so Christopher Robin began to run, first one way and then the next, looking for a tree or stream or path he knew, so he could find his way to his friends. He called out to them—"Pooh! Piglet! Tigger! Rabbit! Owl!"—but none answered, or if they did Christopher Robin did not hear them. From time to time, however, it seemed to Christopher Robin that he *could* hear them, just over a small rise, all his friend's voices, and a new voice he did not know. But when he ran that way he found nothing, just more trees and more leaves.

It was in a small pile of leaves that Christopher Robin finally lay, covering himself with their little brittle hands to ward off the chill of the night in the Hundred Acre Wood. "It's a simple thing, really," he said, bravely. "I've been looking for all my friends, and they have been looking for me! If I stay in one place, they will find me. And then we will go to Pooh's, where I will be warm and have something nice to eat."

And so Christopher Robin lay down in the leaves and went to sleep, shivering only a little, trusting in the love of his friends to find him and bring him home.

I REFUSE TO BELIEVE 9 OUT OF 10 REPUBLICANS ARE COMPLETE TOOLS

Jun

16

2004

"Polls show that nine in 10 Republicans approve of [Bush's] job performance—a level of partisan loyalty unmatched by any president."

— Howard Fineman, "Best advice for Kerry: Be invisible," 6/16/04

There's no polite way to ask this: Are 90% of all Republicans really dumber than a dog drinking antifreeze? How can anyone with an IQ higher than room temperature actually *believe* Bush's job performance is anything more than frog-puking sick? Just today the 9/11 Commission stated there was no credible evidence linking al Qaeda and Saddam, yanking down yet another pillar of Dubya's justification for marching into Baghdad, to put into the pile along with those non-existent weapons of mass destruction. Bush's response was instructive: He pointed to the possible presence of al Qaeda in Iraq today as proof.

Well, Mr. President, not to get *nit-picky* or anything, but we've been in control of Iraq for well over a year now. Maybe you'll want to have Condi brief you on that fact. The presence of al Qaeda in Iraq today says more about the US's inability to keep them out than it says about their supposed—and now evidently mythical—relationship with Saddam. The fact that Bush is clueless enough to believe it doesn't, or simply rather cynically believes if he says it, then people will believe it, should give everyone with the ability to think for themselves the cold shakes. Presumably most Republicans *do* have the capacity for self-directed thinking, even if they've been trained like button-pressing rats by Karl Rove against it.

I know Republicans as individuals; I like Republicans as individuals. I've even voted for Republicans—more than once, even. And this is why I say, with all sincerity, that I find it absolutely *impossible* to believe that 90% of Republicans honestly believe that Bush is somehow doing a good job. Earlier in the year, I asked this, and I think it bears repeating:

We all know why Democrats won't vote for Bush. But let me ask the Republicans: Why on earth would *you* vote for a guy who wants to expand the size of the federal government, increase deficit government spending, curtail personal liberties, bring the government into your homes and churches and then stick your children with the bill? With the exception of Bush's mania for lower taxes, is there anything about the man that is in the least bit Republican? Or to put it in another way: If anyone *but* Bush were planning to expand the size of the federal government, increase deficit government spending, curtail personal liberties, bring the government into your homes and churches and then stick your children with the bill, would you vote for him?

All we have to add to this litany is "and seems to think torture is just peachy keen" and I think we're reasonably current.

In an earlier entry talking about John Kerry's "problem" with an unarticulated platform not actually being a problem, I got some blowback from folks who pointed out that merely not being the sitting President shouldn't be enough to propel someone into the White House. And of course, normally I would heartily agree, but on the other hand the current Bush administration isn't normal. It is, in fact, spectacularly *bad*, the sort of bad that's the presidential equivalent of a 100-year flood. If nothing else, this administration is an object lesson in why presidents actually should be elected rather than appointed by the Supreme Court as a matter of political expediency. John Kerry does not arouse a swelling passion in my chest, but there's really nothing in his political and personal history that suggests he would be a president of such monumental incompetence as the current office holder. Yes, I would agree that "probably not monumentally incompetent" is hardly a recommendation, but really, it's come to that. If all a President Kerry does is not be as blindingly bad as Bush, his four-to-eight will be looked upon kindly.

(For the record, I do imagine that Kerry would be better than "probably not monumentally incompetent," but that's for another time. For the purposes of this entry, "probably not monumentally incompetent" is good enough.)

For me, it's not a matter of Bush being a Republican or a Democrat. It's a matter of his administration being the worst administration I've ever had to live through. It's unfathomable to me that 9 out of 10 Republicans are willing to set aside their ability to think in order to unquestioningly approve of Bush when he's clearly a terrible president, and worse, a terrible Republican. Look, I don't want to suggest I think Republicans should *vote* for Kerry; I think that would be an unreasonable request. But I think Republicans should seriously consider *not* voting for Bush: Just go into the voting booth, go through the ballots for every other position, and then just leave the presidential portion blank. Honestly, the House and Senate are likely to stay safely in the hands of the GOP. Kerry's not likely to get away with much pinko stuff. It's a safe protest.

I mean, if you really *do* believe Bush is doing a good job—a genuinely good job—then vote for him. But if it's just that you can't stand the idea of someone who's not a Republican being in the White House, well, you know. Take one for the team today and get someone new for 2008. Someone who is not incompetent and actually supports Republican ideals—and American ones, too.

AL KISSES TIPPER: A NATION SWOONS

Aug

24

2000

I was wrong about this election. It's actually turning out to be fairly interesting, not because of anything the candidates are doing (they're out stumping stumping stumping and will be doing so for the next three months), but because this is an election that is best showing the fundamental disconnect between the people who are paid to comment on the politicians, and the people who, you know, actually vote. The best and clearest example of this was the ruckus among the commentariat about "The Kiss," the big fat smackeroo Gore placed on Tipper as he was on the way to accept the Democratic nomination.

Apparently (and I say "apparently" because I did not see it; right up until Gore started speaking I was watching the utterly ridiculous martial arts flick "Romeo Must Die") when Gore kissed his wife after she introduced him at the convention, he didn't just kiss her, he, like, *totally* kissed her—one of those kisses that apparently sent the message that maybe later that night Tipper would find out just how stiff ol' Al could really be.

This shocked and appalled the commentators; I believe Robert Novak called it "appalling," though I may have misattributed the quote and I don't want to bother with looking it up. Someone called it appalling, in any event. Some even suggested it was a purely political play, a way to show Al wasn't like Clinton, the implication being that Clinton would never slip Hillary the tongue on the stage at the Democratic National Convention, and were he to try, she might just bite it off right there (and who could blame her). In any event, the pundit reaction to

"The Kiss" was mostly negative. That's just not how things are done in Washington, apparently.

Most of the rest of the Americans that saw it liked it just fine. The fact that Al felt entirely comfortable slobbering all over his wife on national television, right before the most important political speech of his life, says a lot about the man. It says that his priorities are straight, for one thing; while no one doubts Gore is a political animal, one also gets the feeling that if he were to lose the election, he would be okay after a while—the center of his life isn't his political career but his wife and by extension his family.

One couldn't ever shake the feeling that Bill Clinton would push a puppy in front of an Amtrak train if he thought there were a vote in it; certainly when it came to the office or his wife, the wife had to give. Look at the strained, tight-lipped smile Hillary has whenever you see her and Bill in public together and you can't help but think that there's a woman who knows where she ranks on Bill's "Important Things" list. You see the same knowledge on Tipper's face, too, of course. It just signifies a different ranking; Tip ain't exactly the tight-lipped sort, as that kiss went to show.

And, besides all that—Al and Tipper are *married*, for Christ's sake. You're *supposed* to want to lay one on your wife. Al and Tip have been married, what? 30 years? Something like that. If you're a man who can be married that long and still come out and give your wife a snog that makes an entire nation think *man, these two need to get a room*, you know what? That's a *damn fine* marriage you have going there. People like that. People like to see people in love with other people. They especially like seeing people in love with the people they're *married* to—and especially after 30 years.

This isn't the first time the commentators have been off-base regarding Gore, of course. They didn't like Al's speech, either, while the voters apparently went nuts for it—convention bounce or not, you don't leap 16 points in a poll and take the lead in the presidential race if you didn't connect with the folks at home. Either the commentators have it in for Gore (which is possible but unlikely; unlike his boss, Al's not the sort to inspire instinctual vituperation) or they've just been away from actual human beings for so long that they've forgotten how people really are. That, and they're not getting any really good lip action, either. Given the general attractiveness of political commentators, this is quite possibly a seriously relevant point.

I do find it amusing that the commentators seem to feel that the general populace can be swayed by the illusion of sincerity in politics, but when they're presented with the real thing that it somehow leaves them cold. Well, they got the real thing, in both senses of the term, when Al gave Tipper that lip lock. There's a family value for you, folks. No wonder they've got four kids.

MOWING
LIFE LESSONS

I now present **All The Things I Didn't Know I Didn't Know About Mowing My Five-Acre Lawn**, an excerpt of my upcoming (and no doubt soon-to-be-spectacularly-successful) yard care book, *Everything I Ever Knew About Mowing I Learned in Just the Last Two Weeks*. Any resemblance between what you read here and heartwarming lessons about life and love is purely coincidental. Unless it helps me turn this pathetic idea into another *Chicken Soup For the Soul*-like juggernaut. In which case, I meant to do that.

1. You Must Mow Counter-Clockwise. The reason for this is that the blades of death attached to the underside of the lawn tractor take the mulched, decapitated grass stalks and fling them out from the right side of the mower. If you mow counter-clockwise, you get an evenly-distributed dusting of mulch that feeds and fertilizes the lawn much in the same way that beef fats and by-products are used in cow feed to plump up your incipient hamburger (or *were*, until Mad Cow Disease. Stupid Mad Cow Disease). But if you mow clockwise, you blow the mulch into a continually smaller and higher pile of ever more finely chopped grass particles, until what you're left with is an unstable ziggurat of grass motes which will collapse upon you at the slightest provocation, saturating you in mower leavings and making you look like the Swamp Thing's wimpy, suburbanized cousin, Lawn Thing ("Lawnie," as he is known, derisively, to his kin). You will *never* get the grass stains out.

2. You Must Not Sweat the Baseball Diamond Pattern. Look: If the Yankees are paying you 75 grand a year to mow a diamond pattern into the Field That Ruth Spat Tobacco Juice Upon (as I believe it is formally called), then by all means make a diamond pattern with your lawn mower. If they're not, you might as well try to get through your mowing as quickly as possible because you're just going to have to mow again next week (If the Houston Astros are paying you to make a diamond pattern, go the extra mile and make the diamond look like the Enron "E." I'm sure they'll get a big kick out of that one). Any temptation to mow any sort of design into your lawn other than the most utilitarian round-and-round spiral is probably a good sign that you need either to get away from your lawn more often, or you need to be whacked in the head with a sturdy board. It's your choice.

3. Try Not to Think of the Lady Bugs. Over the course of mowing, you will undoubtedly mulch dozens of these friendly, colorful, useful beetles; you'll see them clutching the ends of grass stalks, their red, speckled carapaces winking like a 3rd graders' craft beads just before you run them over and either crush them with your tractor wheels and fling them into the abattoir of whirling blades slung to your tractor's undercarriage to be diced into confetti. Try not to feel guilty about their tiny little deaths, even though you have the sneaking suspicion that killing lady bugs is the only thing that actually enrages Jesus, and that each lady bug you whack gets you a century in purgatory, where demons force Bowflex commercials upon you until your sins are completely scraped away. Try not to think about the lady bugs at *all*.

4. Your Lawn Will Try to Shame You. Your front tractor wheels bend down grass stalks, which keep them from being fully mowed, so when you look back, you'll see little wheel-width-wide rows of slightly taller grass, mocking you to the other grass stalks. Remember your place on the evolutionary ladder, go back and teach those leaves of grass a lesson. Mock *you*, will they. Let's see them mock finely-edged blades of metal whirling at thousands of revolutions per minute! Yeah, who's mocking who *now*? Huh? Huh? *Huh?*

5. No Matter How Much It Seems to Be So at the Time, Those Birds Really Are Not Trying To Attack You And Peck Out Your Eyeballs. They're just after the bugs that are busily fleeing your mower. Honestly, that's all it is. Oh, fine. Wear protective goggles, you baby.

6. When You Are On Your Lawn Tractor, You Must Wave to Anyone Going By On the Road. And if you live in rural America, as I do, you must especially wave at the farmers cruising by on *real* tractors; you know, the ones that make your lawn tractor look like a frisky Maltese next to a Great Dane. The farmers really get a kick out of you waving to them; they sort of chuckle and think to themselves *I bet that idiot thinks he looks real sharp on that toy* as they wave back. Given the sorry state of the American family farm (evidenced by the fact that Congress and the President just sent $190 billion of our tax dollars to prop them up), I feel it's my duty as a patriotic American to give the local farmers at least one thing to feel smug about.

7. You *Will* Eat a Bug. Probably more than one. The sooner you accept it, the sooner you can get past it. Just as long as it's not a lady bug. Jesus is mad enough at you already.

Y'ALL WANT WOOD

Nov
2
1998

I wouldn't want to be the one to reinforce stereotypes, but then, the guy who sold us half a cord of wood this weekend was exactly what you're supposed to expect from someone from West Virginia. He was this good ol' boy named Lon, or Lee, or something, and his sophisticated, market-researched way of determining if'n we all needed wood was to come to the door, tap a couple of times, and then ask: *Y'all want some wood?*

W'all did. Or Krissy did, which amounts to the same thing. We have a wood-burning stove in the front room, which I cleaned about five inches of ash out of last weekend; it's as if the previous owners of the house burned all the incriminating documents before they left. Having cleared the way for additional incinerations, Krissy didn't want to waste a moment. She may be the only pregnant woman in the world who is cold all the time; she was planning to curl up to the stove's blistering hot metal surface and sigh contentedly.

What became immediately apparent is that neither Krissy or I had any concept of what how much wood was in a "cord"; it's one of those units of measurement, like "hoghead" or "fathom," that doesn't have much use in today's zippy, high-tech world. It is, in fact, 128 cubic feet (I looked it up just now). We got a good approximation by watching Lon/Lee/Whom-ever pile a cord of wood on our neighbor's driveway. He ended up with a pile nearly large enough to build a log cabin, with an addition for the in-laws. We decided we didn't need anywhere near that much. The in-laws aren't visiting any time soon. So we got half a cord.

Our pile didn't look any smaller than our neighbors, which led me to believe that the Wood Guy had no idea what a cord really was, either; he just kept piling it out until he felt he had piled sufficiently. And because he was good, decent folk, he'd rather err on the side of generosity. Hell, they got tons of trees out there in West Virginia, just waiting for the choppin'. We paid the man, he thanked us very courteously and then headed off, leaving us with a waist-high pile of wood in our driveway.

About half the wood we managed to arrange on our porch, within easy access for the cold winter ahead, but then we ran out of space. I had to borrow the neighbors' wheelbarrow and take the rest round back to the workshop. It was a big wheelbarrow, but it still took ten trips. By the time I was done, my forearms looked like Popeye's, minus the anchor tattoo. All those trips served to remind me why I had gone to college; it was to avoid doing work exactly like this. Well, guess I screwed up again.

BEING POOR

Sep
3
2005

Being poor is knowing exactly how much everything costs.

Being poor is getting angry at your kids for asking for all the crap they see on TV.

Being poor is having to keep buying $800 cars because they're what you can afford, and then having the cars break down on you, because there's not an $800 car in America that's worth a damn.

Being poor is hoping the toothache goes away.

Being poor is knowing your kid goes to friends' houses but never has friends over to yours.

Being poor is going to the restroom before you get in the school lunch line so your friends will be ahead of you and won't hear you say "I get free lunch" when you get to the cashier.

Being poor is living next to the freeway.

Being poor is coming back to the car with your children in the back seat, clutching that box of Raisin Bran you just bought and trying to think of a way to make the kids understand that the box has to last.

Being poor is wondering if your well-off sibling is lying when he says he doesn't mind when you ask for help.

Being poor is off-brand toys.

Being poor is a heater in only one room of the house.

Being poor is knowing you can't leave $5 on the coffee table when your friends are around.

Being poor is hoping your kids don't have a growth spurt.

Being poor is stealing meat from the store, frying it up before your mom gets home and then telling her she doesn't have make dinner tonight because you're not hungry anyway.

Being poor is Goodwill underwear.

Being poor is not enough space for everyone who lives with you.

Being poor is feeling the glued soles tear off your supermarket shoes when you run around the playground.

Being poor is your kid's school being the one with the 15-year-old textbooks and no air conditioning.

Being poor is thinking $8 an hour is a really good deal.

Being poor is relying on people who don't give a damn about you.

Being poor is an overnight shift under florescent lights.

Being poor is finding the letter your mom wrote to your dad, begging him for the child support.

Being poor is a bathtub you have to empty into the toilet.

Being poor is stopping the car to take a lamp from a stranger's trash.

Being poor is making lunch for your kid when a cockroach skitters over the bread, and you looking over to see if your kid saw.

Being poor is believing a GED actually makes a goddamned difference.

Being poor is people angry at you just for walking around in the mall.

Being poor is not taking the job because you can't find someone you trust to watch your kids.

Being poor is the police busting into the apartment right next to yours.

Being poor is not talking to that girl because she'll probably just laugh at your clothes.

Being poor is hoping you'll be invited for dinner.

Being poor is a sidewalk with lots of brown glass on it.

Being poor is people thinking they know something about you by the way you talk.

Being poor is needing that 35-cent raise.

Being poor is your kid's teacher assuming you don't have any books in your home.

Being poor is six dollars short on the utility bill and no way to close the gap.

Being poor is crying when you drop the mac and cheese on the floor.

Being poor is knowing you work as hard as anyone, anywhere.

Being poor is people surprised to discover you're not actually stupid.

Being poor is people surprised to discover you're not actually lazy.

Being poor is a six-hour wait in an emergency room with a sick child asleep on your lap.

Being poor is never buying anything someone else hasn't bought first.

Being poor is picking the 10 cent ramen instead of the 12 cent ramen because that's two extra packages for every dollar.

Being poor is having to live with choices you didn't know you made when you were 14 years old.

Being poor is getting tired of people wanting you to be grateful.

Being poor is knowing you're being judged.

Being poor is a box of crayons and a $1 coloring book from a community center Santa.

Being poor is checking the coin return slot of every soda machine you go by.

Being poor is deciding that it's all right to base a relationship on shelter.

Being poor is knowing you really shouldn't spend that buck on a Lotto ticket.

Being poor is hoping the register lady will spot you the dime.

Being poor is feeling helpless when your child makes the same mistakes you did, and won't listen to you beg them against doing so.

Being poor is a cough that doesn't go away.

Being poor is making sure you don't spill on the couch, just in case you have to give it back before the lease is up.

Being poor is a $200 paycheck advance from a company that takes $250 when the paycheck comes in.

Being poor is four years of night classes for an Associates of Art degree.

Being poor is a lumpy futon bed.

Being poor is knowing where the shelter is.

Being poor is people who have never been poor wondering why you choose to be so.

Being poor is knowing how hard it is to stop being poor.

Being poor is seeing how few options you have.

Being poor is running in place.

Being poor is people wondering why you didn't leave.

SHAMING THE POOR

Mar
2
2008

One of the things that I've come to expect whenever I write about poverty here in the US is that there will inevitably be people in the comment threads who are under the impression that the best thing to do with the poor, if we must be obliged *not* to let them starve, is to larder the assistance we provide them with an additional heaping helping of shame; the idea being that social disapproval of their condition will inspire them to be poor no longer. It popped up again in yesterday's comments about the kids who pass up on lunch rather than let it be seen that they get free lunch.

Needless to say, I think this is a position that is pretty damn stupid to hold, and here are some of the various reasons why.

1. It's not like poor people—particularly poor children— aren't made to feel quite enough shame already. Indeed, the whole point of the article yesterday is that kids would rather go hungry (and in doing so, jeopardize their futures because it's harder to concentrate on your classes when you are concentrating on the fact your stomach is empty) than to be identified as qualifying for a free lunch. They already *know* they're being judged, thanks much. And the hoops society makes the poor jump through for assistance add more shame, albeit in a largely unintentional way. Adding another *official, intentional* layer of shame isn't going to help.

2. In the case of children in poverty, their being poor is generally not their fault. Shaming the children of poor people for daring to receive a free lunch is tantamount to saying to them, *well, if you had been **smart**, you wouldn't have been born to poor people in the first place.* And, you know. That sort of thinking makes you an asshole. Even if one were to cede there was any sort of benefit to shaming people in poverty, there's not much benefit in shaming children, whose ability either to understand or control the role of poverty in their lives is limited.

3. Shaming people for their poverty generally assumes that the *only* reason for poverty is that people are poor for reasons they can be shamed out of—i.e., poor people are poor because they are lazy and shiftless no good spongers who prefer to be poor, because really, it's just less work. This is a nice little fantasy, which like most fantasies sort of falls apart when it meets up with the real world. People are poor and sometimes become poor for lots of reasons. The number of poor who are poor because they *like* it is, as anyone who thinks about it for more than half a minute may imagine, rather small. Most people would prefer *not* to be poor, as it happens, and would be willing to work to escape it.

4. Shaming as a motivational technique to get people out of poverty is a bit like torturing as a motivational technique to get people to tell you something: It works better in fiction than it does in real life. Shaming, like torture, appeals to some minds because it feels like a tough, no-bullshit approach to dealing with something, and everybody's seen it work in *movies*, so it's got to work in real life. But the reason that shame (and torture) work in the movies is that someone's writing a script; the real word is unscripted. In the real world, attempting to shame people for their poverty isn't going to motivate them much, what it's going to do is create *resentment.* And quite properly so, because per points 1-3 here, in the real world poverty isn't a single-cause, socially acceptable condition.

Which is not to say on occasion shaming might not work on a particular individual, but I think you'd have to look at what the end result there would be. You know, the people who claim to have been poor at some point in their lives and who advocate shame as a useful tool for dealing with poverty come across as people who themselves were shamed about their poverty. These folks have indeed appeared to learn a lesson from the shaming, but what the lesson seems to be is that they should look at those who are poor now with contempt, and say *fuck you, I got mine.* I don't think that's a particularly good lesson.

In the science fiction world, among writers and fans, there's an idea, popularized by Robert Heinlein: "Pay it Forward." Which is to say, you help those who need help, as you can help them, without expectation of personal recompense; what you hope for, and what you expect, is that when those you were able to help prosper, that they will help along the next guy. I'm pretty sure that when Heinlein helped out his fellow writers, he didn't go out of his way to make them feel ashamed that he reached down to help pull them up. That would defeat the purpose of doing it at all.

"Pay it Forward" of course has many antecedents, including both the Golden Rule and the idea of reaping what you sow and, to my mind, the Sermon on the Mount as well. In none of these, it should be noted, is the idea of shame as a useful motivator. There's a good reason for that, although I will leave it to others to deduce what that might be.

However, I will say this. When I was poor, there were people who tried to shame me for it, and people who tried to help me out of it. The names and faces of those who helped me spring to mind without bidding; they are the people whose kindness and generosity let me see how good people can be, and how I should try to be when it was my turn to help, through personal action and through my influence on my government, and how it uses what I pay into it. The names and faces of those who tried to shame me? Gone from me, save for the memory of the smallness of their being, and the poverty of their understanding of how to treat others. I was *inspired* to lift myself out of poverty, not shamed into doing so.

WHAT TO KNOW BEFORE YOU ASK ME TO READ YOUR (UNPUBLISHED) WORK

Perhaps since I give out a whole bunch of largely unsolicited writing advice, I am often asked by readers if I would look at the unpublished story/novel/screenplay/poem they're working on and give them some feedback or advice. Indeed, perhaps you yourself have been thinking of asking me this very same thing. I have two things to say to this sort of request:

1. I'm really flattered that you would think of asking me to critique your work and would trust me to give you valuable feedback. Thank you.
2. No.

And now, all the reasons why I won't read your unpublished work, presented in no particular order.

Reason #1: I don't have the time. As of right this very moment, here are the things I am committed to writing: One novel, a second edition of a non-fiction book (which requires substantial revision and rewriting), a novella, a novelette, several short stories, five blog entries every day of the week, several informational pieces for a book on Ohio, a magazine article on Elvis Presley and other ongoing work for corporate clients. All of this work has to be done because I'm contractually obliged to do it and it pays my bills.

On top of this I write daily for *this* Web site, which does not pay bills but which over time has become incredibly important to my career (and to my sanity). On top of that, I need to read at least a couple of books a week for an interview series I do with authors, occasionally read one with an eye toward giving a blurb, and check out yet a few others to discuss here on the Whatever (pimping writers! Yay!). On top of that, I have a family which would like to see me from time to time, not to mention friends who I would also enjoy socializing with. On top of all of this, I'd like a little time for my own non-work-related recreation. And on top of *that*, I'd like to eat and sleep.

Now, over time the *details* of what I'm doing will change. What is unlikely to change is the *volume* of what I'm doing. That has remained constant pretty much for the last decade and seems unlikely to decrease any time soon, for which I am fantastically and appropriately grateful. But it means that I don't have time to read your work, because critically evaluating work in a way that's going to be useful to the author takes a fair amount of time, and it's time I don't have. I understand that from *your* point of view it may seem like it should be a trivial thing to slip in a little bit of reading and evaluation. But over on this side of things, there's no time. There's just *not*.

(How do I have time to write all this, then? Well, I'm writing it *once*. Saves me from having to write it over and over again.)

Related to the time thing:

Reason #2: I'd rather look like a dick by saying no than look like a dick by saying yes and then not following through. Several months ago and against my better judgment I agreed to look at someone's manuscript for them and offer them an opinion on it. And I still haven't gotten to it. Why not? Because ultimately it's the last priority in my day: I have paid work, I have to respond to clients and editors, I spend time with family, I write on this site, I sometimes travel on business, and so on and so forth. All of this fills up my days, and at the end of the day I'm tired and I just want to watch the goddamn *Daily Show* and then go to sleep. I don't want to give this fellow a half-assed evaluation, so I keep postponing getting to the manuscript until I have time to give it the time it deserves, and that time just never manages to get here. I'm being a total dick to this guy because he's been patiently waiting for me to deliver on what I said I would do and I'm just not doing it.

I'm telling you this for two reasons. The first is that a little self-induced public shaming is just the spur I need to actually get this manuscript read. But more relevant point here is that when I say "no" to you, at least you're not left dangling for months and months like I've made this poor fellow dangle, waiting to hear back from me. Your disappointment is brief and over, not long and lingering and continual. And of course, I'd also personally prefer not to disappoint people on a daily, continuing basis.

Reason #3: You're not paying me. This sounds like me being a snide jerk, but there's actual truth to this. Here's the thing: I get paid pretty well for what I do. When people ask me to read their work, they're usually not including a consulting fee; they're expecting I'll read the work for free. Thing is, giving people a useful critical evaluation *is* work; in effect they're asking me to work for free. And, well. Generally speaking, I don't do that. It makes my mortgage company nervous. And since my schedule is pretty packed (as noted above), any evaluation I do takes place in time I usually allot to paying work. So not only am I not making money doing this evaluation, there's also a reasonably good chance this evaluation is taking up time I could be using to make money. And there's the mortgage people getting nervous again.

Now, let's be clear here: When people ask me to read their stuff, it's not like I fly into a rage at their insensitivity and appalling willingness to take food from the mouth of my darling child; that's just silly. No one who asks me to read their work is saying I ought to prioritize them over actual work; they know they're asking me for a favor. What I'm saying is that all things being equal, whenever possible I'm going to fill up work time with paid work. If someone wanted me to read their stuff and was also willing to pay my corporate consulting fee, I might be willing to make time, and bump something lesser-paying down the work ladder. But I don't suspect many people are willing to pay my consulting fee— nor should they, as there are lots of wonderfully competent editors who would be delighted to give feedback at far more reasonable rates—so generally it's going to be people asking me to do work for free. I'm not likely to do that.

Reason #4: Some people don't really want feedback, and if they do, they don't want feedback from *me*. This works on two levels. First, to be blunt, there are a lot of people who, when they say, "I'd love feedback," actually mean "I want a hug." Yes, most people say they really *do* want honest feedback, but you know what? A lot of them are lying (or, alternately, don't know themselves well enough). How do I know which of these you are? Well, in fact, I don't, unless I actually know you in real life, which in nearly every case I do not.

This matters because, to put it mildly, I'm not a hugger when it comes to critiquing work. I'm not intentionally rude, but I'm not going to bother sparing your feelings or sugar-coating what I think you're doing wrong. In my experience this is hard enough for people to take if they genuinely *want* criticism; when they *don't* actually want criticism—when in fact what they want is some sort of bland positive affirmation of their work or ego validation—it's like being whacked in the face with a shovel full of red-hot coals. I think a lot of folks ask me for critiques because generally speaking I present myself as a nice and reasonable guy, and so they feel safe asking me for feedback. For certain values of "safe," this is wildly incorrect; I don't think it's either nice or reasonable to tell people their work is good when it's not. This has surprised people in the past. Over time I've decided it's usually not worth the hassle.

Reason #5: I don't want to enable you not finishing your work. Lots of people ask me to read the first few chapters or a section of something and offer feedback on it. As a philosophical matter, I think offering critiques on incomplete work is a terrible thing to do to a writer, because what all-too-frequently happens is that writer goes back and keeps rubbing and buffing the same three chapters (or 10 pages, or scene, or whatever) for months and years, and what you end up with is a highly polished useless piece of writing—useless because it's incomplete. Also, the critique is useless because it's only about a part of the work, and who knows how all that fits in with the rest? It's like giving someone a handful of cherries and asking them how they like your cherry pie.

For God's sake, if you're going to hand your work over for critique, *finish* the damn thing first. Even if it's broke, you can fix it. But you can't fix a fragment. All you can do is fiddle with it, and in fiddling avoid finishing it. I don't encourage this; even with friends, I don't read things that aren't finished.

Reason #6: I don't know you. Why does this matter? Well, simple. As noted in reason #4, I don't know if you really want feedback or just a pat on the head. I don't how you respond to criticism. I don't know if you're mentally balanced, and whether a less-than-stellar evaluation from me will turn you into a pet-stalking psychotic. I don't know whether, should I ever critique something of yours and then write something vaguely similar, you'll go and try to sue me for stealing your story idea (you'd lose the case, but it would still cost me time and court fees). There are so many things I don't know about you, they could fill a book.

Now, I'm absolutely sure that, in fact, you're an entirely sane, calm, reasonable person. Most everybody is. But you know what? I actually *have* had someone online go genuinely and certifiably crazy on me. They seemed nice and normal and sane, and then suddenly they *weren't*, and then there were police involved. Don't worry, it was a while ago, everything's fine, and it didn't involve a work critique in any event. However, strictly as a matter of *prudence*, it's best that I don't read your work.

Realize, of course, that the converse of this is also true: You don't know *me*, and while I'm sure I come across as reasonably sane and decent, you never do know, do you? Maybe I *will* steal your ideas. Maybe I *will* be needlessly cruel toward your work because I'm a little weasel of man who needs to feel big by dumping on you. Maybe I am just that big of a twit. You just don't *know*. Maybe this is my way of protecting you from *me*. Flee! Flee!

So, those are the reasons why I won't read your unpublished work. I sincerely hope you understand.

Super Gay Happy Fun Hour!

Feb

11

1999

Of *course* Tinky Winky, the purple Teletubby, is gay. They're *all* gay. That whole *industry* is gay. That industry being, of course, live action children's entertainers.

So we need to out the entire list? Fine. Sigmund *and* the Sea Monsters. All gay. HR Pufnstuf: America's first openly gay mayor (Mayor McCheese only came out after that scandal with his all-too-appropriately named commercial competitor, Jack in the Box). Speaking of Pufnstuf: You remember Freddie, the talking flute? Not *just* a phallic symbol—he's queer as a three dollar bill; his mincing paranoia is widely regarded by insiders as the inspiration for C-3PO. Witchiepoo? *Loves* the Indigo Girls.

Shall we go on? Marlo and the Magic Movie Machine. Both gay. After the show was canceled, the only work the Magic Movie Machine could get was in a gay porno house in Times Square. They cut a slot for quarters into his front panel. The New Zoo Review—some were gay, some were polyamorous, *all* were pagans. The Banana Splits were a rock band in the glam-era early 70s; they slept with *anything* in those cocaine-fueled bathhouse orgies with the Bugaloos. Electro Woman and Dyna Girl—perhaps *the* fundamental lesbian icons of the mid-70s, although Isis gave them a run for the money. I mean, really: An unmarried female high school teacher with a penchant for Egyptian jewelry? Do you need a road map? And let's not even talk about "Captain Marvel": A teen boy that becomes a muscle-bound man in tights with the help of six *Greek* gods. Shazam, indeed.

But what about the commercial characters? Everyone expects the characters in the shows to have some strange lifestyle choices—they *are* performers, after all. But surely advertisers, skittish creatures that they are, would demand heterosexuality. That Mayor McCheese thing was just a fluke, right? Guess again. Look at Grimace. Just *look* at him. The Hamburgler's spent most of his adult life in prison; the things done to him there would give D.H. Lawrence pause. Ronald is gay but studiously celibate; he doesn't want to mess with a good thing.

The Trix Rabbit: Gay *and* obsessive. Toucan Sam has a rainbow flag on his beak. Count Chocula is pure Eurofag; he's been living openly with Lucky the Leprechaun since the early 80s. Tony the Tiger thinks he passes in the straight world, but the bandanna gives him away. And everyone sees the looks he gives Sugar Bear. Snap, Crackle and Pop: *Those* sordid little elves have been at it for years. And as for Cap'N Crunch: Come *on*. No navy in the *world* is going to commission a man whose eyebrows are on his hat. He just likes the uniform.

Every single one of them. Gay like a disco at 2 am. Gosh, it's a miracle that any of us kids grew up straight at *all*.

THE FINAL
JUDGMENT ON
THE FINAL
COUNTDOWN

Jan
7
2008

Thanks to that TV commercial for *Mario & Sonic at the Olympic Games*, in which various chunky Wii gamers train under the watchful eye of their pixellated masters while cheese rock booms in the background, Athena's been exposed to that most hideous of 80s hair metal anthems: "The Final Countdown" by Europe. More to the point, because she saw me wince when the snippet of the song's synth fanfare barfed out of my TV speakers, she's made it a point to torture me with it, coming up to me at inopportune times and singing "It's the final countdown!" and then running away giggling.

Well, I can't *have* that, so this morning before school I finally did what I should have done a long time ago, and made her listen to the whole damn thing, the idea being once she listened to its entire flaccidly vomitrocious length, she would be forever cured of the need to sing any part of it, to me or anyone else. Of course it meant *I* had to listen to it again, too, but these are the sacrifices parents have to make for their children.

Naturally, it was no surprise to me how craptacular this particular song is, but I had largely forgotten the reason *why*, which was, aside from being insipid and banal popcraft in that peculiarly *Swedish* way, instrumentally, every part of the sounds like substandard apings of other 80s rock bands. The synth riff is a clunky transposition of the synth riff from "Only Time Will Tell" by Asia, lead singer Joey Tempest sounds like he spent his teenage years in front of the mirror, attempting to imitoot exarctly Scorpions lead singer Klaus Meine, and the tunelessly finger-mashing guitar solo sounds like a smudged photocopy of every other tunelessly finger-mashing 80s faux-metal guitar solo, which in themselves are smudged photocopies of the fretwork of Randy "I'm the only person who can actually pull this shit off" Rhodes.

Individually it's all crap, but put it all together, and it apparently becomes the sort of *super-synergistic hypercrap* that goes to #1 in twenty-six countries; apparently only the US maintained relative sanity in the face of such musical manure, allowing it to reach only #8. But that was *bad enough*, people. Even so, the next time some smug European starts lecturing you about how America has lost its moral compass, and tortures people, and is turning its Constitution into hamster bedding, you can look them straight in the eye and say "at least *we* didn't let 'The Final Countdown' go to number one, you tone-deaf bastard." And do you know what they will say to that? Nothing. Because there is nothing *to* say. You held the *line*, America. Stand tall.

FATHERHOOD
AND PIE

Apr
22
2004

Today, a two parter from Claire:

> *1. How has fatherhood changed you? What is your experience like as a father? How has it changed your relationship with your wife?*
> *2. Pie or cake?*

Well, first: Pie. All the way. I don't believe this should even be a matter of discussion.

Now that we've got the *important* subject out of the way, let's talk fatherhood.

As a practical matter, fatherhood's changed me in that a large portion of my life is now given over to what can be described as "child maintenance"—the myriad things you do for a kid. For example, later this morning (I'm writing this very early) Krissy and Athena and I will go to the local school so Athena can have her entrance examination for kindergarten, which she starts in the fall. They'll ask her to do her letters and numbers while they also talk to Krissy and me, I imagine primarily to see if we're complete parental idiots that they'll have to work around or not (let's hope not).

Later in the day I'll drive out to Athena's preschool to pick her up and take her home; since Krissy has class tonight, I'll make dinner for Athena, and afterwards we'll probably go out and play in the yard, then Athena will take a bath and afterward we'll either play a computer game together or watch some cartoons. Then Athena is off to bed, and

Krissy and I alternate getting her ready for that (tonight's Krissy's turn). In between all this are the usual conversations, questions and so on that go on between Athena and me on a daily basis. The kid takes up a lot of time, in other words, and I imagine she will for a long time to come. I didn't have to do any of this kind of thing before becoming a father; now I do.

Which naturally leads to the question of whether I miss having the freedom of not having a kid. I don't think so. I mean, I *do* wish sometimes I had more time, especially when I've got deadlines and Athena is bugging me to play with her instead, which I can't do and which can cause me to become irrationally irritated that my five-year-old doesn't understand daddy has to work. As if any five-year-old grasps the actual concept of work—and particularly in my case. When daddy works from home and is sitting around in a bathrobe at 5pm, and he's using the same computer the both of you use to play your favorite pinball game, I think it's fair to say that the already-fuzzy idea of work becomes even more jumbled. So, yeah, a little more time would be nice. Somebody work on that for me.

But otherwise, I'm very happy with the trade. People who don't have have kids often think about children as a matter of what they require from you (time, money, attention), which are resources taken away from other things. And this is of course entirely true, but only half the equation, since you also get something from your kids in return. I mean, having a kid is a lot of work, but having a kid is also a lot of *fun*: The reason parents burble on mindlessly about whatever allegedly amusing damn-fool thing their kid did today is because they're having a ball raising that child, and all those clichéd moments of domestic gooeyness are, in fact, different when they're happening to *you*. Kids are not merely a black hole of needs, sucking away your time, money and youth. They are also entertaining. So long as they're yours.

I don't think fatherhood has changed my personality much. Parenthood is famous for gentling a person's soul, but I don't feel any more gentle concerning the world than I did before. Anyone who's read the Whatever over any space of time can see that the vector of my personality is speeding toward bitter curmudgeonlyness with nary a bump in the road. Nor has having a child curbed my often black and inappropriate sense of humor—indeed, I often use my child as a willing (nay, enthusiastic) prop for my own amusement.

Having said that, I will admit that one of the completely annoying after-effects of having a kid is that I become much more quickly emotional over incredibly stupid things. Hell, we were watching *Brother Bear* last week and I was getting all teary at the ending. I could *die*. I have no doubt that the 25-year-old version of me would be happy to smack around the 35-year-old version of me for getting weepy over greeting card commercials. But at the very least I am aware of how much of an ass I look welling up like a soap star at the drop of a hat. I don't seek out opportunities to have a good cry, you know. And it's not like I don't know that most the stuff gets me *verklempt* is ridiculous and lame. So I don't know that this qualifies as a change in personality, rather than a change in response. If you see me getting all choked up at something, feel free to mock me.

I am happy to say that being a father has confirmed some things about me that I had hoped would be true once I became a father. I was delighted (and relieved) to discover that once I learned I was going to be a father, no part of my brain started looking, frantic-eyed, for an exit (one part of my brain started obsessing about death, but that's not the same thing). I also think it's strengthened my sense of responsibility; I'm still a flake, but less so than before, and if it came down to having to work as, say, a Wal-Mart greeter to keep my family going, I'd be willing to do it (I have a hard time imagining a world in which the *only* job available to me was "Wal-Mart greeter," but that's the point—it's an extreme example). And the love I feel for my child is, as presumed and hoped, unfathomably huge. I simply cannot conceive of having a regret that this child is in my life. Nothing in the world has ever brought me closer to the feeling of a higher power than she has from the very moment of her arrival. Yes, this is probably overdramatic to say. But it also happens to be true.

It's also made me, in public at least, a rather more polite person. If there's one thing that I and the rabidly childfree are in agreement about, it's that there are far too many ill-mannered sloth spawn rooting about places where other humans need to be, and the reason they're ill-mannered is because their parents are complete wastes of protein. Yes, you need to allow for kids being kids, and "public" by and large does not imply "adults only." Even factoring that in, however, there are still too many obnoxious, horrifying children who need to be mulched along with their parents. I don't want my daughter to be a mulching candidate, so I'm generally on her in public to be polite. Which means that *I* have to be polite and set the good example because Athena does definitely cue off what I do. It mostly works in both our cases.

Now, on the flip side, having a child has also made me aware of some of the less attractive aspects of my personality as well. For one thing, I'm lazy and stubborn; sometimes Athena wants to do something with me, and I just don't *wanna*. Sometimes I just want to do my own thing, waaaah. For another, I don't gradiate my anger well; I have a tendency to be very calm as I become progressively irritated and then I suddenly become, well, *not* calm. This is a decent anger response for adults (it keeps me from saying or doing incredibly stupid things, and most of the time whatever's irritating me goes away before I go ballistic), but it's really not great for a kid, especially for kids who (like Athena) take a certain delight in trying to see how much they can get away with before they get in trouble. My problem is that I don't communicate to Athena that she's crossed a line until she's so far over it that she's not only on the way to Trouble Town, she's in fact a longtime resident and running for Mayor. As a result, Athena is confused (and a little scared) by a sudden and to her mind inexplicable confrontation with Angry, Angry Daddy. *Where did he come from? He wasn't here two seconds ago!* It's a failing in regards to my daughter. In this matter, I'm trying to make myself more like Krissy, who shows her displeasure quicker but also doesn't allow herself to get as revved-up as I get.

(In case you're wondering, the appearance of Angry, Angry Daddy is not followed by a series of beatings. I'm not opposed to spanking, but I also think that you save it for when nothing else works and your child is bent on a behavior that's going to get her killed—constantly sticking knives in wall sockets would be a good example. Athena is a child who has a sufficient enough learning curve that I can count the number of times Krissy or I have spanked her and still have fingers left over. We are both unbelievably thankful for this.)

As for how being a father has changed my relationship with my wife: Buckle in, kids, because it's going get sappy. I happen to think my wife is a tremendous mother. For one thing, she's got a maternal instinct that borders on the terrifying; get between her and her kid and she will gnaw on your heart. If you don't think I mean this literally, well, I'll pray for you. For another, she's always smart with, fair to and respectful of Athena, and as such is a positive model for me as a parent. The realization that she is a great parent on top of all her other qualities reminds me that I hit the karmic lottery in duping her to marry me, and that I'd best be spending the next 50 or 60 years making sure she does not experience buyer's regret.

All this mushiness aside, the parenthood aspect of our relationship is something of which we're always mindful. We talk to each other about what's going on with Athena so we can make sure she doesn't get conflicting signals from us as parents; when Athena is stressing one of us out the other will swoop in to give the stressed-out one a break; and (I think very importantly), we make sure that Athena sees how much the two of us love each other and also love her. I don't believe Krissy and I have ever been angry with each other around her (a nice side effect of generally not being angry with each other at all), and any disagreements we do have are generally handled when she's not around. Athena's going to have her own neuroses to develop; best not to add to them if we can avoid it.

As with any parents married to each other, we do have to make sure that our entire relationship and life doesn't revolve around Athena, which means making sure we take the time to spend time with each other. It helps tremendously to have family around for this (family was why I got my ass hauled to Ohio by Krissy, and it was the correct decision on her part), but even just during day-to-day life peeling off some personal time makes a real difference. We also make sure we allow each other time to other things, too. Krissy likes to go out with friends some evenings, and I'll happily watch Athena so she can do that. Sometimes I like to disappear in my office to write or play a game or read or whatever; Krissy keeps Athena amused and distracted so I can have that time.

It's just part of the work of maintaining a relationship. But the rewards are significant, in that I I can honestly say I admire and desire my wife more now today than when we didn't have Athena. All in all, it's an excellent relationship (from my end at least), and if it's been changed by fatherhood, I suspect it's been for the better.

So, in sum: Thumbs up on fatherhood. Lots of work, and lots of reward—the former being integral to the latter. Is it for everyone? Probably not. But it's for me.

"Rules" Woman Getting a Divorce

Apr

4

2001

Ellen Fein, one of the women that co-wrote those ridiculous "Rules" books is getting a divorce, and I couldn't be happier about it. Some of you may recall that my life intersected with the "Rules" women in 1996 when I was on the same *Oprah* as they were, offering the man's perspective on their embarrassingly awful book, thanks to a column I wrote on the subject. I actually had a limo ride with the two of them on the way to Oprah's studio, and I'm here to tell you that there may not have yet been born a more unpleasant pair of vaguely human bipeds; it was inconceivable to me that either of them could have possibly been married, much less dispensing advice on how to collar a man, since any sensible man would have launched himself into a cruise ship propeller rather than to cross either of their paths.

But that's not why I'm happy the woman's getting a divorce. After all, even unpleasant people need love, and far better that they're married off to someone else so they won't think to train their sights on you. No, I'm happy she's getting a divorce because "The Rules" offend the hell out of me. Any relationship that is started under their auspices is inherently dishonest, and the sooner that the relationship unravels, the sooner the woman practicing "The Rules" will realize that she'd be much better off approximating an actual human being rather than the disturbing wedding-seeking man missiles "Rules Girls" inevitably turn out to be. That even one of the alleged masterminds behind "The Rules" can't make "The Rules" work will hopefully be the crashingly obvious sign any remaining "Rules Girls" need to give it up.

The icing on this cake is that these two dreadful women are about to release a "Rules" book on how to *stay* married! And the *icing* on the icing on the cake is that this woman's soon-to-be-ex-husband will now probably get about half the proceeds from the "Rules" books! Ha ha ha ha ha!

I realize it's weak and petty to be having this *schadenfreude* moment at this woman's misfortune. But you know, I don't feel the *slightest* bit bad about it. At all. Primarily because "The Rules" is another one of those periodic attempts to yank women back into believing that they ain't nothing if they ain't got a man. It's not the most recent or even the worst example of this concept—that dubious honor belongs to the "surrendered wife" movement, which states that a woman's response to any cockeyed decree her husband lays down should be *Whatever you say, honey. Here's the checkbook*—but it's bad enough. Anyone who attempts to screw women over psychologically as badly as "The Rules" authors do deserves to be punished. So I'm just peachy-keen about Ms. Fein getting hers.

W

I'm going to talk as a man here for a minute, pleading to any woman out there who might possibly be considering expending a brain cell or two on this whole "Rules" or "Surrendered Wife" angle of things. I will begin by saying that I can't possibly imagine what the Hell is wrong with you that you'd ever possibly be *considering* something like this seriously *anyway*—perhaps some heretofore undetected brain damage or recent ruptured blood vessel in your frontal lobes is starving out your capability for reasonable judgment. Whatever the reason, stop. Just stop. The *last* thing you want to do is put yourself in a position where a man has total control over you.

Why? Well, beyond the fact that it's an irredeemably stupid thing to let *anybody* have total control of your life besides you, there's the more particular matter of the fact that men, invariably, are dumb-asses. Big fat stinky dumb-asses, with dumb-ass ideas about every dumb-ass thing. Why we're allowed out of the house without leashes is beyond me. And anyway, the sort of man who would *enjoy* having a "surrendered wife" is almost certainly exactly the sort of man who should not allowed to be in total control over a woman—he's the sort of guy who will eventually smack her and tell her to shut up and fix him a pot pie. This sort of fellow should have his tibiae crushed by a sledgehammer, not awarded a slave in the form of a wife.

I frankly can't even begin to *imagine* why any man would *want* a wife like that anyway. This morning I was listening to my wife blister the hide of some poor bastard automaton from Sprint, who was feebly trying to argue against expunging some bogus charges from our phone bill, and my heart was welling up with pride and love. My woman doesn't take crap from anyone, least of all *me*. It's one of the reasons I'm married to her, because she's fearless and straightforward and confident and sexy *and* she pays all the bills on time.

Were I to decree that from now on I'd be handling all the finances in the home, first she would laugh at me, and then she'd beat me with an axe handle until I came to my senses. When she first moved in with me, all my bills were on third notices, not because I didn't have the money, but because I was *too lazy to go buy stamps.* Bear in mind that at the time I worked right next door to a post office. The idea that I should be trusted with the finances merely because I'm a *man* is just about the stupidest idea since Crystal Pepsi.

(I don't even want to think about what would happen if I suggested to Krissy that she ought to *obey* me. "Obey" was the one word she specifically had expunged from our wedding vows. To try to impose it on her now, I suspect, would lead to a quick divorce and/or my body being found, bloated and headless, in the creek near our house. And rightly so.)

However, these sorts of dumb-ass movements outrage me most not for my wife's sake, who, it should be evident, doesn't need *my* protection from crap like this, but for my daughter's. Every time a book comes out that says to women that they ought to be tying their self-image directly to a man's pleasure and power, it's saying that my daughter ought to subjugate herself, sooner or later, to some man's will. To anyone who would say this, I have this to say: Bite me. My daughter is already delightfully and gloriously headstrong and confident, she's intelligent and she's gorgeous. There's not going to a man alive who *deserves* to presume to place himself above her, and you can bet that her mother and I are going to teach her to laugh at or break the kneecaps of any man who would suggest such a thing. And to do worse to any woman who suggests it, either.

FELIX HAS COME DOWN IN THE WORLD

Athena's latest toy: It's Felix the Cat, as a golfer. That wouldn't be as in Tiger Woods, incidentally; by the duds Felix is sporting, we're talking something along the lines of Bobby Jones era of things. Which is, of course, entirely appropriate for Felix, since he was also something of a 20s phenomenon.

Most people don't know this, but the very first image transmitted by television was of Felix—some RCA technicians propped up a statue of the cat in front of a camera and let 'er rip. Sure, it's mildly ironic that the first moving pictures on television were of a statue (of an animated cartoon cat, no less), but it just goes to show that history's defining moments need not be inherently dignified.

Alas, Felix has come down in the world since the days of hot jazz and bathtub gin. This particular Felix of Athena's was retrieved out of a coin-operated machine; you know, one of those things with the crane arm—you maneuver the crane arm over the thing you want, press a button, and it drops down and attempts to snag and retrieve the cheaply made object of desire. This particular machine required 50 cents a shot; Krissy shelled out two bucks worth of quarters before snagging Felix by his conveniently enlarged head and negotiating him into the right position for retrieval.

Krissy then presented Felix to Athena, who, while having no idea who he was or the rich but now somewhat denatured cartoon history he represented, nevertheless was pleased to take possession of yet another goofy-looking stuffed animal. One has to wonder how Felix felt about it.

He used to pal around with Bobby Jones, after all. Now he's being slob-bered over, literally, by a kid whose grandparents weren't even gametes when he was in his heyday. Fame is fleeting.

Proof of this fact came when I began to sing the theme song to the "Felix the Cat" cartoon show to Athena, and Krissy looked at me as if I had been suddenly possessed by a jingle-writing demon. She had never heard the theme before. Which was sort of sad. This *is* Felix the Cat, af-ter all. It's not like we're talking about one of the true off-brand cartoons here, like Heckle and Jeckle or Possible Possum. Even in his present humiliated state, he should rate some flicker of recognition. Besides, the tune was catchy:

> *Felix The Cat! The wonderful, wonderful cat!*
> *Whenever he gets in a fix, he reaches into his bag of tricks!*
> *Felix the Cat! The wonderful, wonderful cat!*
> *You'll laugh so much your sides will ache, your heart will go pitter pat,*
> *Watching Felix, the wonderful cat!*

Of course, looking at theme song now, you can see the decline of Felix's popularity all over it. The cartoon show was from the 60s, after all, long after Felix's heyday—his fame had dimmed enough that he had to downshift to the grind of episodic television, not unlike Bette Midler, Geena Davis, and the Sheens, *pere et fils*. This wasn't a glamor shot at the beginning of the TV era; it was a numbing slog through 60s Saturday morning TV.

And it shows. Notice how they oversell his quality; not just a won-derful cat, but a wonderful *wonderful* cat, the phrase repeated twice in the space of three lines. Notice also the guarantee of constant gut-bust-ing hilarity that even someone like the Marx Brothers couldn't fill on such a demanding schedule—not to mention that phrased another way, the fourth line seems more like a warning than a promise of entertain-ment: *NOTICE: Continued use of this cartoon will induce cramping and car-diac arrythmia.* Yeah, give me some of *that*.

Let's face it, the TV show was a desperation stab at a turnaround. And that was 40 years ago. Now he's being fished out of a vending machine.

If it's any consolation to Felix, Athena really seems to like him. He's still got it! Even if "it" has been consigned to the Plexiglas walls of a carnie attraction. It's still show business. He's still got an appreciative audience—it's just a lot smaller. And more apt to chew on his plush little head. Bobby Jones never did that.

THE DICTATOR OF WRITING ANNOUNCES HIS DECREES, PART 1

May
17
2007

Certain events of the past few days have convinced me that most of writerdom has trouble finding its own ass without a claque of workshop buddies to comment on the journey ("I like the way you used your hands to search, but did you *really* need to use the flashlight?"). So in the interest of all writers, who I feel crave strong, confident demogoguery, I have staged a coup, and am now The Beloved and Inspirational Forward-Thinking and Righteous Leader Amongst the Scribes, or, more colloquially, The Dictator of Writing. Having "remaindered" all those who oppose me (or, even worse, sidelined them into SFWA board slots), I am now ready to issue decrees, which all writers must henceforth follow, on penalty of death and/or being eternally blue-pencilled by the sort of officiously tone-deaf copy editor who ate the *Chicago Manual of Style* when she was 14 and has been barfing it up ever since.

The decrees!

1. By Order of the Dictator of Writing, No Writer Will Be Allowed To Write Professionally Without Having First Taken a Remedial Business Course. Because, *damn*, people. You folks don't have a lick of sense about that whole "money" thing. Just as writers can write about anything as long as it's not what they're supposed to be writing, so can they spend their money on anything, as long as it's not what they're supposed to be spending it on (like, you know, bills and rent and taxes and food). Of course, it's not just you. Dostoevsky spent all his money gambling; F. Scott Fitzgerald drank a lot of his (he had help from Zelda) and was in the habit of asking for loans from his agent, which is clearly a trick *I* need to try. However, just because Dostoevsky and Fitzgerald pissed away their money doesn't mean the rest of you get to—at least we got *Crime and Punishment* and *The Great Gatsby* out of *them*.

So: Remedial business courses for the lot of you. You will *learn* how to manage your money, by God. You will *learn* how to budget. You will *learn* how to stretch your income so that you don't end up eying the cat for its protein value during the final days of the month. You will *learn* how keep a ledger of accounts receivable, so you'll know just who is screwing you out of your money and for how long they've been doing it. You will *learn* the tax code, so you can pay your quarterlies on time and you can be clear on what's a business expense and what is not. You will *learn* how to *save*, damn you, so that when life hands you that inevitable surprise gut punch that costs two grand, you don't have to pawn your children. And for the love of Christ, you will *learn* that just because you have a $10,000 credit limit on that plastic rectangle of evil what resides in your wallet, it doesn't mean you have to *spend* it.

You say you don't need remedial business courses? Great! How much credit card debt do you have? How long have you been waiting for that money to come in? How many minutes per pound do you think Frisky the Cat needs in the oven at 375 degrees? And on what notice is your electric bill?

Hmmmm. Well, see. This is why you *need* a Dictator of Writing.

2. By Order of the Dictator of Writing, Undergraduate Creative Writing Programs are Abolished. Really, what a waste of your parents' $37,000 a year. Take a couple of writing courses, if you must (make sure one of them teaches you all the grammar you flaked out on in high school). You can even major in English, if you really want to. But shunting yourself into a writing program at an age where you don't know a single damn thing about life is a fine way to make sure you're never anything more than someone who is clever with words. We've got enough of *those*, thank you kindly. So no more of that. Learn something *else*, why don't you. Something you can bring to the table when you start writing, so what you're writing has something else going for it besides the vacuum-packed pedantry of a creative writing education. Or, heavens forfend, learn something useful and practical, so that you don't actually have to *starve* while you're giving writing a go once you get out of college. Related to this:

3. By Order of the Dictator of Writing, Every Person Intending to Get an MFA in Any Sort of Writing Must First Spend Three Years in The Real World, Hopefully Doing Something Noble and Selfless. Like, I don't know, teaching. Or forestry service. Or the military or Peace Corps. Or taking housecats out for refreshing walks in the countryside. You know. *Anything.* (Except working in a coffee shop. Just what the world needs: Another barrista who writes.) By doing anything else but writing, you will open up your brain to the needs and concerns of other people and things, because, among other things, empathy will make you a *better* writer, and it will also make you a whole lot less insufferable. Also all that craft you're learning won't mean a damn thing if the only sort of life experience you can model is the life of an MFA grad, since among other things, most of one's audience isn't going to be down with that. "His struggles in a setting of academic privilege are eerily like my own!" Well, yes, if all you're doing is writing for *other* MFA grads. Otherwise, not so much. Which reminds me:

4. By Order of the Dictator of Writing, Writing to Impress Other Writers is Punishable by Death. Honestly. You want to impress another writer with your emanations, set a pot of chili between you and then lock the door. Aside from that, think of the poor reader, who just wants to be *entertained,* and does not know or care that you are trying to impress that fellow writer whom you loathe, or want to get into the pants of, or both. Won't you please give a thought to the readers? Especially when death is on the line?

Perhaps to enforce this sentiment, and to cut down the number of needless deaths among writers, we should institute a program like the following:

SCENE: A writer's garret: WRITER is hammering out immortal prose. There is a knock on the DOOR.

WRITER (opening the door to find a large, burly man in the doorway): Who are you?

JOE: I am Joe, sent to you by the Dictator of Writing to help you in your task. I am a reader of average intelligence. Is that your latest work in your hand?

WRITER: Why yes, yes, it is.

JOE: Will you read it to me?

WRITER: Well, it's a work in progress.

JOE: Of course. I understand completely.

WRITER (clears throat): "I blanketed myself with wrath incarnadine —"

JOE punches WRITER in the gut. WRITER falls to the FLOOR.

WRITER (gasping and writhing): Why did you *do* that?

JOE: I didn't follow that sentence. And when that happens, I am authorized to beat you.

WRITER: Let me fix it. (WRITER crawls to DESK, grabs a PEN, and makes an EDIT)

JOE: What does it say now?

WRITER: "I got mad."

JOE kicks WRITER in the TESTICLES. WRITER collapses.

JOE: Now you're just being condescending.

5. By Order of the Dictator of Writing, All Writers Must Be Editors For At Least One Year. Because then you will *understand* why editors suggest changes: To save writers from themselves. Yes, I know it is hard to believe that *your* perfect prose can be improved upon a single jot, but once you've done heroic and dramatic rescues of *other* writers' unfortunate prose pileups, you will at least have an inkling of why those editorial types do what they do.

Also, a good solid twelve months of having to slog through a slush pile will serve to tighten up your own work, because every time something you do reminds you of some piece of crap you found marinating in the slush pile, your brain will actually revulse and your fingers will spasm in the phalangical equivalent of a gag reflex, and you'll find some other way to make your point, one that, incidentally, won't cause some poor bastard editor pain somewhere down the line. And that's good for you.

The Dictator of Writing is now bored with issuing decrees! More will come at a future time, when he has angrily stewed some more! Now go! And bask in my glorious rule!

THE
SPECKLESS SKY

Sep

12

2001

Yesterday, where I live, the sky was perfect: A huge blue inverted bowl, set on top a horizon of trees and rolling hills, and the only things in it were birds and the sun and half a moon. This is notable for two reasons. The first is that my view of the sky is largely unimpeded; from most points on my property, if I wanted to, I could see clear into Indiana. That's a lot of sky to have nothing in. The second is that my property is directly below one of the major flight paths into Dayton International Airport (to say nothing of Wright-Patterson Air Force Base). Combine these two factors and you'll understand why on most days, my sky is never without a plane in it and usually two, and sometimes as many as four or five, punctuating the sky like silvery hyphens.

This is not entirely unusual in my experience. When I lived in Virginia, I lived less than five miles from Dulles International Airport; again, there was never not a plane in the sky. Before that I lived in large to medium-large metropolitan areas—LA, Chicago, Fresno—where again planes were a permanent feature in the urban sky. Nor do I think my experience is notable or unusual. At any one moment, there are typically three to four thousand commercial planes in the skies above the continental United States. Given a reasonable amount of sky to observe, nearly anyone anywhere in the States will spot a plane sooner rather than later. And if you don't see a plane, wait five minutes. One will pop over the horizon, contrails of ice crystals agitating behind it.

Not yesterday. For the first time in my memory, the sky was absent contrails and the steady, implacable progress of airplanes as they crossed the sky, heading from one faraway place to another place equally distant. For the first time I could remember, I saw the sky of my ancestors, the sky of every human but the last three or four generations preceding my own—unimproved by human technology, absent a human presence, unmarred by the human tendency to take the sublime simplicity of nature and yoke it to his own mundane needs. Horizon to horizon, not a thing in the sky but blue, birds and a sun that was only now accepting the end of summer with good and cheerful grace.

Ironically, the thing one really notices about an empty sky is the absence of sound. As frequently as we see airplanes, we hear them even more so; my daughter, who loves to watch planes traverse, knows to look up to see a plane not because she's caught a glimpse of it in the corner of her eye, but because she hears it move—the hollow cavitation of a jet engine, the sound lagging behind the aircraft as if inexpertly dubbed by a bored sound technician. Listen sometime and you'll hear the plane that's above, behind or in front of you in the sky. You hear it so often you don't hear it any more. Planes create the white noise of a mobile society. Standing in my yard, I was overwhelmed by not hearing the planes.

Eventually you get over the idea of not having your sky echo back at you, and you just stare and stare, your eyes looking for the flying machines that aren't there, since you know that even though you won't find any, it's still not normal not to see any at all. I thought that surely my daughter, who (remember) loves planes, would notice that there weren't any in the sky. But she didn't. She was more interested in putting her basketball through her toddler-sized hoop. But then, she's two and a half years old. She doesn't know how exceptional a sky like this was. She doesn't know how very unlikely it is that there will ever be another sky like this, another day like this.

Nighttime eventually fell, and I went out into my yard again. The half-moon set before the sun and wouldn't rise again until well after I went to sleep; the sky was dark and stars were splayed carelessly across it. My wife came out with me, and I showed her the sights: Mars, not as bright as he was earlier in the summer, but still clear and red, an angry horsefly on the constellation Pegasus. Scorpio floated nearby, pincers pointing in the direction into which the sun and moon had fled.

My wife asked me to find the Big Dipper, so we cruised north, and I pointed it out, noting the fact that the Big Dipper is not a constellation at all, but merely an asterism, a smaller chunk of the larger constellation of Ursa Major. We followed the Dipper's guiding stars north again, to Polaris, the star which never sets. Across it all spilled the Milky Way, the cloud of stardust and just plain old dust, a mottled glow that hints at the majesty at the core of our galaxy. It's hard to turn away from a glorious night sky like that. But I did, to go back inside, put my daughter to bed, and reimmerse myself in the horror that was the price of this priceless, speckless sky.

I have to ask myself—and I did ask myself, several times over the course of the day—if it was selfish to celebrate the beauty I have found in that singular sky, that perfect, unblemished sky that I know I will never see again in this life. Was it wrong to appreciate its blue depths, when the cost was gray dust and black soot and red blood, mingled in the Hell mixed up hundreds of miles away? Did the peace this sky brought me mock the pain of thousands, and the pain of the untold number who loved those people? Would the mothers, fathers and children of those who have been lost find it unspeakable that on their cloud of dust and death, I found this sky-blue lining?

I don't know. I think it may indeed be selfish to celebrate that sky. But I can't help myself. Pandora unleashed terrors upon the world when she opened her famous box, but she also released hope, the one thing that was to give people the courage to go on with their lives. In this time, in our time, a new box has opened with all the terrors and pain and suffering we have the capacity to imagine, and more beyond those. You can go insane thinking about them. I spent the day angry and distracted, wobbling between the barely-contained desire to crack dark jokes and the barely-restrained need to bawl like a child. What kept me together was the sky. The one perfect thing on this shattered day. It was my hope.

How I wish I had never had to see that perfect sky. How grateful I am it was there.

FOOTBALL
WITH JESUS

*T*he lord is my receiver; I shall not fumble. He maketh me perform the handoff, and occasionally leadeth me to the Hail Mary pass. He restoreth the point spread; He leadeth me down the field toward victory in His name. Yea, though I thread through the Valley of the Blitzing 350-Pound Defensive Line, I will fear no sacking; for Thou art with me; Thy offensive line of burly disciples they comfort me.

I'm looking through a Christian bookstore catalogue which features Jesus sports figurines, including one in which Jesus, be-robed and sandled, is playing football with some kids. But let me ask the Christians out there in the audience: Would you *really* want your children to play football with Jesus? Before you respond in the affirmative, let me point out a couple of things to consider first.

1. Jesus is heedlessly playing contact football in a robe and sandals, those two articles of clothing being that which visually distinguish Him from, say, the lead singer of the Spin Doctors (who you almost certainly would not let play football with your children). While Jesus is the Son of God, His divinity does not preclude Him from injury; if you doubt this, take a long hard look at a crucifix sometime. Your child could, say, accidentally spike Jesus in His instep, injuring the Redeemer of Humanity and causing Him to be carried off the field, limping and grimacing in pain. No doubt Jesus would forgive your kid, but even so, your kid is going to be known forever as "The Kid That Took Jesus Out of the Game." 4th grade has enough name-calling in it without that following your kid around for the rest of the year.

2. Regardless of his protective clothing situation, Jesus *is* a full grown adult here, greatly outmassing any of His competitors, and offering any Pop Warner team He might play for a distinct (and some would say unfair) advantage. Imagine the terror any 60-pound kid would feel as *any* 180-pound opponent bore down on him, but especially one bizarrely garbed in robe and sandals and who has the power to unleash the Final Judgment upon all of humanity. Even if the kid covering Jesus attempts the tackle, what if Jesus stiff-arms him and keeps on going? What does it do to one's faith when your savior clips you into the turf on His way to the end zone?

3. Angry parents who see their kids hit by others on the field have been known to confront the other player's parents during or after the game. Do you *really* want to try that maneuver in this situation?

4. As alluded to earlier, when Jesus is playing football, not only is he playing for a team, he's playing against a team as well. Well, honestly, who wants to play *against* Jesus? I mean, the kid attempting to tackle the Living Christ has a massive theological quandary on his hands. We all know what happens to those who aren't on Jesus' team, in the larger eschatological sense—they're going to spend eternity in a hot tub filled with kerosene and people who voted for Nader. How is being on an opposing Pee-Wee football team any different? The answer, for your average 8-to-10 year old, at least: It isn't. Jesus' team would win every game by forfeit. That doesn't make for a very interesting season.

Well, you say, simple solution: Just pack the opposing teams with the infidel children of the unbelievers. Those little Wiccan kids shouldn't have a problem tackling Jesus; they're already going to Hell. Okay, but then you have another problem. There are a finite number of spots available on any football team, so only a relatively few Christian children will be able to play in those spots (not to mention that at least a few non-Christians will want to play on the team too, not because of religious reasons but because any kid's football team with a 6-foot, 180-pound receiver has got a real advantage). And as we all know, from a "wrong end of Satan's basting syringe" perspective, simply *not* being on Jesus' team is just as bad as being actively against Him. You see the quandary.

5. We've been making the assumption any team with Jesus on it will automatically win: If not by forfeit, then by Jesus' height and weight advantage, and if not by that then by divine intervention, pure and simple. But intellectual honesty requires us to ask: What if Jesus' team loses? Aside from the psychological toll this would take on the children (whose team is so bad that it can't win even with the direct and active intercession of Jesus Christ Himself), think of the problematic theological issues—especially if, as postulated in the point above, the opposing team was populated entirely by the children of the infidels. If Wotan's Whackers consistently drive down the field, smiting Jesus' teammates along the way, you can bet that's going to have some spiritual resonance, particularly in those parts of the country where Friday Night Football is attended as religiously as Sunday Morning Services.

6. Akin to this, what if Jesus is just a really bad football player? Football was not exactly big in the Middle East 2000 years ago, after all. What if He fumbles continuously? Or is continually offsides on the snap? What if His philosophy of "turn the other cheek" translates to standing there passively while the defensive line pounds the QB into the dirt?

Well, clearly, Jesus will need to be taken off the field to be replaced by a more competent player. But who wants to be the coach that benches Jesus? Who wants to replace Him on the field? And again, there's the larger competence issue. If Jesus can't even handle a hand-off, just how well is he going to guide the souls of the saved to their Final Reward? Both activities are about getting to the goal, after all. You don't want to be in the hands of a bobbler.

All in all, while having your kids play competitive sports with Jesus might seem like a good idea on the surface, in the end it simply raises too many theological and competitive questions. It's probably best just to have Jesus cheering on the sidelines, as long as He's discreet about it and throws in an occasional cheer for the other kids, too. You know. It's the Christian thing to do.

STANDING UP FOR DUBYA, SUCH AS IT IS

Dec

6

2005

People here know I am no big fan of George Bush, but you know, I try to be fair to the man. This is why I'm going to defend him from this broadside from Washington columnist Richard Reeves:

> James Buchanan, the 15th president, is generally considered the worst president in history...he was a confused, indecisive president, who may have made the Civil War inevitable by trying to appease or negotiate with the South. His most recent biographer, Jean Clark, writing for the prestigious American Presidents Series, concluded this year that his actions probably constituted treason...

> Buchanan set the standard, a tough record to beat. But there are serious people who believe that George W. Bush will prove to do that, be worse than Buchanan. I have talked with three significant historians in the past few months who would not say it in public, but who are saying privately that Bush will be remembered as the worst of the presidents.

> There are some numbers. The History News Network at George Mason University has just polled historians informally on the Bush record. Four hundred and fifteen, about a third of those contacted, answered—maybe they were all crazed liberals—making the project as unofficial as it was interesting. These were the results: 338 said they believed Bush was failing, while 77 said he was succeeding. Fifty said they thought he was the worst president ever. Worse than Buchanan.

You know what, that's just a slander on poor Dubya. Yes, he is an awful, awful president: an incompetent of the highest rank, a man of profoundly limited intellectual curiosity who is to the modern American conservative movement what Charles II of Spain was to the Hapsburgs. It's always amusing to read conservative apologists for Bush, who wish to imbue the man with a sort of mystical deep thinking, such as when they suggested that when Islamicist insurgents started flooding into Iraq that it was some rope-a-dope flypaper "master plan" rather than a consequence of the Bush administration having no strategy, or even an *interest* in a strategy, in Iraq once Saddam was hauled out of his rat hole. It ain't happening, people. Bush has all the vision of an Amish buggy horse: If it ain't directly in front of him, he's not seeing it. And let's not forget that an Amish buggy horse isn't exactly the master of his own destiny.

For all that, he's no James Buchanan. Perhaps the Civil War was inevitable—perhaps it was even necessary—but perhaps in both cases it was *not*, had there been a Chief Executive of the United States elected in 1856 whose entire plan for dealing with the sectarian issues rending the South from the rest of the nation had *not* been "well, let's just try to ride this out and let it be the *next* guy's problem." When he finally did become engaged on the issue, it was, as they say, far too little, far too late, and far too incompetently. Let's just say a president whose initial response on South Carolina seceding was to say "They can't do it, but I can't *stop* them" is not a man who deserves the comfort of letting another of his executive brethren front the "worst president" line in his stead.

Say what you will about Dubya, but the Republic will not fall and shatter between now and 2008. There have been other presidents whose administrations have been bad, incompetent, malingering or some unholy combination of all three. But only one president is *unforgivable*, and that's James Buchanan. They knew it at the time; during the Civil War they had to take down Buchanan's picture in the capitol rotunda because they were afraid someone would *deface* it. The deaths of 600,000 soldiers, Union and Confederate, accrue to his account. Dubya's got a while before he gets there.

Again, this is not to minimize the badness of Dubya; he's a bad president, all right, and if one wishes to front the proposition that he's the least competent president *since* Buchanan, that's a legitimate argument in my book. It indeed takes some doing to cut in the line in front of Grant, Harding, Hoover and Carter, but Bush has got the goods, such as they are (Nixon was competent, he was just paranoid to the point of endangering the office of the presidency; he's bad, in a scary category all his own). But let's keep things in perspective: When it comes to worst presidents, Buchanan's the top, he's the Eiffel Tower. He's earned the title in perpetuity, or at least until a president comes along who actually and irreversably destroys the United States of America.

Bush isn't that president, and no one derives benefit in suggesting he is. I mean, honestly, people. Being the worst president since Buchanan is bad *enough*.

THE NEW
SESAME STREET
CHARACTERS SUCK

Oct

2

2000

This makes me feel like something of a heel, but damn it, someone has to say it: All those "new" Muppets on *Sesame Street* really and truly suck. Being a stay-at-home parent, I'm exposed to the Muppets on a fairly regular basis, primarily through Athena's *Sesame Street* toddler software. While the software includes Ernie and Big Bird, the focus of the software is on three newer Muppets: Elmo, Zoe and Baby Natasha. All of them need to turned into terry cloth dishrags as soon as possible.

Elmo, of course, is already at the top of the parental *fatwa* list anyway, thanks to the severe case of financial aggravation known as "Tickle Me Elmo"a few Christmases back. The red, squirmy dolls were disturbing enough to begin with—watch the thing giggle and writhe when you poke it and you can't help but think that this is what methadone for pedophiles looks like—but paying triple and quadruple price for them was even worse. I can't look at Elmo without thinking of him as a monument to parental guilt disguised as consumer mania.

However, that's not the reason I think Elmo bites; Elmo can't be held responsible for the stupidity of America's parental units, alas. I think he sucks because he has no discernible personality. He looks like a Muppet and talks like Muppet, but the thing that made the Muppets work—their cute little needy personalities—is entirely missing.

Think about the classic Sesame Street Muppets and you'll know what I mean. Each of them had his or her own endearingly neurotic quirk. Cookie Monster: Addictive personality and moderate mental retardation. Big Bird: Esteem issues. Bert and Ernie: Co-dependence.

Oscar the Grouch: Misanthropy. The Count: Deviant lifestyle. Snuffal-uphagus: Hell, he didn't actually *exist*. Kermit, well, Kermit was the *worst*, with his veneer of calm control occasionally exploding into random fits of amphibian rage (now you know why it's not easy being green). And as for Grover: Good lord. He's a psychiatrist's yacht all on his own.

Elmo doesn't have any of this. He's merely obnoxious and red and has ping-pong eyes. But get this: He's the most appealing of the new Muppets. The Zoe Muppet, for example, has a personality of the sort that makes you wish that she were real, so you could stuff her in a sack and drown her in a river and be done with her. Baby Natasha (whose existence answers the question of whether having the bottom half of your body as a receptacle for someone's hand is an impediment to reproduction) isn't bad, but I suspect that that's only due to the fact she's a baby. Were she ever to grow up, she'd be as bland as the rest of the new ones.

I know why the new Muppets suck so badly. Most obviously, of course, it's the lack of Jim Henson, who is to the Muppet universe as Charles Schulz was to the Peanuts universe: The engine without which it cannot move. Sure, the Muppet universe goes on, but you can tell something's missing; the spark that animated the earlier Muppets, primarily.

But it's also something else. The first set of Muppets were created in the late 60s, when being freakish and weird held a romantic sort of charm, and there was the idea that maybe we should accept people even with their vaguely neurotic quirks. Today, of course, children's quirks are merely something to be medicated out of them at the earliest possible opportunity. The new Muppets don't have quirks, and without the quirks, they simply grate. This is bad news for our kids, since Muppets more or less reflect their target audience.

The solution is clear: Write to the Children's Television Workshop and demand they make their Muppets more freakish. Do it for the kids. They deserve neurotic Muppets! Years from now, they'll thank you for it.

BEST PERSONAL HYGIENE PRODUCTS OF THE MILLENNIUM

Feminine hygiene products. Toothpaste and underarm deodorants are very well and good. But we don't bleed from the teeth and armpits five days every month.

This is a difficult topic for me to write about. There are several reasons for this, but primary among them is simply that I'm a man. Men are not mentally equipped to handle menstruation. I don't mean this in the sense that we all rush for the remote when the tampon ads are on television. Avoiding those ads is just common sense. No one should be expected to believe that *any* woman is that cheerful about tampons. It'd be like a man, wide-eyed and smiling, extolling the virtues of medicated, cottony swabs for testicular herniations.

No, when I say men are not mentally equipped to handle menstruation, I mean that there is no parallel in the male experience. Men simply do not bleed from their genitals on a regular basis. We can't even *imagine* it. Suggest to a man that his equipment should hemorrhage for five out of every 28 days, and he will instantly drop to a fetal position, clutch his tum-tum and scream for mommy (who, of course, would have no sympathy whatsoever). This is not to say that men can't grasp the *concept* of menstruation. We're aware it happens. It just fills us with a confused and holy terror, like Australopithecenes confronting the Monolith.

Be that as it may, it's just a physical process, and a messy one at that. Something had to be done. Or did it? The most amazing thing about feminine hygiene products is not what they do, but the fact that they weren't commercially available at *all* until well into the 20th Century. This is astounding to me; after all, the onset of human menstruation didn't suddenly occur in tandem with the rise of the radio. What were women doing before then?

Various things. As early as the second millennium BC, Egyptian women were fashioning crude tampons out of available materials. Polynesian cultures created "menstrual huts," in which women would retire for their interim. The "hut" concept is not exclusive to island paradises; similar huts pop up everywhere from the Caucus Steppes to New Guinea (New Guineans, incidentally, having a very complex and disturbing relationship with menstruation; among other things, the men in certain New Guinean tribes would practice genital mutilation, the aim being to imitate the menstrual flow. Women, that sound you hear is the soft *thump* of every man reading this falling to the floor and clutching his groin in sympathetic pain). Mostly, however, women made do, using natural sponges, rags or other absorbent materials. In the 19th century, reusable cotton pads came into existence, but, you know, *ick*.

Then World War I, and the discovery by nurses that a super-absorbent type of cellulose fiber designed to bandage soldiers also made an excellent menstrual pad (blood is blood). Kimberly-Clark, the makers of the cellulose bandages, decided to market the pads, and thus Kotex was born. And almost died, when it was discovered that women of the time were so mortified at the concept of asking their pharmacists for menstrual pads that they would rather go without. Finally, someone came up with the concept of the "honor box"—A woman could discreetly go to a box, drop in a nickel, take the pad (in an unmarked box) and walk away as if nothing ever happened. Clearly this is a far cry from today, in which women are shown on television celebrating the existence of "wings."

Commercial tampons followed the introduction of the pads in the 20s and 30s, though there was some trial and error: Not only did the first tampons not have applicators (that wasn't standard equipment until 1936), some of them didn't even have *strings*. I'm cringing just *thinking* about it. The manufacturers were apparently also blissfully unaware of the bacterial danger of leaving a tampon in too long; the copy of one early tampon box notes that one wearer left hers in for 48 hours with no ill effects. One wonders if it was the 49th hour that killed her.

Not all feminine hygiene products were of such utility and usefulness. As with so many other products women use, some feminine hygiene products seem designed specifically to intimate to a woman that walking around in a natural state is tantamount to scaring babies and dogs. Specifically, I'm referring to feminine odor products, in which the menstrual odor is played up to be the closest thing to raw sewage that ever came out of a person's body, and never mind the *actual* raw sewage located one orifice south.

One memorable 1948 ad shows a husband stalking out the door while the wife cowers in a chair, weeping. "Why Does She Spend Her Evenings Alone?" the ad asks. The answer: Because she's stinky. You know what I'm saying here (although the putative solution—Lysol, of all things—hardly seems much better; if ever there was a place for "minty not medicine-y," this is it). The irony of this is that in 18th Century France, for one, menstrual odor was thought to be seductive, "impregnated with subtle vapors transmitted by the essence of life," according to a commentator of the time. This assessment has to be tempered by the fact we're talking both about the 18th Century (as stench-filled a century as there's ever been) and France, a place full of underbathed people who regularly eat cheeses that smell like gangrenous feet. Still, the point is yet in evidence: Normal menstrual odor is not nearly the worst thing to come out of one's body.

Odor products aside, feminine hygiene products allowed women more control of their bodies, and as an extension, more control of their lives. This is something to which most hygiene products don't aspire; most hygiene products merely make you cleaner. And while there's nothing wrong with that (quite the opposite, in fact), in the race for the millennium's best hygienic products, there's really no contest. So, three cheers for the tampon and the sanitary pad.

And now, you'll excuse me. I need to go and shiver uncontrollably for a couple of hours. I'm just a man, after all.

TORTURE

A German reader who was appalled at my suggestion last December that we make Saddam Hussein spend of the rest of his life in a box into which videotaped depositions of the victims of his regime were streamed endlessly (he thought it would be torture, whereas I would be more inclined to call it karmic justice), wanted to know what I thought about the US treatment of Iraqi prisoners at Abu Ghraib prison.

Well, in no uncertain terms: It is shameful. But more than that, it very simply marks the moment at which I believe the United States has unequivocally lost the larger war for the future of Iraq and of the Middle East, the war, if you will, of the hearts and minds of the Iraqis and of those of good will in the region. Whether one believes that deposing Saddam was a good thing or not, our armed forces have given the enemies of the United States the evidence they need to posit a moral equivalence between us and him, regardless of whether it is true. We have no one to blame for this but ourselves: If one does not wish to be compared to a brutal dictator who crushed and tortured the Iraqi people, one should not, in fact, crush and torture Iraqis in that brutal dictator's most infamous prison.

We tortured Iraqis, and the impassioned appeals that such treatment is not representative of our nation's ideals is utterly beside the point. Those people writing about how noble it was for us to quickly own up to our failings gloss over the salient fact that we have something we need to own up to. Everyone who wants credit for everything we've done *right* in Iraq fails to appreciate that you can't get credit for doing a bunch of little things right if the things you get wrong are so goddamned spectacular. It's *nice* that people are sending toys and school supplies to Iraq. But plush toys and pencils are no match for pictures of US soldiers setting dogs upon naked, cowering Iraqis. It's not even close.

There's a word for this sort of thing: Incompetence, and that word sticks to just about everything this current administration has done in Iraq from the moment our forces stabbed into Baghdad. The military offensive was bold and brilliantly done; the occupation of the country has been utterly abysmal, and everything about it seems to have been designed to squander what good will we accrued by freeing the country from Saddam's grip. This could have been a "good war"—not an easy war—had our administration showed some indication that it actually cared what happened to Iraq and the people within it once Saddam was kicked out of power. But it didn't, and to a large extent still doesn't—which is not entirely surprising to me since I personally never believed that George Bush had any interest in invading Iraq except to avenge his father. I had hoped that those *around* him might show some evidence of long-term thinking once Dubya's limited objective had been accomplished, but I guess I was wrong about that.

I'm still not sorry we went in and got rid of Saddam—it was an action too long in coming. But everything since then has been nothing short of a disaster; Abu Ghraib is not an exception but the end result of systematic incompetence that plagues the entire enterprise. The abuse and torture the Iraqi prisoners suffered is the fruit of lack of forethought, lack of planning, lack of intent, and lack of care. To put it bluntly, this simply wouldn't have happened if those at the top of the food chain actually gave a shit about Iraq. But they don't. Dubya stopped caring the instant they flushed Saddam out of his bug hole; everything since then as been (literally) killing time until we can bug out and claim some sort of moral victory. Well, Abu Ghraib robbed us of that.

Who is responsible? Well, there certainly seems to be enough blame to go around, doesn't there. Those at the top didn't care or didn't want to know or at the very least seem more annoyed that the truth is out there than they are by the fact of the torture itself. Depending on who you believe, those at the bottom were either untrained to serve as prison guards and left without real supervision or instruction, or they were following orders from above which explicitly condoned torture. One is malignant neglect, the other is simply evil. It all stinks, from head to tail, and it seems unlikely to me that anyone is going to come away clean.

Personally, what I wish were that it were November so I could cast my vote and register my disgust with this current administration, which in this as in nearly every other thing it has done has shown little but contempt for anyone and anything that is not of its own narrow ilk. Bush and his people are staggeringly bad at their jobs—they are so bad that even their good ideas rot and fester as soon as they are taken out of the bag. This is what you get when the President of the United States is a man who has a level of self-introspection that is best described as canine, and whose cadre of cronies appear outraged at the idea that they can and should be held accountable for their actions (or lack thereof).

This is the worst president and administration since I've been alive—yes, even worse than Nixon, because as paranoid and bad as he was, some of his administrative policies did more good than harm. Nixon was a criminal, but he wasn't an incompetent. It's rather terrifying to say that I'd prefer a competent criminal in the Oval Office to the contemptuous incompetent who is in there now. But there it is. As I've said before, Bush isn't the worst president ever—Buchanan, Harding and (probably) Grant are ahead of him in the queue—but if someone else wants to be the worst president of the 21st century, he or she is really going to have to work at it.

Abu Ghraib is a defining image of the incompetence, contemptuousness and stupidity of this administration; if it eventually helps boot Bush from office, then some good may come from it. I'm sure that the more agitated Bush supporters will try to find a way to make a parallel between Abu Ghraib and the Madrid Bombing; i.e., that it was an example of terrorists gaming the system to get rid of an adversary. But Abu Ghraib is a self-inflicted wound. Al Qaeda didn't make US servicemen and women torture Iraqis.

I'm sure my German correspondent would want to know how I can declare what happened at Abu Ghraib shameful and yet be perfectly content to inflict what he feels is torture on Saddam Hussein. The answer is simple: I am not my government or my military. It's one thing for me to concoct what I feel are karmically appropriate punishments against mass murdering dictators in the privacy of my own mind; it's another thing for my government and military to condone torture or through incompetence or inaction allow torture to occur. As a private individual I'm allowed my fantasies, but my government and my military exist in the real world. I'm not going to be allowed to mete punishment on Saddam, so I am free to create imaginative sentences. My government and my military *are* meting out punishment, however, on actual people, none of whom approach the high stinkin' evil of Saddam. So I would that *their* creativity be somewhat less terrible than my own.

THE
COMING WAR

Since it looks like we're heading toward one, here's my take on war.

1. It should be done if it's necessary. For now, I'll be vague as to what constitutes "necessary" because it's very much open to interpretation.

2. If you're going to do it, then you should make sure your opponent ends up as a grease spot on the wall, and that his country is reformulated so that it never ever bothers you again.

In the best of all worlds, both of these are fulfilled; you have no choice but to go to war, and you squash your opponent like a plump grape underneath a sledgehammer. But to be entirely honest, if I had to choose between the two of these, I'd pick number 2, if only because if we must participate in an unjust war, 'tis better it was done quickly. That way the stench of our pointless involvement is over quickly, and we expend as little matériel as possible (not to mention, you know, the deaths of those who fight our wars for us are kept to a minimum). Also, if you have the first, but not the second, what you end up with is a longstanding crapfest that you will ultimately have to revisit, whether you wish to or not.

Such as it was with the Gulf War. I'm not a terribly big fan of that war, but I'm perfectly happy to cede the point that it was necessary to some great extent. Yes, it was a war about oil. Thing is, while we can argue about the need to reduce our oil consumption (I tend to think the greatest advance in technology in the last couple of decades is the coming age of fuel cell and alternate energy cars), ultimately we still do need oil, and certainly needed it in 1990.

And of course it's not like it was just a war about oil on *our* side of the fence; had Kuwait's primary export been goat meat, Saddam would have been less likely to get all fired up about reintegrating the lost 19th province of Iraq. The Gulf War also offered the added attraction of the possibility of turning Saddam into a fine particulate mist with the aid of a well-placed smart missile. He's a morally disagreeable enough person, and his regime largely worthless enough to have made the case for its dismantling persuasive.

The Gulf War took place while I was in college, and I remember being at candlelight vigils in the quads, not to pray that the US stopped the madness of the attack, but that we kicked the righteous hell out of the Iraqis and that it would all be over quickly. I had a brother in the Army who was over there in the fight. The longer the fighting went on the better the chance something bad would happen to him. Fortunately, it was over quickly, and we learned what happens when a large but poorly-trained, badly-equipped army goes head-to-head with a highly-trained, massively-equipped army: The poorly-trained army loses people by a ratio of more than 100 to 1. We squashed the Iraqi army, all right.

But we didn't squash Saddam or his regime, and ultimately, I find this inexplicable. Saddam should have not been allowed to continue to rule. His personal detention (to say the *least*) and the dismantling of his political machine should have been part of any surrender. War isn't a football game, after all, where the losing coach gets to try to rebuild for next season. Particularly in Saddam's case, where he was the aggressor; he started it. The penalty for starting a war (which, to be clear, you then lose, miserably) should be a nice 8x8 cell with no phone privileges until you die.

Lacking the will to depose Saddam, we (and by we I mean the US and the UN) should have been willing to back up the weapons inspectors with the immediate and massive threat of force. Simply put, any facility that the weapons inspectors were denied entry to should have been bombed into pebble-sized pieces within 15 minutes of the inspectors leaving the area. Aggressive countries that have been defeated in war do not have the luxury of "national dignity" or whatever it is you want to call it. The fact that we just spent more than a decade letting a hostile regime jerk the world around is angrifying (a new word. Use it. Love it).

Let's turn our attention to the new war we'll be having soon. Toward the first point, is this war absolutely necessary? I doubt it. I think it would be much more useful to swarm the country with weapons inspectors and high-altitude bombers that track their every destination. After the first few times Saddam's precious presidential palaces are turned into powder when the inspectors are turned back, they'll get the clue. I see nothing wrong with reminding Iraq on the point of a missile of its obligation to let us look anywhere for anything. Clearly they won't like it, but, you know. So what.

Many suggest that the purpose of the coming war will to be to assure that Iraq cannot ever threaten any of us, but this achieves the same goal at lesser cost (and without exposing our military to undue chance of death). If indeed containing that threat were the goal of the upcoming war, this works just as well, and will have the additional value of being what was actually the correct response anyway, and only the better part of a decade late.

However, it's clear that Dubya wants a war for purposes not related to weapons containment; indeed, his administration is utterly disinterested in that aspect of the Iraq problem, except as a convenient trope to sell the war to inattentive voters. Dubya wants regime change, and I can sympathize. Saddam has been in power a decade longer than he should have been, and I can think of worse uses of the American military than clearing out bad governments around the world. If Dubya said something along the lines of "First we get rid of Saddam, and then we're going to pay a call to Robert Mugabe," well, that's a barricade that I'd be inclined to rush.

I'm not holding my breath on that pronouncement, however. Ultimately I suspect that Dubya wants Saddam out as part of a father-avengement thing, although what Bush I needs to be avenged for is unclear; Bush I isn't dead at the hand of Saddam, after all, nor injured, nor in fact seriously put out in any recognizable way. I believe at best Dubya is avenging his father's taunting at the hands of Saddam. If that's the case, Dana Carvey had better go to ground as quickly as humanly possible. This is of course a poor reason to send a nation into war, but Dubya does have the advantage of a decade's worth of stupidity in dealing with Iraq providing him with some actual legitimate reasons to plug Saddam.

Let's get down to brass tacks. On balance, the end results of fighting this war will be (cross fingers) the removal of Saddam and the dismantling of his political state and (incidentally) a clearing out of whatever weapons capability that may exist. For those reasons, I'm *not* opposed to fighting a war with Iraq now. Be that as it may, even those people who fully support a war against Iraq are rather painfully aware that the stated reasons that the Dubya administration wants to gear up for war are window dressing for a revenge fantasy. It is possible to fight a just war for less than entirely just reasons. We're about to do it.

Just, necessary or not, let's hope that this war is total, complete and ends with Saddam dead or in chains, his system smashed, and Iraq occupied in the same manner as Japan or Germany was at the end of WWII, with an eye toward making the revamped country successful and benign (the scariest things to come out of Japan and Germany in the last 55 years, after all, were Godzilla and the Scorpions, respectively). Anything less will be, in a word, unforgivable. If we mean to wage war, let's wage war like we mean it.

THE BEST END
OF THE WORLD

Thomas Muentzer's Armageddon, in 1525. It wasn't actually the end of the world, but really. When is it ever?

The history of the human species is the history of a people waiting for the other shoe to drop. The very first human who had the ability to think beyond the next five minutes probably got up one morning, looked around the cave and the savannah outside, smiled briefly and then thought, *you know, this just can't last.* Humans are innately eschatological—looking for the signs and portents that signify that the end of the world is nigh. It beats Yahtzee.

While all humans everywhere seem to have some conception of a final end of our planet and our people, Western civilization has been particularly obsessed with the end time (our Eastern brethren look at the world in a less linear fashion, what with all reincarnation stuff, although even they believe in a eventual, final resting point of the human soul—Nirvana, which is literally the annihilation of desire. That's right, when you finally reach complete understanding, you won't *want* that Ford Expedition! Better stay on that Wheel of Suffering for a while until you get it out of your system).

As a systematic collection of beliefs, the Western end-of-the world mania gets its start in Zoroastrianism, a religion out of Iran, whose prophet, Zoroaster, taught that the world was a battleground in a 9,000 year war between the forces of good and evil. At the end of it, a final savior, called the *saoshyant*, will come and lead the forces of good into triumph. God (or, more specifically, Ahura Mazda, the god of good) will then use him to redeem the world and resurrect the dead.

Sound familiar? It should; elements of Zoroastrianism deeply inform Judiasm and its own messianic writing, as well as Christianity and Islam. Zoroastianism's god of evil, Ahriman, is even the blueprint for Ol' Scratch himself—that'd be Satan, you know.

More recently, the concept of end times and apocalyptic struggle has expanded beyond the usual boundaries of religion. Take, if you will, the political system of Marxism. Marxism is full of the hallmarks of the end times: Belief in a protracted struggle between the forces of good (the workers) and evil (those who would alienate the worker from his labor), a final apocalyptic battle (your worker's revolution), and then, of course, the Worker's Paradise, which is your basic post apocalyptic Millennium, minus of course Jesus (who, however, was well-known to prefer the company of the poor over the rich).

This apocalyptic struggle is even more explicit in Nazism, which had the apocalyptic battle (the eradication of Jews and other non-Aryans), its messiah (Hitler), and, most explicitly, the Third Reich, which of course was also referred to as the "Thousand Year Reich," aping the millennium exactly (the title "Third Reich," though a reference to German history, also fits comfortably into an apocalyptic world view—in the 12th Century, Joachim of Fiore, an Italian monk, interpreted the Book of Revelation and discovered three ages of the world, hinged on the triune nature of the Christian God. There's the age of the father, which was pre-Jesus, and the age of the son, which was the current time, and an upcoming "Third Age," to be ruled by the holy ghost, which would correspond to the Millennium).

Nowadays, of course, most people are repelled by the explicit Nazi/Judeo-Christian parallels, particularly as it implies that the Nazis are the forces of "good" in this world view (the idea of Hitler as the Messiah is particularly odious). But in 1938, I'll bet you a lot of Germans thought it was pretty keen.

Ironically, in this century, it's science that has given us fuel for our apocalyptic fire. There's the atomic bomb, most obviously. Nuclear annihilation, nuclear winter, Mad Max, Godzilla. But it's just the fiery tip of the iceberg. AIDS is a favorite example for the obnoxious

Bible-thumper of the incurable plague that precedes the apocalypse (rest assured other plagues, from the Black plague onward, have also pulled this duty). The advance of technology that allows a global network and near-instantaneous access to vast reams information is also a piece of the end days puzzle.

Global warming, and its twin offspring El Nino and La Nina, contributes to those massive floods and hurricanes and fires we've been having recently. Hell, even meteors from space, the 1990's favorite way to blow up the world, belong in the pot: They didn't call the movie "Armageddon" for nothing, even if they did manage to screw up the reference ("Armageddon" is a battle—and is in fact an actual geographic location—not the actual end of the world).

Ultimately, however, the problem for humans, and particularly Christians, has not been that the end is coming, but that it hasn't come soon *enough*. Christians have literally been expecting the end times since the very beginning of the religion. The earliest Christians fully expected the Kingdom of God before they died; indeed, much of the literature conceptualizing and explaining the second coming (including the Book of Revelation) is about trying to rationalize why Christians are still loitering on earth instead of kicking up their heels on a cloud somewhere.

Subsequent interpretations of apocalyptic literature through this last millennium have filled its days with presumably definite dates in which the world as we knew it would end and the new world would begin. This despite the fact Jesus himself noted that "No man knoweth the day nor the hour of my coming." But you know how people are. They get all excited and stuff.

First and foremost, of course, is the actual beginning of the second millennium, which (for all you math geeks out there), the people of the times took to be 1000 AD. Churches were packed with the cautious expectation that the Millennium, with the big "M," might actually coincide with the millennium, with the small "m." It did not. Later, the previously mentioned Joachim of Fiore, in formulating his three ages of God, pegged the age of the Holy Ghost to begin sometime in the early part of the 13th century, by which time, conveniently, Joachim would be dead and unable to answer for himself if there was a problem with the calculations, which of course there was.

Somewhat further up the timestream, the biggest End of the World event in the new world took place in 1844. Seems a New York farmer named William Miller predicted, after careful analysis of the Book of Revelation, that the Second Coming was on the way in 1843. Through skillful promotion and the use of helpful pamphlets, hundreds of thousands bought in, but when the appointed hour arrived, Jesus was nowhere to be found. Miller checked his records and discovered—oops—he'd dropped a year in the translation of dates from BC to AD. He set the new date: October 21, 1844.

Miller's adherents, the Adventists, sold their worldly possessions and decamped to Miller's farm to await the Lord. Jesus, alas, missed his Second Chance at a Second Coming. This event, or lack thereof, becomes known as the "Great Disappointment," which, all things considered, may be the only time something described that way can be said to be an understatement.

(Adventists are still waiting, by the way. The new thinking is that the 1844 date was the moment Jesus started his examination of all the names in the Book of Life. After that, he'll come down and start his reign. The Adventists have this time chosen not to set a specific date—though it's real soon now—and that's probably wise. As for the fact that Jesus needs 156 years and counting to read a single book, all one can say is: That's *some* book.)

Thousands lost their property and some probably lost their faith in the Great Disappointment, but nobody died. The same cannot be said for Thomas Muentzer's Armageddon, which is why I, after all this preamble, now bequeath it the title of Best End of the World.

Thomas Muentzer was a priest who, at the time of the Protestant Reformation, read into the Bible (newly translated into German by Martin Luther, with whom Muentzer had had some acquaintance) that the Apocalypse was coming, and that the forces of good and evil would be arrayed along social and economic lines. The good folks would be the peasants, who are, of course, the salt of the earth, while the forces of evil were in the form of the princes and landowners of Germany.

As you might expect, this particular interpretation of the Bible was not especially popular with the princes (or with Martin Luther himself—who at one point called Muentzer "The Satan at Allstadt"), but the masses ate it up. And it just happened to fit the mood at the time in Germany, where peasant revolts were popping up all over the lands. Muentzer found himself leading one of those peasant revolts, and in 1525, was at forefront of a peasant army, 8,000 strong, facing the army of the princes at Frankenhausen.

This was the battle Muentzer had been waiting for—he'd been riling up the peasants by telling them that this battle would signal the End of the World, that God himself would intervene and thus, the Kingdom of God would be at hand. The princes, whose well-armed, well-trained forces reasonably expected to wipe the floor with the peasants, reportedly tried to find a non-confrontational end to the battle (they needed those peasants back in the fields, after all). But Muentzer riled up the troops some more, proclaiming that he himself would catch the princes' cannonballs in his shirtsleeves. What's more, as the battle was about to commence, a rainbow appeared in the sky above the battlefield. As it happened, Muentzer's flag featured a rainbow on it. It had to be a sign. Muentzer's peasants marched into battle, singing hymns. Christ was coming, and he was on their side.

It was a massacre. Five thousand peasants died screaming as the princes rained cannonshot down on their heads (the princes' forces lost maybe a dozen people all told). Muentzer did not catch a single one of those cannonballs with his sleeves; in fact he fled the field of battle and was discovered some distance away, hiding under a bed. Muentzer was arrested, tortured, made to recant his various heresies, and on May 27, 1525, executed by the princes. In one sense Muentzer was right, it *was* the end of the world, although the world that was ending was his. It was, alas, a very personal apocalypse.

Somewhat ironically, several centuries later, Muentzer would be held up as a national hero by the communist government of East Germany, who saw parallels in his actions and the actions of the Glorious Worker's Revolution. So I suppose when communism fell, that made Muentzer a two-time loser.

We're still awaiting the end of the world. And let's be clear on this: The end *is* coming, one way or another, for the planet Earth. In the absence of planet-squashing meteors, horrifying viral or bacterial plagues that wipe out all known life, the sudden and unexpected appearance of an alien race that claims Earth in an eminent domain land grab for a wormhole superhighway they're building to Alpha Aquilae, or even, yes, the Second Coming, the sun is *still* going to use up all its hydrogen one day. In burning helium instead, it will swell up like a big red balloon, swallowing the inner planets as it expands. That'll be about five billion years from now. Wear sunscreen.

In the meantime, I will suspect we'll have plenty of time to think about how everything is going get flushed, one day, sooner or later. Or (and I know this is radical idea), just *don't*. Stop worrying about the end of things. Sure, things end: Divine intervention, celestial expansion, network cancellation, or simply an inopportune slip that causes you to crack your head on the toilet will all conspire to bring about the cessation of the things you know and love.

The remedy, the only remedy you have, is to keep at it: Keep doing what matters, keep seeing the world around you, keep loving those who matter to you. Because when the end of the world comes, however it comes, what's ultimately going to matter in your life is what you've made of it.

You've got some time left. Get to it.

ADDENDUM

Scalzi, you putrefied smear of degenerate amniotic fluid. Another book. No, not even, merely a collection of transcribed hoots and shrieks of a Ebola crazed baboon, hammering away on a keyboard and lucky, I say, lucky enough to string letters together into something resembling drivel. Your inspiration, no doubt coming from the electrodes alligator clipped to your dangling testicles, which themselves are only remarkable for the fact that you manage to lick them while exploring the profound (alas, only to you) depths of your own ass.

Enough, I can no longer besmirch my beautiful mind with the contemplation of your execrable insignificance. You bore me.

—C. Rader

Oh, merciful gods and bananas, another magnum opus from Scalzi, the man who singlehandedly settles the "evolution vs. intelligent design" controversy by proving both sides wrong. Listen, you pulsillanimous donkey-fister, I'd rather chew on someone else's hemorrhoids than be subjected to whatever your dental work is picking up THIS week. You have the writing talent and personal hygeine habits of a smear of week-old fish slime on an anonymous street in Minsk. Your prose soars with all the grace of a bilious orangutang, and delivers biting wit to rival Perry Como. Your books–and you–should be pulped and spread on crops as an industrial weed-killer, except that it'd be against international eco-terrorism regulations, you masticating coprophage.

—Nicole the Wonder Nerd

...........................**W**...........................

You suck.

Postscript - since the winner will be published in your book I thought the email should be kept in line with the average attention span and intellectual capacity of your reader base.

—CB